# WHOSE FUTURE?

# WHOSE FUTURE?

## Community Planning in West Maui

Lisa Huynh Eller

North Beach-West Maui
Benefit Fund Inc.

Lahaina, Maui, Hawai'i

ISBN 978-1-9524-6110-1 (pbk : alk. paper)


Published by the North Beach-West Maui Benefit Fund, Inc.
P O Box 11329
Lahaina, Hawai'i 96761

Distributed by University of Hawai'i Press
2840 Kolowalu Street
Honolulu, HI 96822-1888

Every effort has been made to trace copyright holders
and to obtain their permission for the use of copyright material.
The publisher apologizes for any errors or omissions and
would be grateful if notified of any corrections that
should be incorporated in future reprints or editions of this book.

This book is printed on acid-free paper and
meets the guidelines for permanence and durability
of the Council on Library Resources.

Print-ready files provided by North Beach-West Maui Benefit Fund, Inc.

# CONTENTS

# FOREWORD

This book is another project of the HK West Maui Community Fund and published by the North Beach-West Maui Benefit Fund. It was intended to provide a recent retrospective look at the community plan update process for the West Maui Community Plan. The final copyediting process was completed shortly before the August 8, 2023, fires that destroyed Lahaina Town.

More than merely a cautionary tale about the limits of the community planning process, the story of the recent community plan update in West Maui takes on renewed significance for the people of West Maui as the industrial disaster relief and rebuilding complex pulls West Maui communities in multiple and contradictory directions.

From one point of view, the West Maui Community Plan can be seen as a weak compromise regarding appropriate uses of land in West Maui—appropriate as to the desires and wishes of the West Maui people—that over time may likely be ignored in various ways anyway. From another perspective, however, it also serves as a high water mark for community involvement in the community planning process in Maui and Hawai'i.

French philosopher Henri Lefebvre once noted in the *Critique of Everyday Life,* "Everything great and splendid is founded on power and wealth. They are the basis of beauty...Castles, palaces, cathedrals, fortresses, all speak in their various ways of the greatness and the strength of the people who built them and against whom they were built. This real greatness shines through the fake grandeur of rulers and endows these buildings with a lasting 'beauty.'"

As the West Maui community is pressed into making decisions about the future of Lahaina Town, it is hoped that this volume will show the beauty of the West Maui Community Plan update process—allowing the greatness and strength of the community who struggled to create it to shine through.

*Lance D. Collins*
*Wainalu, Honokōwai*

vii

# PREFACE

This book is a chronicle of the conversations and meetings that led to the adoption of the 2021 West Maui Community Plan, beginning with the Community Advisory Planning Committee's (CPAC) first meeting in July 2019.

Writing in journalistic style and relying solely on public record, I pieced together the conversations and decisions that took place over more than 50 meetings, two years, and through the COVID-19 pandemic. Mahalo to my editor Katie Fox, and to Jay Hartwell and Lance Collins, for helping me sharpen the language and content of this book.

What follows is not an exhaustive account of every testimony, decision or opinion. This book does not cover the Planning Department's outreach prior to the first CPAC meeting. Rather, like with any news article, I highlighted the most consequential topics through the voices of those who participated in the process: kūpuna, citizens, Hawaiian cultural practitioners, developers, industry groups, scientists, and government officials.

The conflicts arising from clashing interests—for example, a developer wanting to build in a culturally sensitive area such as Olowalu—is not new. But the times in which this process unfolded were unique. For one, West Maui was acutely experiencing the impacts of climate change: perpetual drought and the loss of coastlines and roadways to rising sea levels. These impacts were becoming increasingly difficult to ignore. Secondly, Hawai'i's isolation during the pandemic put tourism on pause and under a microscope. Tourism, one of the island's largest economic drivers, was always a major factor in planning. In its absence, decision makers had a rare window to rethink their approach to it. Too often the history of community planning processes—who made what decision and why—is lost to time.

I hope this book can be a resource for those involved in planning for West Maui, now and decades from now, when the next plan update is due. And I hope readers see the importance of context to understanding the process and its participants. To consider testimony and decisions, one must understand the person giving it and making them, and who or what is influencing them.

# INTRODUCTION

On August 8, 2023, on the eve of sending this manuscript to production, a massive fire killed an unknown number of people and destroyed Historic Lahaina Town. At the time of this writing, close to a thousand people are still missing. Many of the voices chronicled in this book were people who knew Lahaina intimately. They were people who lived or grew up in the town. Their perspectives on wildfires, disaster response, landownership and other related topics have become more relevant in the aftermath of the tragedy.

West Maui residents had become increasingly aware of wildfire danger in the years leading up to the Lahaina Fire. In August of 2018, a fire in Kauaʻula Valley just above Lahaina burned more than 2,100 acres and damaged homes and property. Residents criticized Maui County's lack of preparedness and response, and warned of a future catastrophe. The following year, another cluster of fires fueled by overgrown brush, drought, and record heat set West Maui ablaze once again.

By the end of 2019, when the people who would come to shape the West Maui Community Plan were just beginning their work, the harm that fires could cause was becoming a more constant concern, and committee members voiced their unease. These conversations are recorded here as part of this chronicle of the West Maui Community Plan. The plan's authors discussed, among other things, their worries about large landowners who did little to manage flammable nonnative grasses on their vacant properties (October 8, 2019), whether developers should be exempt from constructing through-streets for emergency access (September 5, 2019), the safety issues caused by the maze of one-way streets and cul-de-sacs in Lahaina (November 21, 2019), and concerns over continuing to allow heavy industrial land use or fuel storage in Lahaina (February 27, 2020).

In the afterword of this book, Brian Richardson deconstructs the power dynamics of the community planning process, and explores how these dynamics might impact both the short-term and long-term future of Lahaina. The same apprehension expressed throughout this book—wealthy developers capitalizing on unprotected land and residents desperate for homes—has heightened in the wake of the tragedy. How will Lahaina be rebuilt, and for whom or what?

# WEST MAUI COMMUNITY PLAN AREA

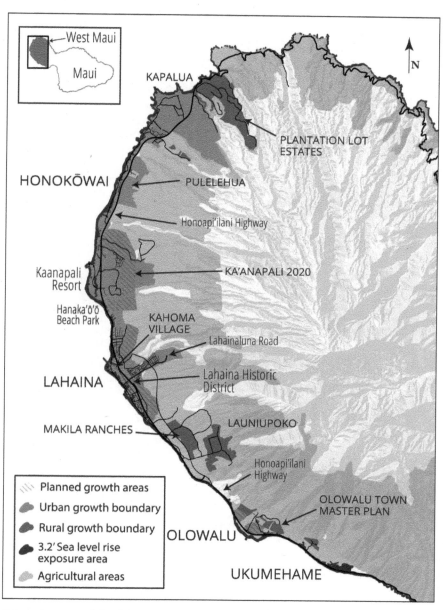

Selected proposed development areas

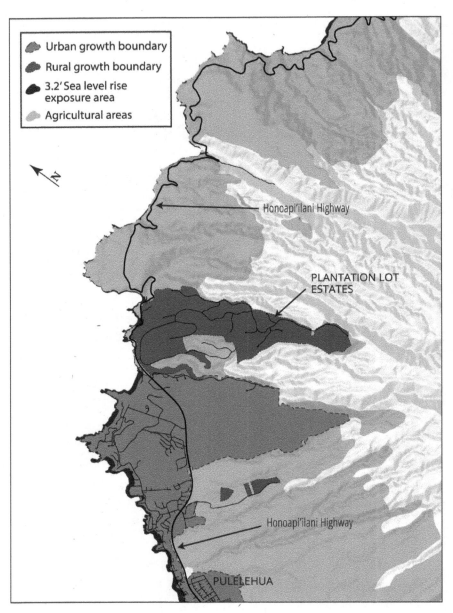

Urban growth boundary
Rural growth boundary
3.2′ Sea level rise exposure area
Agricultural areas

N

Honoapi'ilani Highway

PLANTATION LOT ESTATES

Honoapi'ilani Highway

PULELEHUA

Northern portion in detail

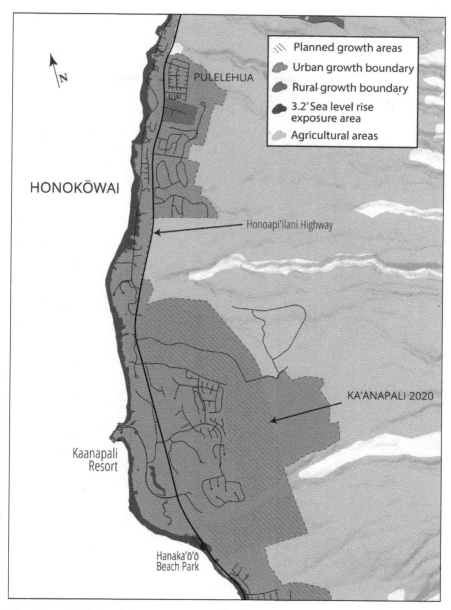

Legend:
- Planned growth areas
- Urban growth boundary
- Rural growth boundary
- 3.2' Sea level rise exposure area
- Agricultural areas

N

PULELEHUA

HONOKŌWAI

Honoapi'ilani Highway

KA'ANAPALI 2020

Kaanapali Resort

Hanaka'ō'ō Beach Park

Honokōwai-Kā'anapali Resort portion in detail

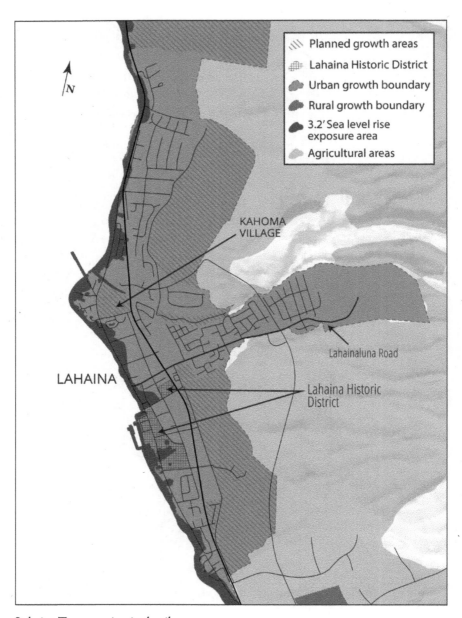

Lahaina Town portion in detail

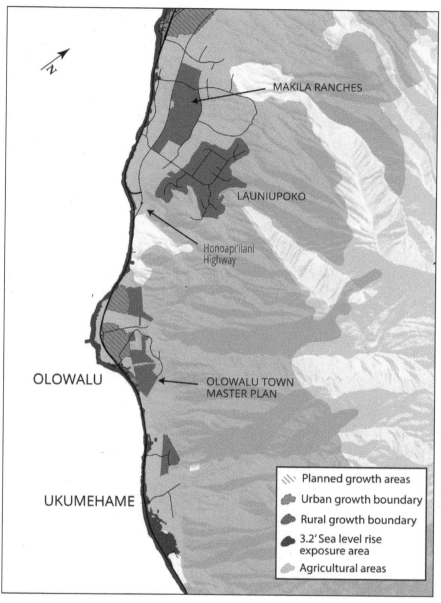

MAKILA RANCHES

LAUNIUPOKO

Honoapiʻilani
Highway

OLOWALU

OLOWALU TOWN
MASTER PLAN

UKUMEHAME

Planned growth areas
Urban growth boundary
Rural growth boundary
3.2' Sea level rise
exposure area
Agricultural areas

Southern portion in detail

# COMMUNITY PLAN
# ADVISORY COMMITTEE

## UNRESTRAINED GROWTH

In 1996, Maui County adopted the West Maui Community Plan despite opposition from the public. Dozens of articles were written about the Plan in the *Lahaina News* over the course of four years, giving a glimpse into a power struggle between a community alarmed over West Maui's growth and the influential group of large land developers capitalizing on it.

The first article referencing the plan appeared on September 23, 1993. "Most of the 22 people who testified opposed the county Planning Department's recommendations for the plan," the article read. It went on to quote David Chenoweth, a member of the Lahaina Citizen Advisory Committee (CAC), as saying: "Our Planning Department's version contains the same unrestrained growth scenario of the past." The article then detailed requests by CAC members to scale back development:

> Chenoweth and Andrea Heath-Blundell, the co-chair of the Lahaina panel, asked the commission to follow the advisory committee's recommendation to get rid of Project District No. 3—a 310-acre plot mauka of north Kaanapali and Honoapi'ilani Highway that would provide for 1,200 units. She said the district is unnecessary in light of the new housing going up at the Villages of Leialii in Lahaina and Puukolii Village in Kaanapali.
>
> Chenoweth said the district is needed like "a hole in the head."
>
> Members of [the] committee also asked the commission to support their call for a park at North Beach, and preservation of beach access and open space.

As the community plan process moved forward, developers were meeting one on one with elected officials to submit their requests. In November of 1993, the *Lahaina News* reported that Richard Cameron, vice president of property management for Maui Land & Pineapple Company (ML&P), met with then Maui County Mayor Linda Lingle and submitted a letter to Maui County Council then chairman Goro Hokama. The company wanted to move the proposed Napili Regional Park to a 50-acre site near Kapalua/West Maui Airport.

Gary L. Gifford, the president and chief executive officer of Kapalua Land Co. Ltd.—a subsidiary of ML&P—said the company's plans to develop the 16.3 acres as part of the Kapalua resort was also a major factor in Cameron's request.... ML&P's vice president stated that they had already discussed their proposal with Mayor Linda Crockett Lingle and County Parks Director Charmaine Tavares, who were considering the request.

"While we do not yet have a response from the administration, I feel it is appropriate to make this request now as you should be receiving the West Maui plan soon," wrote Cameron.

Mayor Lingle said that she was actually "surprised by the letter to the council at this time."

She said she sat down with Cameron about a month ago and listened to the specifics of his plan, but was waiting until she could talk to people involved with the project.

## July 13, 1995

Two years after the West Maui Community Planning process began, community sentiment remained the same. "Residents urge slow growth in community plan" was the headline of a *Lahaina News* article dated July 13, 1995.

Most of last Thursday's speakers urged responsible planning. Fuzzy Alboro said the initial development of Kaanapali had been welcomed because it brought jobs to the area. But further development will bring more people from elsewhere and can no longer be viewed as helping West Maui residents. "There should be a point when we say, 'Hey, brother, how about giving it a halt.' It's time," he told the council members.

Representatives of large landowners were present at the same meeting to "make pitches for their companies' plans," according to the *Lahaina News.*

Amfac/JMB Hawaii Vice President Teney Takahashi argued that growth cannot be controlled.

> "There's a misperception that growth can be controlled," said Amfac/JMB Hawaii Vice President Teney Takahashi. "Growth can only be accommodated." Takahashi reminded the Planning Committee of the contributions Amfac has made to the county and state, including money for the Lahaina Bypass and land for the West Maui Youth Center. He urged the councilmembers to stick with the recommendations of the 1983 community plan, which allowed for the development of the North Beach property. All laws protecting wetlands would be followed, Takahashi said.

The final West Maui Community Plan would determine the fate of some of the more contentious development projects, including plans for new hotel development along North Beach, West Maui's last stretch of undeveloped coast.

### *October 19, 1995*

Not all of the Planning Committee's actions received public opposition. Some were viewed favorably by residents. Among those decisions were the designation of 13 of West Maui's major streams for open space designation, a moratorium on sea wall construction, and the expansion of the boundaries for the Historic Lahaina District. But the benefits from these actions would be eclipsed by the large development projects that would later gain approval from the Council.

The Planning Committee's recommendations were forwarded to the full board for its vote. In the public meetings that preceded the vote, however, both opponents and proponents came out in full force to advocate for their positions. The tourism and construction industry succeeded in rallying a crowd of employees to attend the hearings. The tug-of-war prompted the County Council to send the recommendations back to the committee for further discussion and work.

### *February 29, 1996*

The West Maui Community Plan passed by a vote of 7–2 in February of 1996, according to a *Lahaina News* article. While a few last-minute amendments passed that would benefit the community, including the inclusion of more park space and a zoning redesignation for a preschool, the plan allowed for significant development along the coast. Council Planning Committee Chairman Tom Morrow and Councilman Wayne Nishiki voted against approving it.

In the final vote, both Nishiki and Morrow voted no on the West Maui Community Plan, and complained that the final document now allows for too much development. They were particularly concerned with more development in the Kā'anapali North Beach area.

Nishiki read from a letter from a hotel employee, who said that new hotels at North Beach would hurt the occupancy rate at the existing hotels and create more job instability. "There are 18,443 visitor rooms on Maui. Do we really need any more?" Nishiki asked. "I don't think any of us would agree that we need more hotels."

Morrow said he agreed with West Maui community activist Dave Chenoweth, objecting to the 310-acre North Beach Mauka luxury development proposed by Amfac. That area is among the best crop land in the state, Morrow said, and approving development there counters the idea of protecting the county's agriculture and rural identity.

The Planning Committee chairman said he's been warned by travel agents not to keep paving over Maui or the tourists are going to stop coming.

But the plan had a defender in West Maui Councilman Nakamura, who believes it will bring more economic development.

"Some don't believe I represent West Maui in the community plan," Nakamura said, giving a sideways nod toward a couple of long-time activists who have attended every council meeting on the plan.

Nakamura said most residents favor the final plan and that he was speaking on behalf of those who couldn't attend the daytime council meeting because they are working.

## "The Community's Will"

The 20 years that had passed since the adoption of the 1996 West Maui Community Plan were a time of dramatic change in West Maui. Annual visitor arrivals increased by almost one million people between 2006 and 2019.[1] In 2020, the median price of a single-family home hit a new high of more than one million dollars. The number of visitor units outnumbered homes for residents, and traffic grew worse each year. Residents were becoming increasingly

---

1. Annual visitor arrivals (international and domestic) to Maui increased from 2,235,701 in 1990 to 3,059,905 in 2019. (Source: Department of Business, Economic Development and Tourism.)

concerned about environmental health as drought and sea-level rise persisted. (These issues would later come into focus as the COVID-19 pandemic unfolded around the world.)

This period of rapid change provided the context for the next iteration of the West Maui Community Plan. In 2017, the Maui County Planning Department started to draft a new version of the plan with input from residents through "stakeholder" meetings, open houses and presentations by subject-matter experts. Three distinct decision-making groups—the West Maui Community Planning Advisory Committee (CPAC), the Maui Planning Commission and the Maui County Council—were charged with reviewing, amending and adopting the plan.

The first to take a crack at the plan, and the one that would do the most to shape it, was the West Maui CPAC: a 13-member volunteer committee of Maui residents. Nine of the members applied and were appointed by the County Council, while another four were appointed by then Mayor Michael Victorino. The CPAC held 35 in-person meetings and two virtual meetings—three times the number of meetings that the Planning Commission and County Council held.

A voting majority of the CPAC, some of whom viewed themselves as progressives, fully committed to creating a plan that would put full-time residents' interests above tourism- and development-driven interests. Those CPAC members not in the voting majority, some of whom worked in the real estate industry and had ties to developers, advocated to remove restrictions that prevented more development, especially when it came to "affordable housing." They, too, viewed themselves as working for the will of the people.

Though they sometimes found common ground in advocating for traffic solutions and addressing sea-level rise, more than not, their views clashed. This led to dramatic disagreement, and accusations of unfair treatment and conflicts of interest. In the end, the CPAC's version of the West Maui Community Plan represented the views of the voting majority. It put in place restrictions to slow the pace of development unless that development benefited full-time residents. It resisted changing land designations for agricultural lands despite pressure from landowners who purchased former sugar cane lands and built luxury homes on them. It prioritized the protection of known pre-contact burial sites and other areas of cultural significance to Native Hawaiians. It created more parks and open space in places where developers wanted to build more homes. And unlike the 1996 plan, it addressed concerns over climate change—namely the impacts of sea-level rise.

## "I Don't Feel That This Committee Fully Represents the Community"

### *July 25, 2019*

In the summer of 2019, the West Maui CPAC began the process of reviewing the draft community plan. Of the five areas on Maui to embark on this planning process, they were the first and would set a precedent for how the process would unfold around the rest of the island.

The previous West Maui Community Plan, which yielded an unprioritized to-do list, was adopted in 1996, more than 25 years before the next one would be adopted. The plan had identified 81 implementing actions with assigned county, state and federal leads. The 2021 report from the Maui County Implementation Division reported that only 21 of the 81 implementing actions identified in the 1996 West Maui Community Plan had been completed. Another 43 actions were marked "in progress" or "ongoing," and the remaining 17 were marked "not begun."

A lack of implementation and enforcement, poor planning, and rampant development would all be blamed for West Maui's traffic and pollution problems. Rising real estate prices put homeownership out of reach for many. The median home price in Lahaina rose to more than $1 million in 2022, while Maui County residents earned a median household income of about $88,000, according to 2021 U.S. Census Bureau data. The draft plan would not have the final say in the future of West Maui growth, but it would influence where and how that growth could happen.

Two dozen community members, among them Mayor Michael Victorino, members of the West Maui CPAC and staff from the Planning Department, packed the gym at Lahainaluna High School for the first meeting on July 25, 2019. Over the next three hours, the most pressing issues facing the CPAC would begin to emerge. Public testimony and committee discussion centered on the question of who benefited, who lost and what was lost because of existing approved and proposed developments in West Maui.

Solomon Pili Kahoʻohalahala guided the group in an *oli* (chant) written by Native Hawaiian historian and educator David Malo. Malo was a member of the first class at Lahainaluna School and later served as headmaster. In the oli, Kahoʻohalahala called out to the people in attendance, and they responded in kind. He explained that doing so meant calling out for support. It was a symbolic gesture of the collective effort that they were all embarking upon.

As historian, [David Malo] became a cultural expert. And he spent many years of his life with very important people in Hawaiian culture, who are leaders as well as people of the community who are practitioners. And therefore, his wealth of knowledge was incredible. But he was also a visionary. And in this particular vision, he says that I want to be buried in a location where my grave will not be overwashed by the foreign tide. And think about that—about what it says, and what a vision this man had decades ago. And then now think about the work that you do, and what you have responsibility for, and what is your vision in terms of this place? All of West Maui? So I leave you with those thoughts.

Each CPAC member took a turn introducing themselves and their reason for joining the Committee. Many of the members spoke about having grown up in West Maui, moving away, moving back, raising their families here, watching it change and now wanting to improve life for their fellow community members.

The nine members of the West Maui CPAC appointed by the County Council were Joseph Aquino, Ravi Bugga, Yvette Joyce Celiz, Karen Comcowich, Donald Robert Gerbig, Dawn Hegger-Nordblom, Kai Nishiki, Joseph Pluta and Leilani Reyes Pulmano. The four members appointed by Mayor Victorino were Jeri Dean, Aina Kohler, Hans Michel and Dylan Payne.

Celiz, Dean and Payne all grew up in Lahaina and graduated from Lahainaluna High School. "I've seen it change for the better and I've seen some change not so good," said Kohler, who talked about being born and raised in Lahaina and leaving for a time before being called back.

Kai Nishiki, the daughter of former councilman Wayne Nishiki from the 1996 West Maui Community Plan, said her priority was to provide for the needs of residents and future generations. Pulmano, who had been living in Kahana for the past 16 years and worked at Pacific Rim Land, shared her desire to help balance future growth.

Aquino said he applied for CPAC because he wanted to see the community grow in a smart way. "I don't want growth to be taken over by corporate and the locals being left to deal with the problems," he said.

Other members had spent most of their lives in West Maui, after moving there for work decades prior. Michel lived in Lahaina for 56 years. He came to Maui to work as a pastry chef at the Royal Lahaina when it opened up in 1963. Both Michel and Pluta, a realtor, had been involved in multiple community planning efforts. Donald Gerbig, former employee of Pioneer Mill, spoke about his desire to allow development in a way that could be compatible with existing infrastructure. "We can expand and not increase traffic too much and yet we'll have nice development," said Gerbig.

Rounding out the West Maui CPAC were two relatively new Maui residents. Originally from Colorado, Comcowich had been living in Lahaina for 15 years. Bugga, a former World Bank Group manager, recently moved to Maui to retire. "We don't have an agenda," he said. "I just wanted to help keep this place wonderful, the best in the world."

The main purpose of the first meeting was to nominate the vice chairperson and chairperson for the CPAC. Both would play a key role in moderating the group's discussions and decisions. Planners invited attendees to provide public testimony, presumably about the individuals who might step into the committee roles. But many who came forward to speak questioned the integrity and intent of the new CPAC members. Their concerns were perhaps best summarized by testifier Jeremy Delos Reyes:

> It doesn't matter your ethnicity or nationality. But my concern is with who we elect. I don't feel that this committee fully represents the community. Because a person that lives in a gated community cannot understand a person that lives in low-income housing or subsistence living. And so, with the five people that I saw raise their hand, [they have] associations with a certain entity: Maui Land & Pine, West Maui Land, West Maui Construction—all those guys. I feel it put in favor for a certain type of development that they pushing for in West Maui...But if we are outnumbered by a certain mindset, then I feel that it's kind of faulty already. That's already diluting the community and what the community really wants.

Several testifiers nominated Nishiki as the chairperson. Michel nominated Joe Pluta for chair, and Nishiki nominated Hegger-Nordblom as the chairperson and stated her willingness to serve as vice chair. However, Hegger-Nordblom was not present. State law requires an absolute majority of all members to take action. With 13 committee members total, seven votes were needed to elect a person to a position. During the first vote, six members voted Nishiki as chair, while four voted Pluta as chair. Counsel noted that the group did not have enough votes to move forward. Their options were to either take a second vote, or wait until the next meeting to go through the process again and appoint someone as pro tem to act as chair for the current meeting. The group ultimately decided to recast their votes, electing Nishiki as chairperson with eight votes.

Nishiki then guided the group in the nomination for vice chair. Joseph Aquino nominated Jeri Dean for vice chair and Celiz seconded it. Aina Kohler nominated Pluta for the position. The first round of voting did not garner the seven votes needed to nominate either. Upon re-voting, Dean was nominated to vice chair.

After nominating the chair and vice chair, the CPAC opened up the floor to public testimony on specific items in the draft plan. Two residents of Plantation Estates and Honolua Ridge—subdivisions of multi-million-dollar homes built on two acres or more of agricultural land—requested the CPAC change their community plan designation from Agricultural to Rural Residential. John Kindred, president of the Plantation Estates Lot Owners Association, said:

> Our land is zoned Agricultural, but the nature of our community is rural. We're not opposed to agriculture. In fact, we encourage it, but rather what we're seeking to do simply is to be able to provide peace amongst our neighbors by having similar characteristics apply across the neighborhood in terms of nuisance noise, community design rules, et cetera. We receive water from a private water company; our wastewater is managed through septic tanks. Our community roads are privately funded and maintained, and our garbage is collected by private disposal company paid for by our members. We're grateful to be protected by the Maui Police Department and the Maui Fire Department.

Kindred said the community is made up of retirees, business owners, and second-home owners. There are 103 total lots in the association; half of those lots have been developed.

Michel pointed out that Plantation Estates was originally approved on the condition that part of the development would be set aside as affordable housing: "Affordable (housing) never came—till today we are still waiting. Only planning people know that from way back. Something went very wrong."

Dick Mayer, vice chair of the General Plan Advisory Committee and former citizen advisory committee member, encouraged the CPAC to use words with legal effect: shall, require, prohibit. Doing otherwise, he pointed out, would leave too much up for interpretation. Mayer said he took offense to one section being named "growth framework":

> From the beginning, this draft plan assumes that there will be significant growth of West Maui without leaving it up to you, the plan advisory

committee, to make recommendations on what changes you would like
to see in the district. You may want no growth, or you might want little
growth. A more appropriate title would be "change framework" or "plan
framework." You don't have to put the word "growth" in there if you don't
think the area is capable of handling more growth.

Lastly, Mayer pointed out that the draft plan, as the plans that came before
it had done, relied on Hawai'i's Department of Business, Economic Development and Tourism's projections for growth. The Maui County Code allows for
an alternative planning approach that does not rely on growth projections, but
rather on what the community desires in terms of population density.

> Part of the problem with growth comes from the Planning Department's
> slavish reliance on the state's DBEDT population and housing projections
> that merely continue the trends of the past, even if those trends are not what
> people want. What else could you expect from a [department] established
> to promote economic development and tourism? For example, those state
> projections show a strong growth of population in West Maui, and the
> plan has gone ahead and made those projections a foundation for this plan.

Many testifiers spoke of the nonexistent yet often promised "affordable
housing" for full-time residents. "Affordable" was not affordable for the vast
majority of West Maui residents who earned less than $44,000 annually, testi-
fier Michele Lincoln pointed out.

Others specifically called for the need to fulfill the State's legal commitment to Native Hawaiians. They urged the CPAC to take actions that would
support Native Hawaiians in building safe homes on homestead lands. They
also asked members to be cautious when making decisions where land titles
were in dispute between large land developers and claimants to *kuleana* rights
(laws protecting the entitlement of Hawaiian tenant farmers and their descendants to landlocked real estate parcels).

More broadly, public testimony acknowledged that the 1996 West Maui
Community Plan, the land use decisions that followed, and the rampant growth
and promotion of tourism was destroying West Maui. They viewed the West
Maui Community Planning process as one of the few opportunities to right
the wrongs of the past. Proposed solutions emerged in the process of the first
CPAC meeting: place a moratorium on any new hotel or commercial develop-

ment until the community planning process was complete, and stop approving development entitlements until the ones already on the books were fulfilled.

In so many words, testifiers drove home the point that West Maui's existing roads and water supply could no longer support more development. Richard Iaconetti:

> I believe we're missing a huge point here—and it's been brought up twice already—and that point is water—fresh water. There has not been a comprehensive study done geologically since 1989.... We need to stop thinking about everything else and think about water, because there's not enough, and you don't know how much is left. The mountain looks dry to me right now; I've been living here my whole life. And I don't see it getting better unless we stop everything and test the water out, the water gets back into the stream flow.

The later part of the first CPAC meeting was dedicated to providing members with an overview of their legal obligations per the Sunshine Law. Of particular interest to members were the laws created to address conflicts of interest.

> There are certain prohibitions under that article. There's a prohibition on accepting gifts or money in your position; you cannot engage in any business transaction or activity or have a financial interest that is incompatible with the proper discharge of the member's duties, or that may impair member's independence of judgment and the performance of official duty. And you cannot fail to disclose a financial interest or vote on a matter affected by such interest.

## INDEFINITE ENTITLEMENTS AND UNDUE INFLUENCE

### *August 6, 2019*

At this second meeting of the CPAC, members heard from a handful of testifiers, many of whom would become fixtures at the community plan meetings. Resident and community activist Michele Lincoln opened up testimony by reminding the CPAC that the plan carries the force of law. She called out a number of areas where the CPAC could have an impact on restoring the integrity of the plan:

The West Maui Community Plan will establish precedents for other communities to emulate. Remember, the West Maui Community Plan is an ordinance rather than mere guidance and suggestions. What you were working on is the law of the land. The CPAC could be instrumental in righting the wrongs that have proven to be the source of an unhappy and much-to-be regretted legacy. Start every conversation of updating the community plan with the premise of "love one another." That sentiment was unanimously expressed as the vision of the West Maui community. Until the land issues are addressed and resolved, there's not much hope to achieve the community we desire. Work with legal counsel to put language in the community plan to prohibit quiet title and quitclaim for the next 20 years of questionable title lands: allow for local heirs to reclaim family parcels without expensive appeals to the courts.

Van Fisher, who identified himself as a long-time real estate professional, spoke on the need to prioritize homes for full-time residents. The topic of affordable housing would come to dominate conversations at the CPAC meetings, as would the community's desire to retain land designated as agriculture. Van Fisher:

We don't need any more luxury homes; we don't need any more big ag subdivisions of luxury homes. What we need is affordable housing for people who live here. I would like you to think out of the box and consider maybe perhaps a different type of zoning overlay, which is a resident-only-zoned zoning overlay where only people who live here can live in the area. I think that there's a danger in going to these really small lots, trying to cram people into little 3,000- to 4,000-square-foot areas. It's just not good for their lives, especially now that you've allowed, or know that the county is allowing, 'ohana [family] units on these properties. I think that going with a minimum lot size of around 10,000 square feet, you can put a house on there and a couple of small 'ohana units, and some people can have some nice family areas.

*       *       *

At any point along the process for shaping a community plan, the individuals and groups involved can subtly or drastically change the direction of the plan, whether or not that direction is supported by the community, no matter how well documented the shared sentiment may be. CPAC member Ravi Bugga pointed out the plan's vulnerability to undue influence at the second meeting.

We should continue to stay involved, to make sure that all the work we're collectively doing gets listened to and doesn't get substantially changed somehow. I think it's incumbent upon all of us to just continue our involvement until the final plan is approved. And if someone attempts to change it significantly from what we believe the community wants, we should all be there to stand up and talk about it.

\*　　\*　　\*

Maui County's Long Range Planning Division staff were among the West Maui Community Plan's original authors. As planning professionals, they sought to incorporate "smart growth" principles, recommending that growth occur near existing infrastructure and community services. Their outreach efforts, what they heard from residents who attended planning events, also influenced their decisions on how to designate certain areas, such as whether to keep designated agricultural land or change it for another use. Their recommendations would later put them in conflict with developers who were proposing projects away from infrastructure, landowners who wanted to change their community plan designations (state law dictates that zoning must align with plan designations), and CPAC members who simply disagreed with the Planning Division's recommendations.

County planners Pamela Eaton and Jennifer Maydan explained the West Maui Community Plan's role within a hierarchy of plans. Adopted in 2012, the Maui Island Plan and the County Policy Plan provided the sideboards for the development of the community plans. Throughout the process, county planners advocated for alignment between the plans, especially the Maui Island Plan and the West Maui Community Plan. And they weren't the only ones. Many would later use the alignment argument while advocating for more development. This caused friction among CPAC members and staff who had different interpretations on alignment: if the Maui Island Plan drew an "urban growth" boundary around a given area, did that require the CPAC to fill in that area with development?

"What happens if we come up with recommendations and ideas that are different somehow?" Bugga asked Eaton. She replied that the answer depended on the particular topic, and the laws governing that topic. Most importantly, Eaton said the West Maui Plan should be specific to the area and represent the voice of the community.

"We should try to find areas where there might be some difference of opinion; we should try to be as specific as possible," Bugga said to his fellow committee members. "And also, as someone mentioned in the last meeting, try to be as directive as possible, saying, 'Hey, this is what the community really wants, folks. We know something was talked about X years ago, but this is today.' "

At the same meeting, Eaton and Maydan presented sections of the draft plan to the CPAC for input, review and approval. Along the way, technical subject-matter experts and county, state and federal representatives would also make recommendations that shaped the plan.

Housing and development dominated discussions among CPAC members. Committee member Jeri Dean summarized the challenge ahead by stating that we "are in a crisis on many fronts." The other members, wherever they stood on development entitlements, seemed to agree that meeting the demands for future growth would be a major challenge. They wrestled throughout the process with how to meet these needs in the face of strained resources: water supplies, roads, public beaches and parks.

Decisions made in the past West Maui Community Plan were impacting the quality of life for area residents—that much was clear. Some CPAC members openly questioned whether one of the committee's responsibilities was to rectify mistakes of the past through policies adopted today. Newly elected chairperson Kai Nishiki suggested introducing a tool to expire or "sunset" development entitlements rather than allowing them to be held or sold indefinitely. Members Hans Michel, Jeri Dean and Aina Kohler expressed concern that the CPAC was flying blind if it did not know what development had already been approved and what was in the works. There was a sense that there was an incomplete picture of existing development entitlements, and that that information was critical to what recommendations the CPAC would make.

## A County in Disrepair

### August 20, 2019

By the third meeting, in light of the conversations around strained resources, the idea of placing a hold or moratorium[2] on tourism or new commercial development seemed to be gaining steam. Albert Perez of the Maui Tomorrow

---

2. The Maui County Council voted to adopt a two-year moratorium on new hotels and visitor lodging in January 2022. The moratorium was introduced by councilmember Keani Rawlins-Fernandez. Mayor Michael Victorino vetoed the bill in July 2021. But the Council voted to override his veto months later.

Foundation, a local nonprofit that advocates for the protection of natural areas and open space, offered up language in his opening testimony at the meeting.

> Right now, I don't know how many are proposed in West Maui, but island-wide we have eight hotel proposals. And we don't need any more visitor accommodations. Right now, we're really out of balance. [ ... ] Maybe you can figure out how—if we still have an affordable housing problem in West Maui—then we won't allow any more visitor accommodations or commercial establishments to use additional wastewater. That's just the wastewater example. And you could do the same thing for water or any other type of infrastructure.

Over the next three hours of the meeting, CPAC members delved into the topic of water—how it is used, transported, and treated throughout West Maui. Presentations from water officials reaffirmed concerns over the sustainability of growth in West Maui. The area's aging water infrastructure systems had reached a point in which they needed replacement, and the county was struggling to keep up with the cost of maintenance. "The brutal truth is for the next 20 years, the timeframe of your work, mostly what you're going to see with county infrastructure is going to be a struggle just to keep the status quo," said Dave Taylor, the Maui County Capital Improvement Project director. Interestingly, Taylor framed the discussion in terms of the size of development. He alluded to the fact that larger blocks would be less of a drain on public funds:

> The big decision you make is: are we going to develop West Maui with large blocks, medium blocks or small blocks? And the smaller those blocks are, the more it falls on the county tax dollars, rates and fees to pay for that infrastructure. The more you support larger development blocks, the more that developers have to front all that, and they build that into the mortgages. So the single biggest decision you make about infrastructure, you don't really need to know anything about it—you just need to know that that land use decision you make is going to trickle down and have these huge infrastructure repercussions.

In some cases, the county was still working on projects, such as the Lahaina Watershed Project, that were listed in the 1996 West Maui Community Plan. Funding dried up for the project, said Maui County Department of Public Works (DPW) director Rowena Dagdag-Andaya. Of the 13 implementing actions in the 1996 Plan under the DPW's purview, eight were completed, seven were marked "in progress," and one action was marked "not begun."[3]

Old and uncompleted projects were now urgent matters. One example was the need to repair sinkholes that were being created by the county's aging drainage system that ran beneath the roads. The DPW had recently completed a drainage system inventory of West Maui, and had plans to assess drain line conditions over the next months to years, noted Dagdag-Andaya. With this information, the DPW could prioritize those lines needing repair and then work with the Maui County Council to secure funding for that work.

At the same time that roads and existing drainage systems needed immediate attention, some rural areas around West Maui lacked any proper drainage systems. Not only would funding be needed to maintain existing systems, but funding was needed to build proper infrastructure to deal with flooding.

At the request of the Planning Department's Long-Range Planning Division, subject-matter experts like Dagdag-Andaya, Scott Rollins and others would appear before CPAC over the next several meetings to suggest policies and objectives related to their respective expertise areas.

DPW's suggestions included ensuring drain systems comply with the county's drainage rules, revising subdivision ordinances related to drainage, requiring post-development best management practices, and pursuing other funding streams for all the work that was needed. To this last point, Dagdag-Andaya noted that some areas charged residents stormwater fees to help offset the costs of maintaining drainage systems. She later brought up the possibility of creating a county ordinance that would require property owners to keep their drainages clear of debris to ease flooding. Pursuing such a route would create an enforcement branch or a policy to support the staffing that would ensure compliance.

After the DPW's presentation, CPAC chairperson Kai Nishiki referenced the persistent flooding in the Kahana area and asked whether the county ever

---

3. Source: 2021 Annual Status Report on the Implementation of the Maui County Community Plans. The one action marked "not begun" stated: Modify restrictive building code requirements to allow new buildings and renovations to be consistent with historic designs, such as balconies and canopies that protrude over the sidewalk. "Completed" indicates the program/policy/action has been implemented. "In Progress" indicates the department or agency is addressing the program/policy/action or has addressed it to some extent since its adoption, but has not yet completed it. The "Ongoing" column indicates the program/policy/action is an ongoing effort and will never be 'completed' because of its continuing nature. "Not begun" indicates the department or agency has not taken any action on the program/policy/action.

considered other solutions, such as moving residents out of flood zones, when drainage systems appeared not to be working. Nishiki would later share similar concerns related to sea-level rise and managed retreat.

> I know that our community notices that that area is regularly underwater. And I'm just wondering, at what point do we look at something else besides drainage issues and talk about actually moving people out of these areas?

Dagdag-Andaya did not have a direct response and instead referenced an upcoming drainage study that could point to alternative solutions. While West Maui's drainage system appeared to be backlogged—literally and financially—the area's wastewater treatment plant faced different challenges. The area's plant, built in the 1970s and updated throughout the following decades, had the capacity to handle more wastewater. The problem, in most cases, was getting the sewage to the plant. The system was originally built to service the area between Kapalua in the north down to Puamana in the south. It was not built to serve areas *mauka* (inland) of the highway and south of Puamana, noted Rollins. This is where individuals and entities with financial means had an advantage. They could afford to build lines and pump stations to reach the plant. Others were not so lucky.

Besides the wastewater treatment plant, the county manages a recycled wastewater system that produces R1, the highest quality of reuse water. While the system has the potential to help alleviate the pressure placed on Maui's freshwater supply, it is far from reaching that potential. Currently, it provides R1 water mostly to the Kāʻanapali Golf Course, and secondarily to the Hyatt Regency Maui Resort and Spa, the Hyatt Residence Club Maui, and Honua Kai Resort. Rollins said a second line that had been developed in the '70s to feed a reservoir to support sugarcane and pineapple cultivation fell into disuse.

Treating and transporting water for R1 use is a costly, and sometimes energy-intensive, endeavor. Rollins said the county would need to create elevated storage and find users who can accept the water when the county pumps it. The current system, which recycles about 40 percent of the wastewater it receives, is not a 24-hour system. The remaining untreated 60 percent of wastewater goes into injection wells, which eventually discharge into the ocean. Rollins said the county is looking to build storage by tapping into existing unused reservoirs such as the Honokowai Reservoir owned by Maui Land & Pineapple Company. If that can be done, the recycled water system could eventually provide R1 water to the developments around Airport Beach, North Beach and the Kāʻanapali resort areas. From there, the county could build a loop to reach the upper reservoir owned by the Department of Hawaiian Homelands (DHHL). However, the R1 water is high in chlorides, making it less desirable for plants that are sensitive to high-chloride water. Rollins said the county has tried to address the high-salinity issue over the years but has not solved the problem.

The wastewater treatment plant and pump stations are maintained regularly. But the gravity feed lines need capacity upgrades, which is hard to do without knowing where development is happening, said Rollins. Who should pay for the upgrades? Rollins floated the idea of using impact fees, or requiring developers to pay up front for the infrastructure service. In the past, the county placed conditions on development that required the developers to help pay for the capacity upgrades. They also created assessment districts in which the county developed the infrastructure up front and then charged a fee for every house or gallon that discharged into the system.

It wasn't lost upon CPAC chairperson Nishiki that the current wastewater and recycled water systems largely benefited resorts and properties that catered to tourists and part-time residents. Substantial infrastructure investments were needed to build gravity lines, and ideally additional wastewater plants, to reach areas where residents and Native Hawaiians lived or could live.

Kai Nishiki:

I would just like to see priority given to developing DHHL lands, because as you know, we have a shortage of housing. And if we would provide water for these sorts of projects, we're actually getting local people, native people into homes versus transplants.

Scott Rollins:

It costs between $1,000 and $1,500 per foot to put a pipe in the ground in most places on this island. So it adds up in a hurry. The best alternative for Lahaina would be to build a scalping plant somewhere near the park or something like that, where we could pull water out, treat it there, and then use it there and then send the remaining back to the treatment plant. And that's something we've discussed, we've done a few studies on, but we have not put it in our 20-year plan as of yet.

The Wastewater Reclamation Division gets the majority of its revenue from sewer fees. Everyone who is connected to the system pays to maintain it. The division also receives some funding from recycled water rates and haulers.

The system costs $47 million per year to maintain, which leaves $8 million for capital improvement projects (CIP)—only a fraction of what was needed to complete the $39 million in CIP projects in 2019 alone. The division meets this funding shortfall with supplemental funding from the state's revolving fund, the State Department of Health, grants from developers, and bonds. Bonds are problematic because they need to be repaid with interest. In 2019 alone, the debt service was over $14 million. As was the case with DPW's drainage system, funding is an ongoing challenge for maintenance.

*    *    *

CPAC members asked numerous questions related to water supply and shortages. Nishiki expressed concern over the proliferation of private wells, and what impact those wells would have on West Maui's water supply. The issue Nishiki raised is one of the area's numerous water problems, many of which would be highlighted and discussed in the process of developing the West Maui Community Plan.

West Maui is now a designated water management area. Water users are required to apply for water use permits. As Bianca Isaki and Jonathan Scheuer explained in their book *Water and Power in West Maui* (University of Hawaiʻi Press, 2021), "All water users are required to apply for permits in WMAs, but 'water user' has a specific meaning that excludes, for practical purposes, the everyday domestic user. 'Water users' include county municipal water supply purveyors, well drillers, and other, generally larger scale, water system developers."

Theoretically, water availability is one of the key determinants of whether or not to approve developments, and the primary figure used to determine how much water the state can draw from the aquifer without harming it is "sustainable yield." For West Maui, that figure has been set at 34 million gallons per day. Of that yield, approximately six million gallons per day, or 18 percent of sustainable yield, is currently withdrawn, said Eva Blumenstein, planning program manager at the Maui County Water Department. But relying on this figure is problematic, as Isaki and Scheuer wrote:

> However, administrative predictions of sufficient amounts of West Maui groundwater resources are predicated on 'sustainable yield,' which is meant to describe the amount of water that can be withdrawn without harming the aquifer system. As discussed *supra*, many have criticized 'sustainable yield' as an impractical concept that does not describe on-the-ground realities and

impacts to communities and natural resources. Further, for many decades, West Maui residents have observed that expanding water development would not reduce water needs. This is primarily due to increasing resort and residential development.

Kaleo Manuel, deputy director for the State of Hawai'i's commission on Water Resource Management, recommended that planning staff and/or CPAC review the updated water resource protection plan, one of the five components within the Hawai'i Water Plan, and see "how this plan is or is not inconsistent with the some of the policy recommendations" under the umbrella of the state's plan.

In developing groundwater for future development, the County needs to consider not only current water levels but the impact that uses will have on the aquifer's ability to recharge over time, noted Blumenstein. Some factors decreasing recharge included long periods of drought, low rainfall, and a decrease in irrigation. A lot of surface water was diverted to water sugarcane lands, which increased artificial recharge to the aquifer. On the other hand, factors that increase groundwater recharge include having intact forested watersheds in the upper mountain regions. Such areas foster persistent cloud cover and fog cloud cover, and nearly all recharge (an estimated 96 percent) is natural rainfall and fog. Blumenstein remarked,

> Some of the things that I want to bring to your attention in terms of looking at policies for resilient systems—these are also coming out of the draft water use development plan. There is a need to develop basal groundwater to meet population growth for [the] west side and also because we anticipate there'll be less surface water available for drinking water purposes. [...] Considering also climate change impacts, we may not rely on surface water as we have in the past. Also, well development coordination between the different providers [is important]: it doesn't really matter if it's the county or private purveyor that serves the [planned growth], but it matters how that groundwater is developed.

## Discrepancies Between Plans

### August 22, 2019

An estimated 12,000 commuters drive in and out of the West Maui area on a daily basis. Most of them use Honoapi'ilani Highway as their main entry point.

With only two lanes running parallel to the ocean, the influx of vehicles coming into and out of West Maui causes traffic jams that can last for well over an hour. High tide and surf sometimes flood the highway, exacerbating the congestion. Like West Maui's water supplies and infrastructure, the state of traffic also showed the strain of growth.

Some of the area's roadways were managed by the county, others by state and federal agencies. The CPAC needed to hone in on what they could improve under the county's jurisdiction as well as how they could advocate for their priorities at the state and federal levels.

Their early conversations centered on how to improve Maui's public transportation system with Maui County Department of Transportation Director Marc Takamori. The loop servicing the West Maui area was by far the county's most popular route. He said a recent audit showed that the island's bus service provided only the bare minimum service, meaning it had room to expand. But they needed to conduct research to figure out what additions would be financially feasible or supported by user fees. Marc Takamori:

> Recently, I think within the last year or so, the county council did an audit on our department to figure out how we're doing. The auditors basically came back and said that with regards to our fixed route system, we have the most bare-bones system that you can provide services and community. So as of right now, we take that as we can only do better by adding more service, by adding more routes.... One of the things I think we want to look at is, you know, if we're going to propose reasons, fees changes, then we can potentially propose additional routes in different areas as well.

CPAC members were eager to offer solutions to improve the public transportation system—solutions such as adding a direct airport-to-hotel bus service and allowing passengers to carry surfboards and luggage onto the bus. In the book *Thinking About Traffic in West Maui* (UH Press, 2021), the authors take a deep dive into the various big traffic solutions for the area, including building a tunnel through the mountainside and creating more bike-friendly systems.

\* \* \*

Concerns about climate change, sea-level rise and managed retreat begin to emerge as a topic of discussion in the context of road improvements. Maui County DPW Director Rowena Dagdag-Andaya spoke on the topic at the August 22, 2019 meeting:

We mentioned a lot about sea-level rise and climate change. When we think of future transportation projects, that's always front and center, or what's going to happen to our road, or what's going to happen to our project. In the next 20, 30, 50 years, due to climate change, we got to start planning for that. Are we doing managed retreat in various areas in the coastal areas?

*   *   *

Many of the CPAC members expressed interest in creating safe, walkable communities, and the construction and maintenance of walkways falls under the county's jurisdiction. These early conversations planted the seeds for what would become policies and actions to support walkability and other modes of non-motor transportation. Such decisions were tied to development, as Dagdag-Andaya explained:

> When we look at transportation, we've got to look at land use at the same time—what are we going to put in our neighborhoods? Because whatever you decide with land use, that's going to affect transportation. It's going to affect affordable housing.... We've got to think holistically when we're planning new neighborhoods or even retrofitting older neighborhoods.

Dagdag-Andaya said the DPW was focused on making progress on the West Maui Greenway, a proposed 25-mile, multi-use trail utilizing the abandoned cane haul road running parallel to Honoapiʻilani Highway.

*   *   *

A reoccurring conversation that emerged from the August 22, 2019, CPAC meeting was how the West Maui Community Plan would interface with existing county and statewide plans for transportation, water, land use, housing and other issues. Committee members wondered out loud how discrepancies between plans would be resolved, and how residents and government officials would balance competing interests. "In the development of the community plan, if we come up with things that are different from what's in the transportation improvement plan, how does that jibe?" asked CPAC member Dylan Payne. "Along those same lines, does the state have to consider what's in the community plan?"

A timely example of this overlap was with the Maui Metropolitan Planning

Organization's (MPO)[4] Transportation Improvement Plan (TIP), which was being developed at the same time as the West Maui Community Plan. MPO's Executive Director, Lauren Armstrong, explained that the West Maui Community Plan and other umbrella planning documents provided the vision and priorities for the TIP:

> In terms of planning here on the left, we have our statewide transportation plan, our Maui Island plan, and community plans. And those are really the visionary documents that are guiding the priorities for the network. With Hele Mai Maui, that I'll talk about later, this is our 20-year vision for transportation. That's where we start to dive in a little deeper on specific projects and funding streams that we want over the next 20 years.

By 2019, MPO had already begun the process of compiling transportation project ideas from various existing plans and community input. The priorities they identified, such as the completion of the Lahaina Bypass road project, realignment of Honoapiʻilani Highway, creation of a Lahaina Transit Hub and progress on the West Maui Greenway, were all supported by the CPAC. The synergy between the two plans allowed the CPAC to focus on advocating for shared priorities and identifying ways to fund these improvements.

## Prioritizing a Thousand Action Items

### *August 28, 2019*

The Maui Island Plan and the existing community plans contained more than 1,200 policies and actions, according to Pamela Eaton, Long Range Planning Department staff. She used this number to illustrate the breadth of existing plans and advised against duplicating content between plans. However, some CPAC members such as chairperson Kai Nishiki would later push back against this approach. On key issues, Nishiki insisted the West Maui Community Plan include duplicate or similar actions to emphasize their importance to the community.

The planning staff drafted the section on transportation and presented it

---

4. MPO, a federally mandated agency formed in 2016 by the State of Hawaiʻi and County of Maui, is charged with facilitating comprehensive planning for federally funded or regionally significant transportation systems on Maui.

to the CPAC for the first time on August 28, 2019. Maydan said that in future meetings, committee members would receive draft content ahead of time. Planners used their discretion to include some of the incomplete or ongoing actions from the 1996 West Maui Community Plan in the new plan. County planner Jennifer Maydan:

> [Policy] Seven: support construction of the planned Lahaina Bypass Road in such a way as to promote safe, efficient travel across the region without encouraging further urbanization or impeding agricultural operations. And as we have noted here, this one is a carryover from the 1996 West Maui Community Plan. We didn't edit it, but we wanted to include it in here because we obviously hear that this is still quite a bit of a priority. So this is one where we're assuming you may want to edit it some, but we just thought it was important to note that that came from the 1996 plan. [Policy] Eight: support improvements for the safe and convenient movement of people and goods, pedestrians and bicycles in the Lahaina region, particularly along Honoapi'ilani Highway, Front Street, Lahainaluna Road, Waine'e Street and lower Honoapi'ilani Road and seek to establish a regional network of bikeways and pedestrian paths. This one also came from the 1996 plan. We added in Lahainaluna Road and Waine'e because we hear from you all in the community that that's very important.

This was the first meeting where committee members discussed policy and began to hint at their own priorities and the types of actions they would support or oppose. Some saw the plan as a place to encourage but not require certain practices; others saw it as a document that should use legally binding language to dictate actions they viewed as beneficial to West Maui.

The earliest example of how CPAC members diverged on their approach was with a policy intended to encourage the use of energy-efficient vehicles. Though most members expressed their desire to take actions to address the impacts of climate change, they could not agree on whether or not to require electric charging stations for new commercial and multifamily developments.

Dylan Payne and Ravi Bugga leaned away from words like "require" and "shall" that would legally require compliance, while others, such as Joseph Aquino and Kai Nishiki, favored the use of unequivocal language. On the issue of requiring electric charging stations for new developments, however, a majority of the CPAC ultimately voted in favor of requiring them with a caveat: "until future technological advances make this unnecessary."

# A Pause on New Developments

*September 3, 2019*

In a move that surprised some of her fellow members, CPAC chairperson Kai Nishiki introduced a letter to request Maui County halt approvals for new visitor and large commercial developments until after the West Maui Community Plan's adoption. She said the draft letter, which appears below in its entirety, was modeled after a similar letter submitted by the Maui Island Plan's General Plan Advisory Committee.

> *This is not intended to be a moratorium of any sort. It is simply a request to the various departments to please respect the process of the West Maui Community Plan and hold off on big, large developments or more visitor accommodations just until we're finished, which is not that long—six months—and then some time for the County Council and Planning Commission and the Mayor to sign off.*

---

To: Mayor Michael Victorino    September 1, 2019

Maui County Council, Kelly King, Chair
Maui County Planning Department, Michele McLean, Director
Maui Planning Commission (Maui Island)
State of Hawaii Land Use Commission
From: West Maui Community Plan Advisory Committee

RE: **Approval Of Developments prior to Adoption of an Updated West Maui Community**

Despite the enormous number of changes that have taken place in West Maui, the **West Maui Community Plan** has not been updated since it was adopted in 1996. We finally have in place a Community Plan Advisory Committee (CPAC) is expected to recommend a long-range plan for West Maui in the next few months.

Our Committee will have an opportunity to examine past trends and the cumulative impacts of the many changes that have taken place. We will evaluate the adequacy of our water quantity and quality, housing needs, highways and traffic, schools, parks, medical facilities, etc. Thereafter, the Committee will advise you on the future directions and approach that the residents Of West Maui would like to pursue.

Currently, many developers are assertively trying to gain approval for their large projects **before** the CPAC has completed the West Maui Community Plan process including an in-depth evaluation of West Maui's needs, infrastructure, carrying capacity, etc. On a regular basis, we read about proposed major projects from Kapalua to the Pali.

We empathize with your dilemma in being approached by developers who ask you approve their specific project. We know that you are interested in trying to meet the needs of our residents. You may even feel that you must make decisions granting approvals and entitlements long before adequate infrastructure is funded and built.

Therefore, **our CPAC sincerely requests that until AFTER our community plan process has been completed and the new West Maui Plan is adopted, that any visitor accommodation expansion and all new large (over 20 units) developments will NOT be approved or entitled, except for 100% "affordable housing" and perhaps those projects already having complete community plan and zoning entitlements.**

Our committee's request intends to give you confidence that if you wait until after the West Maui Community Plan has been approved, you will be able to make far better decisions as to which projects/developments would be most beneficial and appropriate.

We do **not** believe this will be a moratorium on housing because there are many thousand units on Maui Island including West Maui already having received some level of entitlement; and that does not even include small sub-divisions, ohanas, and many potential agriculture subdivisions.

We will support you in your effort to implement the new West Maui Community Plan as it was intended to be,—a comprehensive guide to thoughtful and balanced community planning. Please take any necessary action, for example, to inform the public that you will not be approving West Maui developments prior to the West Maui Community Plan adoption. Let the public know that Maui will be developed in an orderly manner in the best interest of residents today and in the future.

———————————

CPAC members Joseph Pluta and Dylan Payne sharply criticized Nishiki's proposal. Their sentiments provided an early indication of how committee members would clash over West Maui's development. Pluta, a longtime community volunteer and realtor, was the first to speak up: "This is kind of like an unnecessary step, or almost saying that (the) Planning Commission and Department doesn't know how to properly process applications and permits. I think they know what they're doing. I don't think this is necessary." Dylan Payne, too, disapproved of the letter:

> I strongly oppose this letter. I don't support it. And I think to kind of echo Joe's sentiment, I think the planning process is robust, and it has to go through all the various channels. I think this is not the right move. And I think it's a bit disingenuous to say, "Oh, that community planning process is going to be done real quick," because we've seen in the past, like on Molokai for example, it took several years for them to get their community plan approved. So I think this is the wrong thing to do. I think the planning process, as it sits, is more than enough of a gauntlet for anybody to need to run without putting up these types of additional barriers and obstacles.

Nishiki pressed on despite their objections: "Do you feel that we need more visitor accommodations or housing that's not affordable in the next six months to a year?" Pluta said he didn't think West Maui needed more visitor accommodations or non-affordable housing; he simply believed that a process was already in place to properly vet development proposals. Payne responded, "I think this letter is misguided. I don't think we need more hotel rooms. I do think we need more housing. And as I read through this letter, the only thing that I see this doing is making it harder to do that." Affordable housing is the most needed type of housing, but all housing helps, Payne said.

The three committee members continued to argue their positions while other members interjected briefly to offer their perspectives. Ravi Bugga suggested replacing the reference to affordable housing with "any housing for residents" in response to Payne's concerns. He said he would support a letter with changes. Karen Comcowich supported Nishiki's letter as proposed:

> I don't have an objection. I wish we'd gotten this letter earlier. But to say that we're just allowing a hundred percent affordable housing gives the Planning Department an extra something to look back on and say, "This letter is also from the West Maui CPAC; they want a hundred percent affordable housing." So if we're only putting a damper on luxury developments, basically, and hotels and timeshares, we don't need any more of that. If you support affordable housing, and you want to prevent our land from going to people who have the money to develop estates, essentially, you should support the letter as a way to temporarily say that we're not going to do anything except affordable housing. If you really support affordable housing, this letter helps that.

Hans Michel said he opposed the letter because he believed it would negatively impact a pending commercial project in Lahaina and hurt local businesses.

At Nishiki's request, both Planning Department Director Michele McLean and Deputy Corporation Counsel Michael Hopper offered their opinions on the matter. Neither of them was concerned about its substance, and neither found any legal or practical issues with it. But their opinions would do little to dissuade CPAC members from changing their positions.

McLean explained that the letter would not interfere with her department's responsibilities to process requests, but rather it would serve as another reference for decision makers:

> Comparing this letter to the letter that was sent by the GPAC [General Plan Advisory Committee], this letter is not as extreme, doesn't ask for as much, isn't as far-reaching as that one. When I first heard about this idea, I was concerned about how far that letter went. But looking at this, realistically, as the chair said, this is a request. It's not binding. And so, for the Planning Department, if projects come and fall under this request, we still have an obligation to process them. The kinds of projects that this describes aren't ones that the Planning Department has full authority to approve in any way. The project would go to the Planning Commission, or to the Council. And so, we would still feel an obligation to process that unless the law changes. But what we could do is include this letter in our analysis and make sure that this letter is presented to whoever that decision maker is—Planning

Commission or the Council—so that they're aware of this request and can factor that into their final decision making.

Similarly, Hopper had no legal objections to the letter, though he cautioned against using any language that would exclude any one particular group.

I don't see a legal issue with this request. I think it's something that you can make. You've pointed out several times, this in and of itself does not change the county code. So the county code stays in place and all laws stay in place unless they're amended at some point. So this would deal mainly with discretionary approvals—unless there's laws amended, it would be you're basically urging the policymakers to adopt this policy.

The CPAC spent the next hour of their meeting discussing edits to the letter in what was sometimes a tense exchange. Committee members said they were concerned over the possible unintended consequences of the letter.

A number of suggestions were floated by members, including removing the "100 percent" before affordable housing and adding the term "owner occupant housing." CPAC member Jeri Dean, who said she supported the intention of the letter, shared her concern that some folks did not qualify for affordable housing[5] under the current definition.

I definitely appreciate the effort put into the letter. And I appreciate the intention of the letter as well. There are many points that I agree about it. And it's an agreement that I think we mostly generally share as far as the development of—especially—hotels. Like, my jaw just dropped when you said that there are actually proposals for more hotels in Kaanapali. I think the only section that I'd like to see some tweaking is the "100% affordable housing." And the reason for that is I absolutely support affordable housing a hundred percent. However, I also know that there is a large number of residents who live here that don't qualify for affordable housing. They're part of the middle- to low-class.

Though Payne said he found the discussion interesting, he reiterated concerns that the letter fell outside of the CPAC's purview: "Our job is to advise

---

5. Housing is considered "affordable" when costs are at or below 30% of household income.

on the community plan, and I think we're wasting our time doing this. I think we should be focusing on the community plan."

Nishiki strongly disagreed:

> We have this on the agenda; we have adequate time to discuss it this evening. And I do think that it's important for us to convey to the Council and the various departments that we want our time to be respected. And why would we want the Council or the Planning Commission—prior to us even being able to come up with a plan and communicate what our needs are—why would we want an outside agency approving something for our district that we may not desire in our community? So I do think it's very valuable. And I respect everyone's time here and your opinions. However, I really feel that this is a very important issue for us to say, 'Hey, affordable housing is a priority for us."

Hopper presented CPAC with their options for moving forward. They could take a vote on approving the letter and later change its language, or they could defer action, come back to the committee with a revised letter, and then take a vote. But in light of sunshine laws, he advised against communicating with each other about suggested changes outside of scheduled and publicized meetings. Nishiki opted to defer a vote and present a revised letter at a future meeting.

*                    *                    *

The next section up for review, "Ready and Resilient Systems," covered a broad range of issues related to natural resources, including drought, water supplies and sea-level rise. Here again, as Jennifer Maydan explained, the Long Range Planning Division drafted a set of policies and actions, with input from various government agencies, for the CPAC to review.

> A lot of the policies we pulled from the presentations of the various subject-matter experts provided to you folks over several meetings, some of them we pulled out of your discussions and questions with those folks. Some of them came out of technical resource papers, especially regarding sea-level rise and shoreline hazards, really came out of the presentation as well as the more in-depth technical resource paper.

A challenge in this approach, which became apparent in early discussions, was that committee members sometimes struggled to understand the terminology used in the recommendations. For example, a draft water use policy included the terms "optimize pumpage," which refers to efficient pumping and not more pumping.

*   *   *

The impacts of climate change, namely sea-level rise and drought, featured prominently in a way they had not in the previous plan. There seemed to be a growing recognition that Maui County needed a better understanding of how these impacts could potentially harm county infrastructure.[6] Sea-level rise and the concept of "managed retreat," or moving buildings inland, emerged as an important ongoing conversation.

One of the first policy recommendations related to this topic was to "reserve existing golf course facilities as future receiving areas to transfer existing development impacted by climate change." Kate Blystone explained its origin:

> This is a discussion we've had in the planning department in the Long Range Division, thinking about places where we can put uses that are currently occupied on the shoreline. We need a place for them to go, and that might be a good place. And we wanted to bring it to you to have that discussion to see whether or not this is something you resonate with.

As he would throughout the planning process, Joe Pluta wondered about whether the policy would infringe on private property rights.

> I guess I had a problem with the way that says "reserve existing golf courses." It looks as if somehow we have the right to put restrictions on them for a specific purpose. And do we have that? Is that even lawful for us to do that?

---

6. The findings from the first phase of a vulnerability assessment of Maui County's parks was released in November 2021. Researchers concluded: "All 65 parks in the study will experience long-term shoreline change due to sea level rise, some parks more than others. Seventy-eight park facilities (restrooms, parking lots, picnic shelters, etc.) or 36 percent of facilities in parks included in this study are expected to be exposed to sea level rise within the next 30 years or earlier if high tide and wave events and storm surge impact the shoreline as has occurred at Baldwin Park. Access to most parks on State and County roads will be impaired by sea level rise. Approximately 32 miles of State and County roads will be inundated by sea level rise impairing access to 40 percent of County parks. Finally, flooding and land loss due to sea level rise is likely to occur within the next 30 years for 46 parks or 72 percent of the parks in the study without action."

The policy would not restrict existing uses, county planner Jennifer Maydan explained.

> Joe, this policy would not restrict the existing use entitled to them for golf courses on those properties. It wouldn't stop that use. It's just identifying those golf courses as potentially good receiving areas, as the sea level rises and uses need to retreat from the shoreline, that the golf courses might be appropriate areas for those users to retreat to but not restricting their current use as golf courses today.

Fractures emerged on the CPAC as policy conversations progressed. Some members advocated for a hands-off approach to what they viewed as private property rights concerns; others wanted to aggressively manage what they viewed as irresponsible growth.

*        *        *

Built into the process of community planning are conflicts of priority. In the case of the West Maui Community Plan, county officials and advisory members argued over writing implementable policies that would also address the community's concerns. The ongoing conflict revealed itself early when one suggestion to modify language of a draft policy bubbled into a disagreement about what is and is not a realistic goal.

Citing concerns over water quality, chairperson Kai Nishiki suggested changing the word "decrease" to "eliminate" in a draft action aimed at managing injection control wells. But eliminating the wells was not a realistic goal, said Eric Nakagawa, Maui County Department of Environmental Management director. His response triggered a discussion among county officials and CPAC members about how wastewater is treated or disposed of in landlocked states. The point members were making was that Maui County did have alternative means to dispose of the waste—the real barrier was money and prioritization. Nakagawa's response opened up a philosophical discussion about whether actions were truly "unattainable" or whether the county simply did not want to deal with them. Planning Director Michele McLean offered her take:

> These plans don't get implemented, and one of the reasons they don't get implemented is because they're not realistic. And in terms of goals, one of the Planning Department's goals is to end up with plans that are realistic and truly implementable. You're hearing from the director of the department

saying that elimination is unrealistic. You could say "strive to eliminate," but to just say straight out "eliminate"—that's not a realistic implementing action. If that's what you folks choose to do, that's your prerogative to make that recommendation.

At the time of the meeting, the community was very concerned about untreated sewage harming local beaches and threatening the health of residents. Maui County was being sued by several environmental nonprofits for violating the Clean Water Act. In July 2021, the Hawai'i Federal District Court would rule that Maui County was required to get a Clean Water Act permit for its injection wells at the Lahaina Wastewater Reclamation Facility in West Maui. The decision ended a nine-year legal battle. Nishiki, who became upset over the conversation, continued to challenge officials on the issue:

> I really feel like our committee members are looking out for what's in the best interests of our community. And sometimes we hear from the directors and from the departments, and they're mostly like, CYA—you guys are just trying to make it so you can get out of implementing an action that our community really wants. And we as a community are tired of hearing about injection wells and knowing that our kids are swimming in poop water every day. And our visitors are coming here, and we're selling them vacations while they're swimming in poop and pee and pharmaceutical drugs. And at some point that has to end. And, you know, I don't appreciate the director coming up here and saying that this is an unrealistic goal. It's not an unrealistic goal. It's just one that the county is unwilling to implement.

Following Nishiki's remarks, Dave Taylor offered to provide comment to help with discussion but she cut him off, saying, "I know you also support injection wells, so perhaps not." Later, CPAC member Dylan Payne invited Taylor to share his thoughts. Taylor responded,

> My comment is not about any specific infrastructure. It's not just about injections. It's very general. One of the difficulties we have in implementation, when specific technology is mentioned, is we're locked to that specific technology. I would suggest that you might want to think about the end results you want. . . . In this case, the chair mentioned her concern about ocean water quality. Rather than talking about a specific technology, you could frame that by saying all West Maui water should exceed state standards

by 50 percent. And whether that means we change the wastewater system or drainage or something else, let the technical people figure that out.

## SIGNIFICANT FUNDING AND SAFETY NEEDS
*September 5, 2019*

The mauka realignment of Honoapi'ilani Highway and the completion of the Lahaina Bypass project have long been priorities for West Maui. The bypass, once complete, could significantly ease traffic by allowing commuters to make a straight shot into town. The highway's realignment, however, had become an urgent need in recent years as rising sea level and storms periodically flooded parts of the highway. CPAC member Joseph Pluta spoke to the urgency:

> How do we divert [the traffic] right now so that these areas that are currently critical, we don't have to wait till a bypass happens? [The realignment] should be happening right now; we need to plan to be able to not have us cut off from the other side.

Though the CPAC, state, county and federal officials agreed on the transportation priorities for West Maui, the projects required significant funding. The bypass completion would cost an estimated $70 million, according to Robin Shishido, Hawai'i Department of Transportation engineering manager. The realignment of 4.5 miles of Honoapi'ilani Highway was estimated in 2021 to cost $90 million. With the cost of the projects on the table, the CPAC's conversation with Shishido shifted to how the county could generate additional funding through user fees and other creative methods. Advisory member Aina Kohler mentioned this in her remarks:

> I feel like the Department of Transportation really does know what needs to be done. And it's just a matter of prioritizing and finding funding for it. And it's just going to be time. So for me, I would hope that maybe we could be open-minded about other ways of finding funding.

The advisory members offered several ideas for generating additional transportation project funding. Their suggestions included creating toll roads, charging parking fees at select county parks, and fundraising to cover the cost of environmental impact statements. Shishido questioned whether some of those ideas would generate the level of funding needed to support the projects. He highlighted instead the potential of a rental car surcharge and mentioned a pilot project to collect fees based on miles versus fuel.

> Early this year, we started a demonstration project called the Hawaiʻi Road User Charge. This is just a project to look at an alternative way to collect revenue, rather than the gas tax...other states are realizing that as cars get more fuel-efficient, the gas tax money is going down. So right now, we collect about 35 percent of our funding from the gas tax. So we're looking at a project, or demonstration project, to look at collecting revenue by the miles you drive instead.

Maui Metropolitan Planning Organization Director Lauren Armstrong agreed that the rental car surcharge was the easiest and most direct way to generate additional funds.

> Originally, the legislators had asked for an additional $4.50—they got $2. And the requirement to keep the funds on the island in which they were generated was also removed. As we know, as bills go through the legislature, they change significantly. I think it would be wise to see the funds from this recent additional surcharge be used by the department to implement projects. From a practical standpoint, I know we've had a lot of discussion about the mauka realignment versus the Lahaina Bypass north....I think if you can't get to Lahaina, it doesn't matter if there's a bypass north. On the other hand, both of these projects are critically needed—the bypass north is a lot closer to ready to implement. I think it's really important for Maui to make use of the rental car surcharge funds that we have if the DOT is ready to work with the community to build that project in the next three years.

Later in the meeting, the conversation shifted toward the connection between roads and fire safety. Drought, hot weather and fallow farm lands contributed to an unusually high number of wildfires on Maui in 2019. The fires, combined with limited water supplies and inadequate escape routes, worried many CPAC members and other residents. The Lahaina fire station is the busiest of all Maui County stations. Battalion Chief Kaulana Kino spoke about the fire outlook for the area and advocated for the fire department's inclusion in considering development proposals:

With our changing weather conditions, we can expect to see a lot more wildland-urban interface and brush fires moving forward in the future. So how, as the West Maui CPAC and as the Maui Fire Department, can we both support that? For West Maui development, some of the things that can be considered over the lifespan of this plan . . . a lot of the driving factors will not necessarily be through my fire department. [They'll] be through development, through growth, through access. From our point of view, one of the main things that we want to highlight is that we're included in planning so that we can provide valuable input into how our transportation infrastructure looks when we go to design these new communities. What are some smart approaches we can take towards development? For example, before I left the office today, [someone] pointed out a good idea is, in most subdivisions, we put the park at the center. If we were to put the park on one of the ends of the development [instead], that right there gives us a one- to two-football-field-sized abatement area where we can much easier defend homes.

Committee members understood the nexus between safety and development design, and they would take steps to develop policies to support safer neighborhoods. Chairperson Kai Nishiki pointed out, "Developers are also asking to get exemptions for through streets in subdivisions that want to do cul-de-sacs, and I just want to hear from your point of view: is that in the best interest of our community?" He responded: "From the point of providing emergency services, through streets will always provide better access to neighborhoods. . . . Cul-de-sacs can always present challenges as far as access, turnaround time, or location to stand pipes and hydrants." Kino also advocated for building a new station at Olowalu because of its proximity to large fires, high collision areas and ocean rescue occurrences.

## "We Have a Dirty Water Problem in West Maui"
### *September 24, 2019*

Kai Nishiki's letter to the county was on the agenda once again. The letter requested that new developments be put on hold until the West Maui Community Plan was completed. Though a vote on how to proceed would be deferred to a future meeting, seven people testified in support of the letter, citing concerns over poorly planned growth. Gordon Firestein and Tom Landrigan were among those voices. Firestein commented:

You all have a very, very demanding job. And you're making a valuable contribution with your service on this committee, which is in large part why I'm here to urge you to approve the letter to the county item on your agenda tonight. This is a critically important step in assuring that your hard work counts for something in the end. Case in point, the Makila Farms project: if County Council approves it next week, this will amount to spot planning based on the 201H Fast Track[7] rules in an area which the community, through this process, has explicitly said ought not to be developed in this way.

This is completely antithetical to the values underlying the CPAC process, which is all about long-term planning, about looking carefully at the bigger picture, about considering the needs of the community. Now everyone agrees that we need more affordable housing. And your letter includes an exemption for 100 percent affordable developments and other projects already entitled but not yet built. The draft letter is a completely reasonable request to the county to respect what you are doing and exercise a little patience until you've been able to complete your work, while at the same time allowing projects to go forward that are clearly needed by the community.

Like Firestein, Landrigan expressed concerns about developer Peter Martin's proposed Makila Farms project. In his opinion, developers like Martin were abusing the expedited permitting process to advance projects the community clearly opposed.

Basically, Fast Track is being abused. The volumes of paperwork dropped on the county with the 45-day deadline to act is unreasonable. It is reminiscent of the worldwide tourist scam Three-card Monte, or shell game—or for that matter, any con game that you've experienced where a decision has to be made immediately, and odds are slanted against you. There's time to consider affordable housing. Reject these developments now and seek other developers willing to partner with the county. Look for sincere business people who care so much that they do not demand the cash windfall for appearing to be altruistic.

---

7. Fast-track permitting is an expedited review process that may be granted to "a project comprised of 100 percent residential workforce housing units with a fully-executed residential workforce housing agreement between the developer and the County, recorded in the bureau of conveyances or registered in the land court." Maui County Code 2.96.160.

With cultural resources slated for the day's agenda, testifier Dina Edmisson spoke about protecting *kanaka maoli* (native Hawaiians) as a cultural resource.

> I would like to speak to the preservation of another very important, in fact vital, part of our culture: kanaka maoli. If kanaka maoli cannot afford to live here, thrive here, raise families here, grow old and retire here, then protecting every architectural and cultural and spiritually sacred site is for nothing. If we don't act on immediate and significant solutions to create lasting affordable housing for local people, then you're just going to have a bunch of immigrant mainlanders standing around looking at historical sites—no one practicing the culture, no one perpetuating the culture, no one teaching the culture and no one leading us to protect the culture. Therefore, I propose the following in the spirit of kuleana lands: I would like to see increased access to and families able to live and farm upon agricultural-zoned lands.

In her testimony, Maui County councilwoman Tamara Paltin floated the idea of revoking development entitlements from projects that have been held by developers for decades with no end in sight:

> When guys sit on their entitlements for 10, 20, 30 years, it just, in my opinion, hurts planning and hurts the community and hurts our abilities to have a livable, workable community. I'm not sure what can be done about that, but I would just encourage the strongest policy language that you can come up with for environmental reasons to have a sunset time on entitlements. If folks aren't making any kind of progress in 10, 20 years or any kind of trying effort, then we need to give somebody else a chance. Because not doing that has led to the situation we're in now, where we're fighting over 19 affordable units that is sprawl in the middle of the transit corridor.

After public testimony closed, CPAC members heard from environmental and cultural resource professionals about West Maui's lands, water and culture. Their scientific data showed an increase in water pollution, a decline in live coral cover, and worsened drought.

Their concerns were nothing new. Environmentalists had long sounded the alarm about the trajectory of West Maui's environmental health. Back in 1995, in an article titled "County plans for West Maui scrutinized," the *Lahaina News* reported:

[Mark] Howland, a wetland biologist, called the ecological changes he sees in West Maui "alarming." The concrete drainageways he sees all over this side are 1940s technology which allow large amounts of nutrients to enter the coastal environment, contributing to seaweed problems. "It's not ocean upwelling [causing heavy algae blooms]," Howland said. "It's shoreline development being unchecked and unregulated."

Howland's calls for better planning were echoed by environmentalists more than 20 years later.

"We have a dirty water problem in West Maui," said Tova Callender with West Maui Ridge 2 Reef, an organization that works to find and address the sources of land-based pollution impacting nearshore waters. Every area from Honolua to the Pali was failing state standards for water quality, based on their high levels of turbidity and nutrients.

A number of factors were contributing to poor water quality: legacy sediment from plantation-era lands, stormwater runoff, coastal erosion[8] and injection wells. These were all dumping excessive amounts of nutrients onto West Maui's coral reefs, contributing to their sharp decline.

Nutrient levels, a measure of water quality, exceeded state standards in Kapalua Bay, Ka'opala, Pohaku, and Canoe Beach. And because West Maui had not reached the population threshold to trigger permit requirements for water discharge, much of the water entering the ocean was untreated and unmanaged. She encouraged the CPAC to put measures in place to reduce stormwater runoff and carefully consider development.

At this point, there is not a lot of additional management that happens. When [the sign] says, "This drain runs into the ocean," it really does. But something to bear in mind as we go forward: as you allow more development and increase that impervious surface, it's more water moving more quickly, driving more pollutants into the ocean.

"Ridge 2 Reef" implies that we're also concerned about the reefs. And when we talk about the reefs in West Maui, we have this USGS mapped effort. You can see there's a concentration in Kā'anapali around the corner to Honokowai, as well as the Olowalu stretch, that are the biggest chunks of reef we're looking at when we're talking about reef here. Thanks to the

---

8.  "Scientists say West Maui is one of the regions hardest hit by coastal erosion—and many residents are growing increasingly alarmed by the impacts." *Hawaii News Now,* September 27, 2022.

Department of Aquatic Resources, there's a very long data set that tracks, on a transect, the percent [of] live coral cover. So if you had a meter-by-meter square, and you plumped it down and counted how much of that was live, you would have this data that would then populate these graphs. Red is bad. Red means declining precipitously. And you'll see in Honolua Bay, [live coral cover] went from 42 percent to nine percent over the timeframe of this dataset. That's pretty scary. In other areas it's not quite so bad, but overall, we are seeing a loss and decline.

Callender's presentation and that of Jennifer VanderVeur from the Coral Reef Alliance bolstered some of the policy decisions the CPAC would later make, such as protecting streams and gulches as catchment areas for sediment.

Up mauka, the forests were not faring too much better. Pomaikaʻi Kaniaupio-Crozier of Puʻu Kukui Watershed Preserve poignantly spoke about the impacts of climate change, the increase in severe storms and intense but brief rainfall events, and drought in areas once abundant with water.

Remember that pretty picture with the waterfall? Well, Puʻu Kukui averages nearly 400 inches of rain per year. Sometimes it's one of the wettest spots on Earth. Not wettest spots in Hawaiʻi—one of the wettest spots on Earth. Sometimes we're ranked number two—we actually pass [Mt.] Waiʻaleʻale [on Kauaʻi] sometimes with over 700 inches of rain. This data right here is from the beginning of this year, January 1 to September. We've got just a little bit over 140 inches. That means we're hoping in the next three months we're going to get 240 inches to hit normal. Okay, so sometimes it's a bit depressing, because you get right up to the waterfall, and it's dry. You look down in the stream, and it's dry. And you hope that you don't have to talk to your keiki [*children*] and your grandchildren, really have a heart-to-heart, and say, "We never do nothing. We never do nothing for you folks." I believe we put people on the moon in the '60s. It's a fact. We did. I believe we can do it. But we would need everybody to get together and support.

## "CANCEL FURTHER DISCUSSION AND CONSIDERATION OF THIS LETTER"

### *October 1, 2019*

Even though tourism was slated as the main topic on October 1, 2019, almost all public testimony was about affordable housing. CPAC chairperson Kai Nishiki's proposed letter, which sought to halt all development except for "100 percent affordable housing" projects, was slated for a vote. Testifiers unanimously agreed West Maui suffered from a severe deficit in homes that average-earning families could afford.[9] But their opinions were evenly split on whether the letter would make matters worse or better. Those who opposed the letter said it would scare away developers by creating more restrictions. Those who supported the letter said it would allow for more thoughtful development and prioritize projects committed to constructing a higher percentage of homes that locals could afford.

Perhaps the most moving testimony came from Tricia Higashi, who tearfully spoke about her family's struggle to stay afloat despite her earning $65,000 a year as a speech pathologist for local schools. Higashi, as well as testifiers Linda Garcia and Buz Moffett, opposed the letter because they believed that it would slow the construction of new homes.

> I'm the fourth generation of my family to be on the Island of Maui. And I am not in support of this letter to be sent out. It says West Maui community plan has not been updated since it was adopted in 1996. You folks all know—and thank you so much for your time—but we are so far behind in what is necessary. You know, I have so many friends that are sandwiched in between this generation of elderly parents who have worked for the state their whole lives and now have to live on a fraction of the income that they used to. And it's so expensive to already live. You know, I live with my mother—she's on retired teacher's salary. My son lives with me; we share a bedroom. I make $65,000 a year with a master's degree, after 12 years, and I have to live and sleep in the same bed as my son. You know that time for our housing is now. We cannot do it. I'm telling you, there's so many other people in the same situation. It's difficult to go to work when you know you're living paycheck to paycheck, and you're only an accident away, or some kind of episodic circumstance, that's going to put you in a situation where you're not going to know where you're going to get whatever for it to rent. Rent is so high.

Higashi's testimony received applause. Immediately after her, realtor and builder Van Fisher, who was involved in Martin's proposed Makila Farms

9. Maui County home prices rose more than 280 percent between 1996 and 2021. U.S. Federal Housing Finance Agency, All-Transactions House Price Index for Maui County, HI [ATNHPIUS15009A], retrieved from FRED, Federal Reserve Bank of St. Louis; https://fred.stlouisfed.org/series/ATNHPIUS15009A, September 30, 2022.

project, took the opportunity to criticize Nishiki's letter and advertise his project.

> I didn't plan to come back and was literally stunned to find out about this letter that's being proposed to the county. I'm also involved with Makila Farms and one of the real estate agents that's handling all the sales. That project should be approved. My heart breaks for that girl that just testified up here. I don't have to do this. I have a house. I'm very fortunate. But so many people don't. I've heard from hundreds of people exactly like her, calls that leave you in tears when you hang up the phone. These people need a home. Makila Farms, $161,000 for a starter home, okay? A one hundred percent affordable project can't offer that.

CPAC members Joe Pluta, Dylan Payne and Leilani Pulmano, as well as testifier Tom Blackburn Rodriguez, said that Nishiki's proposed letter was an overreach of the CPAC's responsibilities. He commented:

> I'd like to conclude by saying that the proposed letter is not within the mandate of the CPAC. Although I appreciate the passion behind the arguments to address the true needs of West Maui, the CPAC can focus on its mission as advisory and not a regulatory body and finish on time within the 180-day framework given to you.

In support of a halt on certain developments were CPAC members Ravi Bugga, Dawn Hegger-Nordblom and Karen Comcowich. Those testifying in support included Jennifer Mather and Dina Edmisson. Mather commented:

> I think the letter that you drafted and then amended with everybody's help is relevant and respectful and directed to the administration to pump the brakes and wait for this process—at least the CPAC part—to be done. And I think it echoes the sentiments of our community members who have been at council meetings and state policy meetings who said that they want us to respect this process and not make any decisions on entitled developments until you folks are done with yours. So I would urge the committee to vote in support of that letter being sent off as soon as possible.

Edmisson shared a conversation she had the night before with a man who, three months prior, had become the recipient of workforce housing in

Kāʻanapali. He said he was already looking forward to renting out the house so he could travel. She placed blame not on the man, but Maui County for not putting enough restrictions in place to control the market.

> As a community, as a county, we have not instituted enough laws or limits to control this way of thinking and possibility. Now I'm all for people getting ahead in life, but not at the expense of our community. However, we can change this conversation through legislation. [ . . . ] We cannot build ourselves out of a housing crisis; we must control the current market—or at the very least, all new developments moving forward. And don't let developers tell you they can't put these types of restrictions because no one will buy. That simply is not true. There are plenty of local people ready, willing and able to purchase an affordable or workforce housing home that would not flinch at these types of restrictions. And that is exactly the type of buyer we are trying to attract—the people who have every intention to be a long-term resident and working part of this community.

Following public testimony, Pluta introduced a motion to "cancel further discussion and consideration of this letter." He commented, "We have no legal right to interfere with the existing lawful process of the Planning Department." The motion was seconded by Payne, but failed to pass in a vote of 5–5.

In attempting to reach a compromise, Bugga suggested changing the language to "51 percent" affordable housing rather than "100 percent" and adding a clause that the development should not be on agricultural land.

At first, opponents of the letter refused to support it regardless of what it stated. But when it became clear the CPAC could not move forward from discussing the letter, Pulmano and Payne relented to revised wording. Pulmano made a motion to amend the language. Both the revisions to the letter and a subsequent vote to adopt the letter passed by majority vote.

> I will redo my motion to read: "Therefore, our CPAC committee sincerely requests that until after our Community Plan process has completed our review period, no new visitor accommodation or expansion [be approved . . . we] strongly encourage affordable housing.

Mufi Hannemann, a longtime Hawaiʻi politician and CEO of the Hawaiʻi Lodging & Tourism Association, took the opportunity to tie tourism back to the topic of affordable housing. He said that the industry's efforts to root out illegal transient vacation rentals would help make more homes available to residents. He also encouraged the CPAC to involve the visitor industry in its policy discussions.

> We believe the best way that we in the industry can bring about more afford-able housing is leading the crusade to root out illegal transient vacation rentals—that has been a big goal and objective. People think the hotels are doing this because it's all about competition for short-term rentals. I want to make it clear we don't mind the competition if they compete with us on a level playing field. They want to compete with us in resort areas, but not pay the four taxes that the state and the counties assess...Those unwilling to operate legal rentals would have to make the decision to rent or sell to a local person.

*   *   *

In recent years, the ratio of visitors to residents has grown. While the Maui Island Plan and the Maui County Plan call for no more than one visitor per three residents, that number has grown over the past decade. Currently, islandwide, about 41 percent of the people on island are visitors. In West Maui the ratio is closer to 1:1, said Dick Mayer, a retired professor at Maui Community College and former committee member for the Maui Island Plan and the General Planning Advisory Committee.

This disproportionate number of visitors to residents is worsening traffic and putting a strain on infrastructure. "The only way that you can support that large number of tourists here is by importing [help]—seven, eight, nine thousand people commuting from the other side every day," said Mayer.

> What you need to look at is: how do we get back into balance in this community of yours so you have a healthy community that is not overloaded by tourism and tourism impacts? One way, obviously, would [be to] say, "Let's not build any more tourist accommodations." But that's very tricky, because there's a type of tourist accommodation that comes in that isn't listed among tourist accommodations, and that's second homes. All the people who live up Kapalua and Kā'anapali, almost all of them, this is their second home. So they're here for two months or three months of the year. It takes up water resources to irrigate the lawns; it takes up wastewater. And those people are not counted as tourists.

Mayer urged the CPAC to examine the true impacts of tourism and figure out ways to get some of the spending dollars reinvested into maintaining county infrastructure. He said both the Maui Island Plan and the county's plan contained tourism-related policies that CPAC could incorporate into the West Maui Community Plan. Lastly, he appealed to committee members to continue to stay involved in the process.

> With the Maui Island Plan, which I was the vice chair of, the [Maui County] Council went ahead and was trying over and over again to change things that we had recommended as a citizen body of 25 people from all over this island. [CPAC member] Hans [Michel] was one of the members of that committee, and several other people as well. And [it's] absolutely necessary [to] follow up—otherwise they will divert. And they did divert—they put in a whole bunch of changes in there that were very bad, I think. But we didn't have the power to stop [it].

## The Fight Over Agricultural Lands
### *October 8, 2019*

Hawaiian culture and how to preserve it in West Maui was the focus of the first half of the October 8, 2019 meeting. Presenter Keʻeaumoku Kapu provided an overview of place names and significant events that took place in Historic Lahaina Town, once the capital of the Hawaiian kingdom. Such names embodied the values of the community and imparted knowledge about the natural environment. Kapu suggested adding Hawaiian place names below current names on the same signs to bring back these values. For example, the original name of Shaw Street was Alanui ka mamo, meaning "the pathway of the people," and the original name of Front Street was Alanui ka moʻi, meaning "the pathway of the king."

> But the possibility of putting Ala ka moʻi below Front Street or Ala ka mamo below Shaw Street, you start changing the methodology and bringing everything back and reapplying those values. You create a code of conduct by identifying these things. People would have more respect to know that this is the original name of this place.

County planners recommended a long list of policy and action items related to the historic district as an interim step in eventually creating design guidelines. The CPAC deferred taking votes on any of the proposed policy for this area until they could consult with the staff person who oversees planning for the district. County planner Jennifer Maydan presented on her behalf.

> As far as the long list of design policies for Lahaina Town, you'll see that there's four different sections: there's rehabilitation, additions, new construction, and streetscape. And it seems like a long list, but it really gives—as far as permit review—it gives the department the ability to tell an applicant, "Hey, this is what you need to do." It really gives it teeth, which the department doesn't have, right now, in their toolbox. So, the intent is that this would be an interim fix to have it in the community plan, but to eventually develop design guidelines.

\* \* \*

In West Maui, where water supplies are declining and where developers can make millions off "gentleman's estates" or "ag subdivisions"—lands zoned for agriculture but used for luxury home development—Maui County struggled with how to handle both existing and proposed ag subdivisions. In an article titled "Farming finds no home on agricultural land," (*Honolulu Advertiser*, 2005), reporter Andrew Gomes wrote:

> With rapidly rising prices and overwhelming demand for homes in Hawai'i over the past few years, there is much pressure to develop houses on farmland that historically has been quicker and less costly to subdivide for residential use. Among ag subdivisions or condominium lots under development, the majority are on Maui. Some derided as having little to do with agriculture—such as Pu'unoa, Launiupoko and Ukumehame—have been challenged as violations of state land-use law.

The owners of Plantation Estates, an ag subdivision, petitioned at every opportunity to have their community plan designation changed from agricultural to rural residential. And the fight over whether to keep the lands in agriculture or change them played out until the West Maui Community Plan was officially adopted.

At the same time, Hawai'i's elected officials touted their support for growing the state's agricultural sector. Governor David Ige's administration introduced an agriculture plan, which included an objective to develop a plan to increase local food production from the current 10 percent to at least 20 percent by the end of the decade. But little progress was being made toward food independence, and in order to increase local production, agricultural lands must be protected for farming, said Kaipo Kekona, a Maui farmer and presenter.

> This is a picture of West Maui just taken off of Google Earth today. As you can see, we have a lot of fallow open lands that are agriculture, but are not being used at all for any agriculture. It's pretty sad and depressing and disappointing. [...] There's a lot of sprawl in there. It's not ideal for what I would like to see the place that I come from, and where I'm proud of. If you know the history of Lahaina, and you look at that food forest photo that I sent you, you know at one point, Launiupoko, which is way down on the right hand over there, and Mala, which is the end where the water comes down, was all very lush and full of agroforestry.

He recommended the CPAC adopt policies requiring large landowners to manage excess brush and maintain ditches and reservoirs on their lands. He also suggested retaining locally grown agriculture for feeding the local community first.

> All produce shall first be sold to fulfill Hawai'i's demand, then any surplus can be exported outside of all these markets. [...] We farm a lot of stuff, and it's not happening. It's going out. And most of it is exported to places that have no investment [in Hawai'i], or see no value other than the fact that they can brag they got food from Hawai'i.

Farmer and presenter Vince Mina suggested planting cover crops on fallow lands while Maui County decides how it wants to handle agricultural land in the future.

> While everybody's deciding on what to do with these agricultural lands, my suggestion is that we plant cover crops[10] [in fallow fields]—and we not

---

10. "A cover crop is a plant that is used primarily to slow erosion, improve soil health, enhance water availability, smother weeds, help control pests and diseases, increase biodiversity and bring a host of other benefits to your farm." Sustainable Agriculture Research and Education (www.sare.org).

only plant cover crops, but we use some of those alleys to harvest the seed to have a cover crop seed industry. That would be really a vital thing for these islands. We could ship here for our farmers, first of all, and then ship across to the mainland. They are in dire need of quality cover crop seed.

While presenters offered a number of recommendations to bolster the agricultural community in West Maui, Dylan Payne commented that their suggestions did not address how to make agriculture an economic driver, which was supposed to be the focus of the meeting.

The context of this discussion was economic opportunity through innovation and collaboration, through the lens of agriculture. And while I am appreciative of all the comments, I don't really feel like I heard any suggestions or recommendations as to how we as a community can use agriculture as an economic driver. And that we need to figure out. I don't have the solution. I don't know what the answer is. But I didn't hear anything tonight. Vince had some comments about cover crops and seeds. But the reason that there's no ag on the west side is because it's not an economically viable enterprise, or we need to find solutions for that.

Mina addressed Payne's comment by stating that economics can come through improving agricultural production by rebuilding soil health in West Maui.

But the economic driver I was talking about is by building our soils—we're making them resilient. And the economics can come from seeds, a cover crop seed industry, that could be developed, that could be an economic driver for agriculture. And at the same time, unless our soils are resilient to production, you run into all kinds of problems: too many inputs, too much water. That's why agriculture fails—because we forgot about growing the soil first before we started growing the plants.

## "Redefining How we Solve this Crisis"
### *October 10, 2019*

The conversation about how to make more homes available to long-term West Maui residents shifted away from constructing new affordable housing to tapping into existing home inventory. Kanani Higbee, who testified at the meeting, expressed disappointment that homes for Native Hawaiians were not discussed by the CPAC. She said approving new-construction affordable housing diminished the state's ability to award lease claims on Department of Hawaiian Home Lands (DHHL) land.

> All this affordable housing is taking water away from the Department of Hawaiian Homelands projects that we have over here. They had 250 lots planned, and they said they can only do 75 because of the water, which I feel is really sad. Hawaiians aren't getting prioritized here.

One area of discussion and focus for Maui County is how to regulate the short-term rental market in a way that could free up some of those homes for long-term renters. The challenge is that contrary to popular belief, the vast majority of short-term rentals are operating legally in West Maui, either because of zoning or because such uses were "grandfathered" into the property. Only a few hundred rentals are operating illegally, and the County has spent a lot of money and time to find and issue warnings to them. Any effort to roll back legal short-term rental provisions would certainly be challenged in court, as it has in the past. Planning Director Michele McLean:

> The grandfathering provisions that are in the County code [are from] a legal opinion that was issued several years ago that the Planning Department followed. And then the County Council over a couple of years sought to codify that legal opinion to put that grandfathered-like status into the County code.

Councilmember Tamara Paltin, who testified at the meeting, asked the CPAC to consider including policies or actions that would help phase out short-term rentals outside of the hotel or improvement districts. Thousands of short-term rentals are currently allowed to operate with no permit or oversight, which is exacerbating the availability of rentals for local residents.

> We need a multi-pronged approach of phasing out some of these [short-term rentals] so that there's more options, as well as building affordable homes, as well as building on DHHL lands. It needs more than just one way, because we can't really build our way out of the mess if people keep coming from the continent and buying houses here. [...] There comes a

time when you got to put the affordable housing crisis in perspective and say, "Are we going to be planning for our residents' needs? Or are we going to be planning for foreign speculation needs?"

CPAC member Ravi Bugga, too, was convinced of the need to tap into existing housing stock. New affordable construction cannot happen at a pace fast enough to meet the demands. Even if new homes are built, they come with a price tag that many locals cannot afford.

> It's very clear, at least to me, that we can't build our way out of this. It's because of all the regulations and everything else. And just the sheer number. We can't build new units fast enough. We haven't been doing that in the past. I don't see us honestly doing it in the future. Anyway, if we do build them, a lot of them aren't really affordable. I mean, the place right on the highway, those are half-million-dollar affordable units, and they're 1,200-square-foot houses. [...] Therefore, what we absolutely have to do, which I think we're all talking about, is to use existing housing stock that's being used for short-term rentals legally or illegally, either to rent or to buy.

CPAC member Dylan Payne asked McLean whether actions to phase out short-term rentals could be construed as a "taking" and have legal implications. She responded that owners would likely make such an argument in objection to the actions.

> We would rely on Corporation Counsel to defend against that. I'm not an attorney. I'm not an expert on takings. My general understanding of takings when it comes to something like this is that they would have to demonstrate that they're being deprived of economically beneficial use of their property. And to a degree, they might be deprived of a *more* economically beneficial use of their property. But certainly, a condominium in Maui has economic benefit even if it's restricted to long-term.

\* \* \*

West Maui needs to provide housing at all levels under the 140 percent average median income (AMI) level, said Linda Munsell, deputy director of the Maui County Department of Housing and Human Concerns. Among these levels, her estimates showed the greatest needs in West Maui are for households within 50 to 81 percent and less than 30 percent of average median income ranges.

We need housing units at all AMI levels. One hundred forty-one percent and above, which are the market and luxury units, the market takes care of that. They produce enough market homes to meet that demand. But it's those units that help pay for the lower AMI units as well. Whenever you say to a developer, "You have to sell a product less than it costs," you have to make up that money somewhere. And typically, it's made up in these market and luxury units. If you're looking at the 81- to 140-percent [AMI] units, those are typically what we call workforce units. West Maui is projected to produce only about 30 percent of the units needed. For the 80 percent and below AMI, you're projected to produce less than 12 percent of the units that are needed in that category. And of course, pretty much everything that's 80 percent and below requires some kind of financial subsidy from the state or from the county.

Many of the current policies aim to generate affordable housing at the 80 percent AMI or higher—far too high a level to help those most in need of housing. Munsell's presentation made the case for a tiered approach when it comes to affordable housing policy—something the CPAC would discuss and consider in later meetings.

Housing advocates seemed to agree the county needed to play a more central role in development if it wanted to create more affordable homes. Life-long Maui resident and housing advocate Stan Franco said that for every five market homes being constructed, only one workforce or affordable home is being built. "We're not building for the majority of our residents. And if we continue down this road, we're never going to catch up or even get close to building for our people. We need to change direction here."

Mike Williams, a fellow housing advocate, explained that the county would not actually be the developer, but would help set up a nonprofit public housing authority whose sole focus would be to develop affordable housing. A nonprofit organization would have access to private funding, through charitable foundations, that are not available to the county. Mike Williams:

The idea would be the county would acquire the land it needs in West Maui to build the low-income rentals, which is the bulk of what you need here, and then lease the land to this housing authority, which would have the expertise to hire the developers to build the homes at an affordable rate. The county would end up owning the land forever; the homes would stay as affordable rentals forever. And the bulk of what you need...I think it's clear it is 80 percent [AMI] and below—frankly, 60 percent and below—you're never going to get developers to build those. It's going to have to be county money.

Although he applauded the CPAC for their ideas to convert short-term rentals to long-term rentals, Williams said such homes would never be low-income rentals. Further, he said the county should take action to discourage high-end housing and hotels and do everything it can to subsidize low-income housing. Franco added that the county needs to put a time restriction on the construction of entitled properties.

Housing policy advisor for former councilwoman Elle Cochran, Autumn Rae Ness, challenged the ways the county has tried to deal with affordable housing. She agreed with Williams and Franco's assertion that truly affordable homes could never be created by the private sector.

> I will also say that nowhere in the U.S. has big development industry provided the solutions for [the] affordable housing crisis. Anywhere that communities across the U.S. have pulled themselves out of a crisis like this, they've done it in spite of industry, and by over-regulating [the industry], and by making their own rules and telling the industry to conform. That's the only way we're going to get out of this. We have to do better.

She took issue with the use of HUD guidelines to determine what people can afford. She argued these numbers should be used as a starting point, but should not be relied on as fact because they were not always grounded in reality:

> HUD says that our average median income is $10,000 more than three years ago. That has skewed our entire affordable housing grid and what developers are allowed to charge our residents for housing. So what does that mean in practice? Here's two examples in 2017. If your family was 100 percent of AMI, and you made 74 grand, you're expected to be able to afford a $408,000 three-bedroom house. Or you could pay $1,600 for a two-bedroom rental. We are also, in that same time, allowing developers to build for 140 [percent] of AMI and call it affordable. That means for somebody who makes $103—almost $104,000, we're calling that subsidized housing, and they're allowed to sell that housing for $571,000. That's three years ago.

Beyond the income levels targeted by existing policies and practices, a number of barriers to building affordable homes surfaced in discussion. Under the current process, developers independently create a plan the county takes or leaves. Ness said this approach is backwards and involves the county too far down the road. Instead, the county should be setting the parameters for the project based on its needs, and invite interested developers to offer proposals that meet these needs.

CPAC member Joseph Pluta supported Ness's ideas and acknowledged the county's failures: "I just 100 percent concur that this area median income is ridiculous the way it is now. I love your suggestions and the way you're going about that. We have failed. And we've got proof."

Ness responded, "You guys are really on the frontlines of redefining how we solve this crisis, because the way we've been doing it is broken. And we're actually making things worse every time we build, like I said, a fake solution. We're actually digging ourselves deeper into a hole."

## "THERE'S A SHORTAGE OF BEACH PARKS AND NEIGHBORHOOD PARKS OF ADEQUATE SIZE"

### *October 17, 2019*

In the same way data from marine scientists supported the case for new or strengthened policies to protect coral reefs, figures shared by county officials pointed to a need for improved accessibility in the form of more parks, open space, walkways and the like. Such spaces support public health, said Lauren Loor from the Healthy Eating Active Living (HEAL) Coalition.

> When we have inaccessibility or non-existent sidewalks, bike lanes, walking paths, this can lead to or contribute to sedentary behavior and habits. And this contributes to poor health outcomes, such as the downstream outcomes that we looked at before. And this is a snapshot of Hawai'i: you'll see [the] adult obesity rate for Native Hawaiians is 40.8 percent statewide. Eleven percent of workers commute by active transportation. Seventy percent of our middle schoolers do not meet national physical activity recommendations. And we are the first ranking, most dangerous state for pedestrians over the age of 65. Approximately two-thirds of Americans are overweight today. According to the CDC, Maui's adult obesity rate is 27 percent. Our state rate is 23.8 percent. Our teens and preteens are at 14 percent. And it is predicted that this generation of children will not outlive their parents.

Loor recommended the integration of public health considerations in the planning of new communities. Would the CPAC push to ensure accessibility features be included in future developments? Committee members would soon argue over whether or not to adopt policies to require or simply encourage these features.

West Maui has 12 beach parks, four neighborhood parks, three pocket parks, one community park and 11 special-use facilities. The size of these parks, however, are inadequate for the population and uses of area residents, said David Yamashita, Department of Parks and Recreation planner. Park facilities need to be viewed as essential as any infrastructure, he argued.

> When you look at West Maui, as we noted from the other graph, you don't have a lot of neighborhood parks. And as someone else mentioned, I think on the committee, they're small, or [there are] not very many improvements. And when I looked at the map and looked at the facilities, what jumped out at me is you've got a lot of people living here. Neighborhood parks are one of the main ways that people [recreate . . . ]. But you look at these sites, and there's just not a lot to do. That's why this is a really important issue. We need to think about a variety of improvements in facilities and parks. There's a shortage of beach parks and neighborhood parks of adequate size. If you look at the size of the beach parks, a lot of them are narrow and/or [need] a big upgrade. But there's a lot of demand for it, as we see from the survey. So what you have—I mean, you all experienced this, right?—There are a lot of people crammed in a very small space. So it's something that needs to be addressed.

Yamashita's data seemed to support the idea that more land should be set aside as park, a position that current and past committee members supported. Back in 1995, the *Lahaina News* reported the Citizens Advisory Committee urged, unsuccessfully, for the creation of more public parks.

One key idea that came out of Yamashita's presentation was to integrate park planning with land use planning. If the CPAC wants to see a trail system created, that trail system should be spelled out in the zoning code and added to transportation planning maps, he said. The parks system also should be adequately staffed and funded. Committee member Dylan Payne wondered where that funding might come from:

> What I'm hearing you saying is that we have a lot of land and resources, but we have very little funding for maintenance of those sites. And you can see that when you walk around the parks that we do have, I think they could all be improved upon. So before we even start thinking about adding new

parks, how do we make the ones that we have better? And how do we make them what they ought to be in order to serve the people that live here? So I'm just kind of like racking my brain, thinking: how do we get you guys more resources to do that?

The Department of Parks and Recreation was working on administrative rules that would allow fees generated by concession standards and sponsorships to go back to funding park maintenance, said Karla Peters from the department.

## To Require or to Not Require?
### *October 22, 2019*

In the few days remaining for the committee to review and approve or amend draft policies and actions, alliances were forming. Chairperson Kai Nishiki and member Karen Comcowich were often in agreement with one another. They both advocated for restrictive language such as "shall" and "must," while members Dylan Payne and Joseph Pluta leaned in the opposite direction, preferring less restrictive language like "encourage." This broader issue was so important that local leaders in their public testimony at the CPAC kickoff implored the committee to include language with legal bearing, or else the final plan would be useless.

The other, broader issue causing friction among members was whether to include policies and actions that already existed in another plan. In one instance, Nishiki wanted to use a policy and accompanied actions from the Maui Island plan to phase out municipal and private injection wells. Responding to objections from fellow CPAC members, Nishiki replied, "Yes, we don't want to duplicate everything. But things that our community want to be addressed, and that are affecting our community and water quality—I think that it's always good to double down [on issues] that we feel are really important to our community."

Though the CPAC agreed that providing truly affordable housing is the top priority for West Maui, they debated over how to define "affordable," and whether or not to require conditions with their construction. One draft policy read:

Support the development of pedestrian-oriented complete communities that meet residents' needs for daily living by providing a mix of land uses, housing close to jobs, services, schools and recreation, and convenient and safe mobility options, including walking, biking, and transit options. Require affordable housing projects, including projects using the state 201H or county 2.97

process, to be near jobs, schools, transit and services, and include sidewalks, parks, bus stops and other infrastructure and pedestrian-oriented design elements that create walkable and livable communities for all.

CPAC member Dylan Payne, a realtor with the West Maui Land Company, took issue with the language: "I think that the use of the word 'require' in that second sentence is a little problematic. I think we could say 'encourage.' I think it just gets a little nebulous there. And then where it goes on and says that these projects need to be near jobs, schools, transit and services: how close is 'near'? I don't [think] it's specific enough here."

Karen Comcowich, who works in the hospitality industry and volunteers for environmental causes, argued for stronger language: "If we don't 'require,' what's really the point of saying anything? I mean, right now, it's 'encouraged' that all these things are in the affordable housing projects, and it doesn't happen."

Pluta, who is also a realtor, voiced his concerns over the restrictive language. "I like Dylan's concern about the word 'require.' I wouldn't want to have an affordable housing project that can pass—and everybody's been supportive—but now it can't happen because it's not close to bus stops, doesn't have sidewalks, and some of those things like that. So, I would take out that word 'required' and also say 'encouraged.' "

While Yvette Joyce Celiz, who works in the hospitality industry, shared concerns over how "near" is defined, she pointed out that new affordable housing development should be required to provide sidewalks and other livable features—features that public officials recently testified contributed to public health.

Comcowich and Pluta debated over the draft policy, with Comcowich arguing that sidewalks and proximity to public transit were basic needs. Pluta, meanwhile, continued to assert that placing conditions on affordable housing would delay their construction, further limiting the availability of homes for those who needed them. By the end of the meeting, Nishiki tabled the discussion on the language of the policy and moved onto the next policy.

Nearly every affordable housing policy solution presented to the CPAC caused debate among members. One draft policy read:

Support projects that provide housing for resident households earning 140% area median income and below according to the need identified by the Department of Housing and Human Concerns, and that are consistent with other community plan policies.

At 140 percent of median income, a household would be able to buy a $650,000 home, which CPAC member Ravi Bugga argued was far too high of a threshold to help those most in need of housing. Jennifer Maydan, who wrote the policy based off of the information provided by housing officials, suggested adding "in each AMI category" to target all the in-need income levels.

As members voiced their rationales for where to set the threshold in the policies, Payne reiterated a point he made at previous meetings that making housing available at any level would help address West Maui's housing needs. "I would submit that any house bill helps the shortage because it generates a number of moves. That kind of cycles through, and it helps a bunch of families down the line as well." Comcowich objected to his point with one of her own: "I disagree that any housing helps down the road, because if you have a million-dollar home being built, it's not going to help anybody who's earning $120,000."

Taking a step back from the proposed policies, CPAC chairperson Kai Nishiki called to question their validity and whether the committee should take action on them or propose other options:

> I have a bit of a problem accepting the Department of Housing and Human [Services'] concerns. I do feel that it's important to look to our nonprofits and other people who are experienced in addressing the needs for affordable housing. I'll definitely be working on some additional policies and action items—and I would encourage my fellow members to do the same—so that we can really provide for the needs of our community and not just take an obviously broken system and take their recommendations when they have not been able to, in my opinion, do their job.

At the close of the meeting, Bugga took the floor to question the morality of what he viewed as affordable housing loopholes. Such policies allowed developers to circumvent their affordable housing commitments by making in-lieu-of payments or trading credits with developments in other locations.

> If you're selling each of these timeshare units, 300 units, you're making revenues of six to $700 million. I have trouble with [them] making a relatively small payment. Again, I don't know what that was; I will find out tomorrow. If it's a small payment in lieu of building 75 affordable housing units, I have a real problem [with that]. I'm sorry; I don't think we should allow in-lieu-of payments unless it's a seriously large amount. That's not what this

is intended to be. This becomes a sham. How can you pay a fine and get away from providing the actual unit? So then we have no units, and I don't know where that money went.

## "That's a Crime. We Can't Allow That to Happen Anymore."

### *October 24, 2019*

Up until this point, the CPAC's meetings were mostly informational, with subject matter experts speaking on topics such as environment, public health, agriculture and culture. October 2019 marked the beginning of the committee's review and adoption of policies and actions. Almost all of this material was authored by county staff, with some carryover from the previous plan, planner Jennifer Maydan noted. How the CPAC voted on these policies and actions was important because their votes would be viewed as the community's endorsement.

The October 24, 2019, meeting attracted a larger crowd and more testifiers than previous ones. They spoke on a variety of issues including fire fuel reduction, water storage, native Hawaiian rights and emergency response.

Kimo Falconer, president of MauiGrown Coffee, Inc. and former manager of Pioneer Mill, pressed the CPAC to find ways to tap into old water reservoirs. These structures, once used by commercial farms, could now be reclaimed to store water for fighting fires and to revive agriculture in West Maui. Instead, they have been allowed to fall into disrepair. Once reservoirs become decommissioned, as was the case with the Wahikuli reservoir, they are lost as a resource for the community, said Falconer.

> There are ways to bring [water] in and keep those reservoirs full to at least have another tool to fight [fires] so that [firefighters are] not running down to the ocean and pulling saltwater and dumping on lands and therefore killing the land. You can't grow anything anymore after that. A lot of times we are putting water in the upper watershed on our pristine land, where their water comes from, dumping salt in there. That's a crime, we can't allow that to happen anymore.

Falconer also spoke about lack of water as a limiting factor to expanding agriculture in West Maui. The community would need to find a way to fund the cost of pumping groundwater hundreds of feet to the surface to use for agriculture. He estimated such pumping to cost around $70,000 to $80,000 per month. Committee member Don Gerbig wondered whether a cooperative could be set up to maintain such a water system. Falconer said that idea was worth exploring. But if the county couldn't figure out how to get agriculture running again, former farmlands would be used for development.

> If we get to the point where this land is never going to be ag, the irony is it's going to go to highest and best use, which is going to be houses. And they're going to need that fresh water, and they're going to go back and put the diversions back in. And then—because they thought this out a long time ago—when they put the water treatment plant in at Mahinahina Weir and they put the water treatment plant right up here, they knew what they were doing. That's going to happen again if we don't figure out some kind of agricultural use. We will overwhelm ourselves with houses, and we're definitely not going to have enough water for that.

A handful of people testified on protecting native Hawaiian rights through the community planning process. Keʻeaumoku Kapu, Aha Moku CEO and cultural resource presenter, reminded the CPAC of its legal obligation to protect these rights.

> The Hawaiʻi Supreme Court has provided a framework by which the state must fulfill its statutory and constitutional obligations to affirmatively protect the native Hawaiian traditional customary rights and practices under this framework. The state and county agencies, when reviewing land use applications, must independently assess. So when I talk about assessing, if you not doing your job and you passing these kinds of things before it goes to the council, you gotta make sure the t's are crossed and i's are dotted. If not, I will be in front of this body and attesting to everything that was created.

\* \* \*

The committee moved quickly through the first set of draft policies and actions developed by county staff related to fire safety and emergency management. All but one of the items were adopted by consensus, with some changes suggested by testifiers and CPAC members. The committee also added a new policy to develop a resiliency hub for West Maui, which was a suggestion made earlier in the meeting.

One policy receiving broad support was to require large landowners to actively manage fire hazards on their lands. The draft policy stated: "Amend the Maui County Code to require landowners of large vacant land in high fire hazard areas to prepare and carry out a fuel management plan." Kapu suggested expanding the policy to ensure historical and cultural sites are protected if and when fire breaks are considered. The policy was revised to include his suggestion and was adopted by consensus.

Minor changes were made to the remaining policies related to fire hazards and emergency management. The newly adopted actions included building a new fire station along Honoapiʻilani Highway and providing annual funds for a GIS database for fire and emergency response infrastructure such as hydrants and stations.

## Save Agricultural Lands, Revive Farming
*November 5, 2019*

West Maui lives with the legacy of intensive sugar cane production. When environmentalists testified at an earlier meeting, they presented data linking coral reef decline to "legacy" runoff—soils laden with pesticides and fertilizers from the plantation days. This industrialized farming caused immeasurable harm to Maui's natural environment. Testifiers acknowledged the need to support local agriculture while also farming in less destructive ways. Throughout the planning process, the community voiced their support for retaining and reviving agriculture using sustainable methods.

The CPAC reviewed policies to support the agricultural industry in a section called "Economic Opportunity through Innovation and Collaboration." One of those proposed policies stirred much debate. It stated:

> Prohibit conversion of agriculture, agricultural lands, outside of the Maui Island Plan's growth boundaries, and limit conversion of agricultural lands within the growth boundaries to urban and rural designations in West Maui unless it can be demonstrated that a conversion that's required to accommodate the population or employment projections for the region or conversion will facilitate shoreline retreat by directly replacing an existing development of similar size and character that is threatened by climate change.

Leilani Pulmano asked why the policy references already established growth boundaries. "Where it says, 'and limit conversion of agricultural lands within the growth boundaries,' I thought that's why we have the growth boundaries—that's actually where our areas are going to grow." Planner Kate Blystone said the policy was drafted in response to public concern over the conversion of agricultural lands and the size of the growth boundaries identified in the Maui Island Plan.

> This would be an opportunity to say, "Do we actually need to develop at that intensity in those growth boundaries?" And also, there's a requirement in 2.8OB to phase development of land. This would be a way of getting at that, if those units are necessary to meet these employment and population projections, or if they're replacing areas that are being affected by climate change. Then we can move into those areas. It's part of development phasing. It's a way to protect agricultural land that is still in agriculture.

Pulmano suggested removing the part that limits conversion of agricultural lands in the growth boundaries. The CPAC chairperson disagreed with her, stating: "I believe that it is important for us to protect agricultural lands. And I would not support striking that. We've heard over and over again that we need to protect agricultural lands." Pulmano held firm in her position, saying a long process led to the creation of the growth boundaries in the Maui Island Plan. The CPAC's role was not to redraw those boundaries, but to define how the growth should look.

At member Dylan Payne's suggestion, the committee decided to postpone a final decision on this particular policy until they could view maps. However, members continued to discuss the language, revealing a diversity of opinions on the matter. Joseph Pluta and Pulmano wanted to remove the reference to development of a similar size and character. Payne said he found the two criteria for conversion in the draft policy too limiting. He used the Plantation Estates Lot Association's request as an example of a request falling outside of these criteria. CPAC member Yvette Joyce Celiz said she supported limiting conversion of ag lands and retaining all of the draft language. Pluta agreed with Payne regarding the need to accurately identify existing uses and taxing these uses appropriately: "There are ag lands that are not active—they're being used for residential purposes, and there's some phony ag going on. And it's not real at all. It doesn't reflect the actual use. They get lower taxes; they've got a higher use. There's going to be some existing development in ag that needs to be reclassified and call a duck a duck instead of calling it an ag parcel." Nishiki wanted to add wording to the policy to prevent the conversion of agriculture lots for the purpose of building "McMansions" or luxury estates.

County planner Jennifer Maydan spoke to the bigger issue of agricultural lands being sold to developers and developed for non-agricultural purposes. "This obviously is not an issue unique to West Maui. This is an island-wide issue, and it is addressed quite a bit in the Maui Island Plan. With the rewrite of our zoning code that we'll be starting very shortly here in the new year, this is one of the primary issues that the consultants will be working on: strengthening our zoning to actually protect ag land."

Immediately following the discussion over limiting the conversion of agricultural lands within growth boundaries, Nishiki floated her idea to include a policy to "disprove the subdivision of agricultural lands or phony agricultural McMansions." Payne laughingly asked how one would define "phony" or "McMansion." Pluta called the wording "too strange." Blystone suggested using, "Discourage the subdivision of agricultural lands for non-agricultural uses." Comcowich proposed a new policy to require owners of agricultural lands in West Maui to develop and implement a farm plan appropriate to the microclimate of their property.

Confusion ensued among committee members as each new proposal raised made it more difficult for them to keep track of what they were reviewing. Maydan pointed out that members were talking about four different policies at one point. With Nishiki's guidance, the committee decided to postpone its discussion of agricultural policy and instead shifted to reviewing policies three and four, relating to the tourism industry.

*   *   *

Though the majority of CPAC members agreed on the need to halt new hotel development to focus on housing for residents, they could not reach consensus on how to do that. Policy three, which attempted to address their concerns, stated: "The number of visitor units in West Maui shall not exceed 33% of the total units in West Maui."

The draft policy would, in effect, prevent new hotel development until enough housing was built to offset it. A version of the policy was included in the Maui Island Plan, but proved difficult to implement because it focused on the number of people, not the number of units, said Blystone. That policy stated, "Promote a desirable island population by striving to not exceed an island-wide visitor population of roughly 33% of resident population."

Committee members questioned whether 33 percent was a realistic goal since the majority of visitors who come to Maui stay in West or South Maui. Resource person Terryl Vencyl agreed, saying she believed the goal "cannot be

accomplished," and the county should focus on keeping visitor units in appropriately zoned areas. CPAC members objected to the proposed policy for other
reasons. Leilani Pulmano said she was concerned about impacts to the tourism
industry workers and neighboring communities. Nishiki debated against both
of these points, saying neighboring communities could address the issue in their
own respective plans and that employment would not be impacted.

After a half hour of spirited exchange between members, Pluta accused
Nishiki of violating Robert's Rules of Order by debating other community
members from her position as chairperson.

> Debating from the chair, as I understand that, is not permitted. If you
> want to debate something, you are not supposed to be the chair. The chair
> is supposed to be an impartial party. You can express your point, but you
> can't argue with our opinion or points as being incorrect from the chair and
> dominating the conversation. That's the point of order. I'd like to see that
> clarified by staff, and if necessary, get a legal opinion.

Pluta then moved to delete policy number three. Donald Gerbig seconded
the motion. Members were divided over the language in the proposed policy.
Moments before taking the vote, Jeri Dean commented: "I am in support of
this policy. I think regulation has to be put in place on any further development, whether it's at the door or not. Visitor development needs to come to
a halt until local people are taken care of in the community." Aina Kohler,
Payne and Dawn Hegger-Nordblom agreed with Dean but said the policy
needed more work.

The group could not gather enough votes to adopt or delete the policy.
They reached the first of many impasses. Planner Kate Blystone offered to
bring back alternative language for the CPAC to consider at a future meeting.

The next policy related to tourism was adopted by consensus after a brief
discussion. It stated:

> Visitor-related development shall minimize the impact of tourists on West
> Maui residents, infrastructure, parks, environment and cultural resources.
> The visitor industry shall focus on quality rather than quantity.

Members Kohler and Dean questioned how the policy could be enforced,
with county planners responding that such a policy would be considered as part
of project proposals. Maydan explained that the policy was a direct response

to the community's concerns over tourism's impacts to residents, resources and infrastructure.

*   *   *

Committee members wanted to broaden the concept of economies in West Maui. Although the CPAC spoke mostly about tourism and agriculture, members had other ideas. Payne:

> Kate said ag is the number two industry or economic driver on the west side. I don't know if that's entirely true, but if it is, that's a sad commentary on how dependent we are on tourism. I really applaud Leilani for getting us to think about how we can encourage other economic opportunity here on the west side, whether it's through small business or promoting wellness as an industry or trying to grow a technology sector here. I know there are a lot of people that are able to, because of the internet, telecommute. They might work for Google or one of the big companies on the West Coast, but they can live here and work full time. What are things we can do to encourage that type of economic growth?

Pulmano recommended the addition of wording to encourage small businesses, and arts-related, historic and wellness-focused industries. Kohler and Nishiki followed with new policies to encourage small-scale renewable energy and climate change response. All were adopted by consensus.

## Truly Affordable and Livable Communities
### *November 7, 2019*

The group's attention turned away from the economy to public health and affordable housing, where they would find much agreement. In the first 15 minutes of the November 7, 2019 meeting, committee members passed a handful of policies for "Safe, Healthy and Livable Communities." Even a policy that members grappled over in a previous meeting passed easily by consensus:

> Require affordable housing projects, including projects using the state 201H or county 2.9 process, to be near jobs, schools, transit and services and include sidewalks, parks, bus stops and other infrastructure and pedestrian-oriented design elements that create walkable and livable communities for all.

Their action aligned with public testimony from resident Angela Lucero, who advocated for the use of "required" in the policy. Such a statement speaks to the importance of equity and inclusion in providing housing to different segments of the population, she said.

An item that continued to cause concern to members was one supporting housing projects:

> Support projects that provide housing for resident households earning 140 percent area median income and below, according to the need identified by the Department of Housing and Human Concerns, and that are consistent with other community plan policies.

The CPAC's Joseph Pluta wondered whether the area median income level should be lowered to 100 percent. Karen Comcowich agreed with him and asked to change "support" to "prioritize." However, Jeri Dean said she wanted the policy to remain at 140 percent AMI to help more buyers. A large percentage of middle-class people make too much money to qualify for the affordable housing, but not enough money to purchase the million-dollar homes, she said. Resource person Linda Munsell offered her thoughts on the policy:

> As far as the 140 percent that you guys are talking about prioritizing certain projects: often, a developer actually needs those market-rate units in order to make the lower-income units feasible for them. When you're saying "prioritize," does that mean you're not going to allow other projects or that somehow they're going to put at a disadvantage? I would discourage you from trying to limit that. Our deepest need truly is at 80 percent and below, and it is true that the higher percentages are very close to market. But I think that you have to have a wide range. And when we calculate what's going to be built, those lower units really do depend on those upper units to make them balance out.

Munsell also took issue with the policy adopted to require livability and walkability features of affordable housing projects. Such features would drive up the cost of a project. This requirement, coupled with a policy that lowers the income bracket for potential buyers, could prove problematic, she contended.

> Now in number 10, you're asking them to be close to jobs, to all these things, which is going to drive up the cost. Now you're going to say, "Maybe we're less interested in those higher-income bracket units that actually will make

the lower-income units feasible." I would caution you. I'm not going to say we shouldn't, because we should. We desperately need these lower-income units. But I'm just afraid the more restrictive you become, the more difficult it is to build.

Member Yvette Celiz suggested including both income brackets in the policy. Such a statement would both prioritize 100-percent AMI projects and support 140-percent AMI projects. The committee agreed to incorporate this wording. They adopted the revised version with no further discussion.

Hans Michel chimed in to say the committee was focused on the wrong target—the county actually needs affordable rental control more than affordable housing. But he did not propose a new policy or action to his point. "People have to start rent out before they can dream of buying a house. Majority of the people around here are broke. If we have a recession or something go wrong, we have a lot of problems with foreclosure."

\* \* \*

Tensions flared between committee members and planning staff when Comcowich proposed several policies and actions that already appeared in the same or similar form in the Maui Island Plan (MIP). For example, one of Comcowich's proposed additions was, "Promote the use of sustainable green building and development practices, such as the Leadership and Energy and Environmental Design standard." The MIP included a number of actions to promote LEED certification, county staff Kate Blystone pointed out. Similarly, when Comcowich suggested a new policy to address light pollution, several people cited existing policies in the MIP, county code and natural resource management plans.

CPAC chairperson Kai Nishiki repeatedly pushed back against the staff's advice not to replicate wording across plans. "Also, since things are in the Maui Island Plan, that doesn't stop us from being able to put them in the West Maui Community Plan as something that's important to our community," she said. Though they would not be prevented from duplication, Maydan said doing so would make the plan less focused, clear and concise. For staff, duplication was a matter of sound planning. For Nishiki and others, inserting the same or similar wording added another level of protection for the community on priority issues.

\* \* \*

The section on "Safe, Healthy and Livable Communities" included the topic of shoreline access. Many in the West Maui community were upset over attempts to close off the public's access to the area's beaches. Both Jim Buika, county shoreline planner, and Nishiki proposed a policy and action to tackle this problem: "Support public and private efforts to inventory, evaluate and expand public shoreline access. Require shoreline access to now-privatized shoreline areas by gates and walls, such as 'Alaeloa, Nāpili and Puamana, Lahaina." The action read: "Evaluate which sections of coastline are gated and privatized and develop a plan to provide public access to these shorelines for the West Maui Community Plan."

\* \* \*

The CPAC quickly voted on and adopted several policies aimed at making more homes available to residents. Building off the advice of affordable housing advocates in October, Nishiki proposed a new policy to "require that the county of Maui actively support an inventory of affordable homes and rentals that are bought and sold among Maui's workforce."

The committee also took its initial steps toward freeing up rentals. One adopted action would propose revisions to the real property tax structure to incentivize long-term rental and owner occupancy and to discourage short-term rental.

## A Laundry List of Actions

### *November 19, 2019*

The committee passed a number of new items impacting the Lahaina Historic District in late November. The first item adopted by consensus was a detailed policy on design guidelines for the Historic District. The Cultural Resources Commission uses any current plan to evaluate the appropriateness of development within a National Landmark District. "Putting these design principles in the community plan is an important intermediate step" until new guidelines are developed, said Annalise Kehler. Their other approved actions included the installation of interpretive street signs with traditional Hawaiian place names, and creating a county Historic District officer position for enforcement and education in the Lahaina Historic District.

The CPAC also supported the phasing out of short-term rentals in the Historic District and prohibiting additional vacation rentals in the area. However, members still had concerns about how to implement these actions. Dylan Payne wondered about whether the actions would negatively impact current and future properties zoned for hotel use. The West Maui Community Plan also called for the expansion of the Historic District boundary, which raised questions about how vacation rentals in this expanded area would be impacted. County staff revised the language to allow existing hotels, such as the Pioneer Inn and Plantation Inn, to continue operating as they had been. The committee adopted the revised policy by consensus.

\*     \*     \*

After reviewing the items brought forth by the Planning Department staff, the group presented their own ideas, many of which were adopted without objections. Jennifer Maydan reminded the members to consider prioritizing their requests:

> If we're creating a laundry list of actions, the plan can get very unwieldy. When you're doing this, [consider:] who is the primary county agency that's going to do this? And are they going to understand what you're asking them to do to put this into a budget item? And is this going to be a priority? We will be bringing back to you all of the actions that you have. And I think you'll start to see that there's a lot, and you're really going to have to make some choices as far as priorities, because there's only so much money.

Undeterred by the county's advice not to duplicate language within the plan, Nishiki pressed for the inclusion of policies related to water quality in multiple sections of the community plan. "I think it's important for us to state that we want to protect them in the Resources section, as well as Ready and Resilient Systems," said Nishiki. Specifically, she wanted to include an action stating: "Transition from use of wastewater injection wells to appropriate environmentally sound methods of wastewater disposal and promote the beneficial use of wastewater effluent" in both the sections on ready and resilient systems and protecting natural resources. Fellow CPAC members Payne and Ravi Bugga encouraged Nishiki to avoid redundancy in favor of focus.

\*     \*     \*

Chairperson Kai Nishiki asked the committee to approve a letter that would grant a six-month extension so that the CPAC could fully review the draft plan. She cited the upcoming holiday schedule as a reason why members might need more time to do their due diligence. At this point in the process the committee had not even reviewed the proposed zoning map, which everyone agreed would be the most important piece of the final plan.

Payne expressed concern that requesting an extension would set a precedent for other Maui communities to delay their processes, even though Molokai requested and received approval for a six-month extension for their plan. However, he was the only member who voiced concern. The CPAC voted to approve the request for an extension with member Pulmano offering a concise version of the letter.

## A Maze of Dead-end Streets
### *November 21, 2019*

The county received much testimony in support of improved pathways for pedestrians and non-motorized vehicles during the community planning process. A grassroots effort was underway to create a 25-mile multi-use trail in West Maui. The Maui Metropolitan Planning Organization had just completed Hele Mai Maui, a long-range transportation plan for the island. By the end of November, the CPAC had played its role in lifting these efforts.

Since the transportation section was one of the largest under review, committee chairperson Kai Nishiki moved quickly through the Planning Department's draft. The group adopted seven policies and 16 actions by consensus before fielding new policy ideas from members Karen Comcowich and Leilani Pulmano.

Comcowich introduced a policy to require new streets to be through streets, and to prohibit cul-de-sacs and gated communities. Joseph Pluta supported her proposal, citing the safety and traffic issues caused by the maze of dead-end streets along Lahainaluna Road: "That is absolutely the worst planned highway or street system I've ever seen in my life. And because of those dead ends and cul-de-sacs that lead to nowhere, you got to turn around and go back and try to find your way out." Planning administrator Pam Eaton said she wanted to allow the Department of Public Works to review Comcowich's proposed policy, because it could potentially conflict with Title 18, the county ordinance governing subdivisions and the county streets and ways created with them. For suggestions relating to Title 19, the county's zoning code, Eaton advised the committee to consider writing direct language to amend the code: "We can make a suggestion in the community plan saying something such as 'Title 19 should be amended to include....'"

Pulmano proposed a new policy to provide shoreside facilities to support boating activities at Mala Wharf and Lahaina Harbor. "We have such a huge boating community on this side of the island, and really not many facilities to provide them." Eaton said boating facilities were under the purview of the state's Department of Land and Natural Resources. She suggested revising the policy to state, "Support or work with DLNR." Pulmano also proposed a policy to support the continued use of Kapalua Airport for emergencies and other needs.

\* \* \*

Only a few proposed action items generated discussion, among them Number 15:

> Discourage at-grade intersections along the planned Lahaina Bypass Road in order to maintain safe and efficient flow or safe and efficient traffic flow without traffic signals. Consideration should be given to safe passage of agricultural equipment and vehicles where appropriate.

Comcowich objected to this item because she believed such intersections would take away from the small-town feel of Lahaina.

> I like on-grade intersections because they slow traffic down. I don't really like the way the bypass makes Lahaina feel like Honolulu or a city. We don't really want to turn into Honolulu, right? We want to maintain the small-town character. This policy to me is actually encouraging making the west side more of a city.

On the other hand, Ravi Bugga argued that slowing traffic would defeat the purpose of having a bypass at all. Pulmano suggested removing the policy because the bypass design was already complete, making such an action irrelevant. Nishiki deferred making any changes to the action item.

Another item that triggered discussion was one that stated: "Amend to improve the county's Chapter 2.97 fast track process to include sidewalks, multi-use paths and access to public transit for affordable housing." Dylan Payne, who consistently voiced his concern about any requirements that could stall affordable housing developments, said he was unsure whether he would support the action:

> If you're trying to create a 100-percent affordable housing project, sometimes having all these amenities makes that difficult because it increases the cost of a project. I don't know that I would support amending the code to include these things. I think it's something that should be addressed on a project-by-project basis, which is to say I don't think a project that oth-

erwise could be really good for the community should be rejected because it didn't include those things. I think it should be up to the council, right? Because they have the right to grant exemptions to various things per 2.97. I don't think I would support this.

Nishiki disagreed with his take, stating the people and families who would be moving into these affordable housing units needed these features most of all.

If we're talking about providing affordable housing, we're talking about people who are in the low- to moderate-income levels. Those are the people who most need access to public transit—they would most likely use sidewalks for walking to work, multi-use paths for biking to work...I fully support this amendment. I think we do a great disservice to those who are most needy if we do not provide access to public transportation, walking, biking, because that's another way for people to save money when they're already struggling to pay their mortgage.

Though Payne said he agreed with Nishiki, he said it would be challenging to require such livability features. He asked staff whether the County Council could allow exemptions to this requirement, to which Eaton responded:

The council can, Dylan, but I can also tell you having this in a community plan would encourage the county departments to not be intimidated and to be a little more proactive, because this is a very strong measure for quality of life. I think it would also encourage council, because they do look to community plans with regard to whether or not to grant an exemption.

Immediately following Eaton's remarks, Nishiki discouraged Payne from commenting on projects that were connected to his employer. This exchange was one of many in which the plan's reviewers—including Nishiki, Payne, and Planning Commission Chairperson Lawrence Carnicelli—would be accused of conflicts of interest.

Dylan, I know that you work for West Maui Land Company, and that West Maui Land Company may be involved in projects such as this. Perhaps this is a place that wouldn't be appropriate for you to participate in discussion or vote on things like this because you work for a development company and you're concerned that these amenities would increase development costs.

I'm just not sure that it's appropriate. I know that you are going before the
Board of Ethics to review conflict of interest.

In October of the same year, Payne asked the Maui County Board of Ethics
to review whether his employment as a licensed realtor with West Maui Land
Company conflicted with his role on the CPAC. In its opinion issued in February 2020, the Board said his employment "is not a financial interest that is
incompatible with his duties as a member of the West Maui CPAC." However,
it advised Payne to disclose his employment and refrain from voting on matters
affecting the interest of the company. He would still be allowed to vote on the
entire or final recommendations for the West Maui Community Plan.

Pulmano, who sits on the Hawaiʻi Housing Finance Department Development Corporation (HHFDDC), supported the proposed action. HHFDDC
also has a fast-track process called 201H. In this process, she said developers can
and do exercise their rights to request exemptions to meeting livability requirements. Pulmano also responded to Nishiki's comment about Payne's conflict of
interest: "I am a developer as part of what I do. I am going to suggest wording in
here that may help me as a developer and I don't think I need to recuse myself
from that discussion."

## AMEND THE COUNTY CODE

### *December 5, 2019*

By the end of the year, the CPAC needed to review the remaining draft policies
and actions covering economic growth, transportation, natural resources and
other issues tied to "healthy, livable communities." Members were mostly supportive of the policies and actions originating from both the CPAC and Maui
County agencies.

However, they continued to wrestle over wording involving the phasing
out of injection wells, a topic that led to lively debate in previous meetings. On
one hand, chairperson Kai Nishiki advocated to use "eliminate injection wells."
County staff continued to voice their concern over the feasibility of "elimination" within the timeframe of the plan. Scott Rollins suggested "minimize"
the use of injection wells. Ultimately, both sides agreed to "strive to eliminate
injection wells."

The final meetings of the year also brought back the challenge of whether
or not to include language in the West Maui Plan that either addressed county-wide issues or appeared in other state or county plans. Those who supported

inclusion emphasized the need to accurately represent community concerns. Opponents of this approach said they were concerned about making the plan cumbersome or causing conflicts down the road.

One example of how this disagreement played out was when CPAC member Karen Comcowich suggested the following policy: "Amend the county code to require permeable surfaces and other low-impact development standards be used in new or redeveloped parking lots and streets to mitigate runoff or and help with groundwater recharge."

Fellow member Dylan Payne questioned whether the West Maui Community Plan, or any other community plan, should include policies like Comcowich's. He wondered whether West Maui policies requiring amendments to county policies could create contradictions and implementation issues down the road. What if a neighboring community wanted something different than West Maui? What would the county do then?

Planning Program Administrator Pam Eaton acknowledged Payne's concerns while also pointing out that all area plans would be reviewed and approved by the Maui Planning Commission and the Maui County Council. If contradictions surfaced through this vetting process, they would be dealt with later. Community plans are appropriate places to recommend amendments to code, according to a recent audit of Maui County's Title 19 zoning ordinance: "One of the things that came out of the audit in terms of recommendations, Dylan, is they said, should the community have specific suggestions as to what should be included in the new code, to make those suggestions in the community planning process."

Dave Taylor, then Maui County's capital improvements project coordinator, reiterated a point he made in an earlier meeting: the committee should focus on the intent of a given policy versus spelling out specific solutions to problems and then requiring the implementation of those solutions.

It's something that I address almost every time I talk to you guys. Rather than implementing [an] act, [focus] on what you're trying to achieve. This was rephrased to say something like, "take actions to minimize offsite runoff and maximize the water that soaks into the ground." [...] You guys don't really need to get that into the meetings; you just say what result you want, then some of the staff experts will take that, and maybe it's implementing some sort of technology that exists.

In response to Taylor's suggestion, Nishiki showed she was uncompromising on the specificity of language. "While I can appreciate the comments of our resource people, I do think that it is important for us to be specific about certain action items. Just saying what we want doesn't always equal someone carrying that out, versus when we say this is how you do it."

Member Ravi Bugga, who often straddled a moderate approach when presented with conflicts, suggested a compromise that would both spell out specific implementing tools and include language that allowed for other approaches. Nishiki was ready to concede on this issue, but Comcowich did not yield, stating, "This is actually something I feel very strongly about because I've watched West Maui be concreted over by both small and large landowners." Nishiki stood with Comcowich, no one objected and the original proposed language was adopted.

## No Expansion of the Tourism Industry

### *December 17, 2019*

Up until the last meeting of the year, West Maui's large landowners or their representatives were largely absent from public testimony. The exceptions to this were John Kindred and Brad Paulson, who represented the Plantation Estates Lot Owners Association. The gated subdivision in Kapalua, Maui consists mostly of luxury single-family homes built on agriculturally zoned lands; the average home price for Plantation Estates was listed at more than $5 million in 2021. Representatives of Plantation Estates sought to change their community plan designation from agricultural to rural residential, a new designation category.

But many community members objected to the conversion of agricultural land for gentleman's estates. Paulson, a full-time resident and association board member, testified against a proposed policy to "prohibit conversion of ag lands within the Rural Growth boundary unless it can be demonstrated that conversion is required to accommodate population or employment object projections." He said such a requirement would be impossible, and the Maui Island Plan already allowed conversion. "In conclusion, we believe that policy should be either deleted or amended."

\*    \*    \*

The committee revisited a policy to halt new visitor development units until the supply of residential units improved. West Maui at the time had an estimated 11,884 visitor units, and residents were concerned over the insufficient supply of housing located near jobs. The CPAC had deferred action on this policy at a previous meeting to allow planning staff to propose new wording.

Planning staff came up with two wording options for the policy. The first offered a one-for-one approach: "No additional visitor units except bed-and-breakfast homes shall be permitted in West Maui unless an equal number of workforce housing units are currently developed in the same sub area." The second option was more restrictive. It included a clause requiring residential units to equal visitor units before any new visitor units would be permitted:

> No additional visitor units except bed-and-breakfast homes shall be permitted in West Maui until the supply of residential housing units equals the supply of visitor units. Once the supply of residential units exceeds the supply of visitor units at West Maui, new visitor units shall be permitted only if an equal number of workforce housing units are concurrently developed in the same area.

The CPAC's newest member, Angela Lucero, took issue with allowing bed-and-breakfast homes as an exception. Lucero, executive assistant for Maui County councilmember Tamara Paltin, had been appointed to replace Joseph Aquino after he left the CPAC. "I don't care for either of these options. It's because I feel our community has made it very clear they do not support any expansion of the tourism industry, especially investment properties and things like that." She wanted the exception removed, or a condition added to require adequate infrastructure needs be met before any new units are developed.

But beyond whether to allow bed-and-breakfast homes as an exception, the committee grappled with how strict they wanted the policy to be. Karen Comcowich advocated for option number two because it would theoretically correct the "horrible imbalance" of residential to visitor units before even considering the addition of more visitor accommodations. Ravi Bugga aligned with Comcowich, voicing his concern that West Maui was facing a tipping point toward "overtourism."

Members Dylan Payne, Joseph Pluta and Hans Michel backed the first option as a more simplified way of addressing the shortage of workforce housing. "Option one would incentivize those people that want to add visitor units to create resident housing," said Payne. "Option two, I think, is so unwieldy that those folks aren't going to do anything to help the housing stock here on Maui."

After several minutes of discussion, chairperson Kai Nishiki called a vote to adopt the second version of the policy. The motion fell one vote short of passing. Pluta then introduced a motion to adopt the first version of the policy; he was seconded. To Pluta's ire, Nishiki proposed the addition of language to the first version that would essentially make it the same as the second version. Visibly frustrated, Pluta claimed Nishiki violated Robert's Rules of Order by proposing an amendment to his motion. However, Pam Eaton clarified that Robert's Rules do allow proposed amendments as long as a vote is taken to accept the amendments. Ultimately not enough votes were garnered to incorporate Nishiki's amendment, which brought the group back to option number one without amendments. This option passed with eight of the 13 committee members voting in support.

## "You are Not Obligated to Designate it for Growth"

### *January 7, 2020*

At the start of 2020, as the world was beginning to deal with COVID-19, county planners presented the CPAC with an aggressive three-month schedule to complete their review. The hardest and most important work lay ahead. The committee would define its preferred growth alternative map for West Maui, which guides the character of future growth and influences the county's zoning decisions. The map would provide more specificity than the Maui Island Plan, and it would act like a traffic signal, allowing projects to move, or causing them to stall or stop altogether. As such, developers and related industries followed this part of the planning process closely. Large land developers would soon have the opportunity to present their projects to the committee. But before they did, county planners would describe the laws, principles and tools the CPAC would need to consider as they moved forward with creating the West Maui Community Plan.

The county introduced new community plan designations for the CPAC to use on their new map. A recent zoning audit recommended revisions to make the designations more descriptive, said planner Jennifer Maydan. Some designations used in the 1996 West Maui Community Plan, including agriculture and conservation, remained the same. New designations, such as "rural residential," "rural village," and various new commercial designations were created. One of the biggest changes was the phasing out of the "project district" designation. "The purpose of the project district was to provide flexibility for larger developments that didn't quite work with the zoning code that we have. And with our new community plan designations and our soon-to-come new zoning code, project district designation and zoning become obsolete," Maydan said.

Planners encouraged CPAC to use smart growth principles to guide their decisions. Such principles aspire to build communities where people could live, work and play, all within their neighborhoods. Smart growth encourages new development in already developed areas, leaving more open space in other areas. By contrast, the county's current zoning and planning practices did the opposite, Dylan Payne pointed out. Planning director Michele McLean agreed: "You're right that the land use designations and our zoning have led to that distinct segregation of uses. That's what we're trying to get away from so that smart growth can be facilitated." Leilani Pulmano, who worked at Pacific Rim Land Company, said she appreciated the changes.

> It's very difficult when you're doing a development, trying to do mixed use with getting a special neighborhood designed with our current zoning code and our current Community Plan. You actually are forced to do a project district and then come up with your own ordinances for development standards. It's really hard to create that, and then the implementation of that, where you have 10 project districts versus something like this. And the update with the zoning code will definitely help.

In setting the stage for the committee's task of developing the map, planning administrator Ann Cua described the layers of permitting that all developments must clear in order to gain approval to build.

> In the State of Hawai'i, and in Maui County, we have a pretty complex, multi-layered land use regulatory system. And many times, a project has to meet all the different layers to be able to be approved. We talked about how we have the state land use districts: basically conservation, urban, and rural. There's the Maui Island Plan layer, the community plans, zoning—which primarily I'm going to talk about tonight—and then environmental review, plus other designations like special management area, historic districts, FEMA or special flood hazard areas. The general objectives of all these different layers is to encourage appropriate uses of land, conserve and stabilize property values, prevent uses that would be detrimental to existing uses—the example of not having a heavy industrial use right next to a daycare center; that's what all these layers help to protect—and finally, to promote the health, safety and general welfare of the community.

Cua said many developers come to the Planning Department for input well ahead of submitting their applications. The department works with the developers to identify potential issues and also encourages them to seek community input. While developers are legally required to notify the public about their application and public hearing, they are not required to meet with the community, she said.

> A lot of people think that when a project goes to Planning Commission, and the department is recommending approval, that we're just rubber-stamping what an applicant wants, and that is the farthest from the truth. One of the things that I felt it was really important for me to mention—anybody who works in the department knows this—there's a lot of this back and forth. But a lot of people from the public don't realize that. There is a lot of going back and forth with looking at Community Plan language, looking at the zoning classification, looking at what people want to do, and advising people that, you know, this is not something that's going to be acceptable. And another thing that we've encouraged people to do for years now is before you come in with an official application, go out to the community—because that is going to save you a lot of time and heartache.

\*   \*   \*

The need to align the Community Plan with the Maui Island Plan was a common rationale for those who leaned toward allowing more development in West Maui. The islandwide plan defined the urban growth boundary for West Maui, and some believed that all or much of the area within this area was fair game for development. Committee member Jeri Dean, a school administrator, spoke to this point during an exchange with Ann Cua and Jennifer Maydan.

"As the planning representative, would it be your ideal goal to have the Community Plan aligned to the Maui Island Plan?" Dean asked.

"Yes, and I believe that's the intent. I don't think that what is being proposed to you, in terms of the Community Plan, is inconsistent with the Maui Island Plan," Cua responded.

"Okay, it could just be me; maybe I'm just seeing gaps. So I'm just trying to understand that alignment. I wanted to just hear that. That is the ultimate goal. So if we anchored our conversations to the Maui Island Plan, we're on the right track," Dean responded. Maydan added:

> Yes, absolutely. The Maui Island plan provides guidance for your process here in the community plan. But you also have to keep in mind that plans are not precise. Plans are plans—plans are looking forward 20 years and

saying, "We're probably going to grow like this; we're going to have these needs. Let's set these boundaries." But time does pass. Things happen. The Maui Island Plan was adopted in 2012. When we come to the stage of doing a Community Plan amendment, there may be more growth that has happened and with the need to potentially to look at the growth boundaries. And maybe a community plan would say, "Wow, these growth boundaries don't accommodate what we need." Or there may be the opposite, that growth hasn't happened much. Maybe the growth boundaries are providing us with too much inventory. Maybe we don't need to put urban-level community designations on all of these. And that's really what this time is—to really look at it and say, "Where do we need to grow?" There could be the opportunity to, if through this process you identify that you don't need all of the growth boundaries, there could be an opportunity to shrink to do a concurrent amendment to the Maui Island Plan.

Planning Director Michele McLean expanded further on this conversation, specifically addressing a question Dean had earlier about resolving inconsistencies between zoning and the community plan. Creating inconsistencies, McLean said, is part of the nature of the community planning process. She also pointed out that the law requires zoning to align with the community plan but does not require the community plan to be consistent with zoning.

Because we have existing development in West Maui. And you have to decide where future development is going to happen. By doing that, you're saying, for example, "On vacant ag land, we want that to be residential; we want that to be neighborhood commercial." So you will be creating inconsistencies. And that's what you are supposed to do. [...] When the time is right for that development to occur, then the zoning comes in, goes through its approval process that Ann described. Neighbors are notified. It goes to the Planning Commission and goes to the Council. The zoning has to be consistent with the community plan. That's in the law. The community plan doesn't have to be consistent with the zoning. The community plan, as you said, really needs to follow the Maui Island Plan. You don't want to start creating growth in the community plan that's not designated for growth in the Maui Island Plan. But you guys don't have to worry about creating inconsistencies with the zoning because that's what you're going to be doing. And that's what you're supposed to do.

Following McLean's comments, Karen Comcowich asked whether areas within the urban growth boundaries of the Maui Island Plan must be developed. She used the example of the area above Hanaka'ō'ō Beach Park. "The community really came out saying they would like to see that not developed; can we designate that as a park?" McLean replied, "It's in the Maui Island Plan growth area, but you are not obligated to designate it for growth if you do not think that that area is where this group wants to see growth."

*   *   *

Kai Nishiki asked McLean whether she thought comprehensively zoning areas for affordable housing and creating actions that prioritized infrastructure for those areas would help develop more housing. "Do you feel that would support affordable housing actually getting developed if there was an action item and the community plan designation?" McLean replied that doing so would help, but the tricky part was to ensure those developments remained affordable: "I would recommend doing that for the parcels you want to see comprehensively zoned and supported by infrastructure. Otherwise, just changing them and saying this should have that income restriction without any other supporting actions seems pretty strict."

Dylan Payne questioned whether the county could restrict uses in the manner that Nishiki described. "What if the property owner says, 'I don't want to do that'? What are their options? And that kind of speaks to a bigger question, right? If we only have so much power in creating the community plan, the landowner has to be on board with that as well." McLean said the support of the property owner is helpful, but not necessary, should the county seek to make changes. In cases dealing with entitlements, landowners are often very involved in the process.

Whether the developer, county or a group of landowners initiates a zoning change, that process can take anywhere from one year to 10 years, said Cua. A project that prompts concerns from the county or the community takes longer. Projects with support across the board can happen more quickly.

I've had a project where it went to Planning Commission, and there were two people that testified they had concerns about the project. By the time it got to County Council, it had exploded with all these people against it. [ ... ] All these things can affect the timing of a project. There can be a lot of agency concerns; it can just be a lot of community opposition. Then there can be a project the community loves, the Planning Commission supports, the County Council supports and it can just sail right through. So it varies.

Nishiki wondered whether a county-initiated zoning change, which would take less time and money than if a developer initiated a change, could be used to help incentivize the creation of affordable housing. When she asked whether the savings in time and money would be significant, McLean responded:

> It can be significant. When you look at the requirements for a change in zoning, there are a number of studies that need to be done. When the county initiates it, when it's typically for a public purpose, you don't have as rigorous a package that the Commission and Council review. There would still have to be some degree of understanding of infrastructure and other potential impacts, but it wouldn't be as extensive nor as costly as when an individual applicant does.

## How Much Growth Does the Community Want?

### *January 9, 2020*

Five growth alternative maps were given to the CPAC for their consideration. These maps would determine where and how growth could occur in West Maui. They would also help guide the county's zoning decisions.

Among the first to testify on the maps were Lawrence Carnicelli, Maui Planning Commission chairperson and then-managing director for Olowalu Elua Associates; and Peter Martin, vice president of West Maui Land Company and owner of Olowalu Elua. Martin was a controversial figure on Maui, vilified by those who accused him of exploiting the county's expedited planning processes at the expense of the community, and praised by others who believed he provided much-needed homes for locals.

Carnicelli, who said he felt nervous to testify before the CPAC, expressed his frustration with the growth maps presented by the Planning Department. His main issue with the maps was that they did not reflect the ones approved by the General Planning Advisory Committee (GPAC) in 2012. "When I looked at these growth maps, I looked at all the alternatives. They're not what the GPAC members thought that they voted on and decided on. That's not what's being presented." Carnicelli went on to give a pep talk to the committee members: "You guys get to make the difference. You guys get to say what, where that goes or not. You guys are the decision makers. You guys matter."

Martin reminisced about his decades of work on Maui, and declared his desire to build housing for residents: "I think I've been involved in building houses or selling developing land [and developed] about a thousand units. A lot of happy people have had houses from me, so I understand that customer. I'm very fortunate to be involved in land here. And my goal is to provide housing for local people. I feel we're taking huge steps backwards." When questioned by Hans Michel about his project at Waineʻe, Martin said he would pursue the 201H fast-track process—a process he had been criticized for misusing—to develop the area. "We still have to go through all the process. So if you don't do 201H, it could take 10–12 years. If we go 201H, which is what I would like to do, it's way more housing for locals. I don't see why people all of a sudden go, 'Oh, this is terrible.' It's a public process, and it's good."

Neither Martin nor Carnicelli liked the growth options presented by the Planning Department. When asked directly by committee member Dawn Hegger-Nordblom which growth scenario they preferred, Martin responded, "[The GPAC-approved plan] had more areas for housing for our local families. I respect you. You make the call. The planning department can't lead you around by the nose." Carnicelli dodged the question.

I'm going to answer like Brian Schatz did when somebody asked him about impeaching Trump. He said, "I'm not going to weigh in on that because one day, I'm going to have to make a decision." You know, so I don't think it's fair for me right now to do that, even though I can't quite take off that Planning Commission hat. I don't mean to skirt your question, but I just think that's kind of where I think I should make the decision—when all the information is present.

Ravi Bugga later asked Carnicelli to share his opinion about how the CPAC could "avoid the same fate that befell GPAC." Carnicelli contradicted the tone of his public testimony, in which he told the committee they were the decision makers and their actions mattered.

Unfortunately, you guys are advisory, right? You're not the final decision. Because it goes from you guys to Planning Commission, and then it goes to the Council. And if things hold true to how they've been, historically, the Council is going to rewrite the whole thing anyways. My frustration is what GPAC came up with is what was approved. And that isn't what was given to you guys. [...] Do the best you can. Vote your own conscience—you're one of 13. And as they say, there's your business, other people's business and God's business. Take care of yours. You guys can do the best you can. And then you trust. That's what GPAC did.

Two other governing bodies would influence the content of the West Maui Community Plan. After the CPAC finishes its review and work on the plan, it would be reviewed by the Planning Commission, where Carnicelli served as the chairman. Angela Lucero asked him what he thought the Commission's role was in reviewing the plan. His vague response hinted at the likelihood of the plan changing while in the hands of the commission.

> I personally don't want to be another CPAC. I don't want to go and do the same thing that you guys did. I think the Planning Commission—and again, I'm only one to nine—I think we should look at it from a completely different lens. What that is, I'm not sure. Admittedly you guys all live here in this community. Not everybody on the Planning Commission lives in Lahaina. I think the Planning Commission also has to be sensitive to that, too, and say, "Okay, some guy in Wailuku is going to make a decision for Lahaina." I think the Planning Commission has to be really real about who they are, what they are and what they are going to do.

Though the maps from the Planning Department were different than what the GPAC advanced in 2012, they reflected the current wishes of the community, Karen Comcowich argued. Carnicelli acknowledged this point but suggested that the community may have found the maps confusing. Comcowich pushed back against what he insinuated: "The maps may have been confusing, but do you think the community understands what they're currently living in and how much growth they would actually like to see in the community? Or do you think they can't comprehend that because they're on the ground?" He said the community did know what it wanted, but its opinions and actions were contradictory: "The number one thing this community wanted was housing. [...] And you go over here, what's the one thing that we don't want? Growth and development. So we're a little bit schizophrenic as a community."

*       *       *

West Maui's population has grown over the last two decades at a slightly faster rate than Maui County as a whole and the state of Hāwai'i, said planner Jennifer Maydan as she set the stage for the committee's review of the maps. Almost 60 percent of the population growth from 2004 to 2016 was from natural increase or from residents having babies. The other 40 percent was from migration, mostly internationally. West Maui's daytime population swells with visitors and residents who work in the area. About 31 percent of the daytime population is made up of workers from outside the region, and 53 percent is made up of visitors. Although the county could not predict the rate of population growth, it could nevertheless expect growth. Maydan remarked,

> We obviously don't have the crystal ball to predict the future population, and unexpected events happen that impact population growth. But we know the region is growing, there's a workforce housing shortage, and families are doubled and tripled up. Housing of the right type and in the right place is needed to address these critical issues.

Based on the State Department of Business, Economic Development and Tourism projections, which rely on trends and models, the County Planning Department came up with a projected growth of 33,754 people for West Maui. Planners used this figure as their target for creating the maps, which illustrate various development patterns that could produce enough housing to accommodate the anticipated growth.

Even though the projections created pressure for the CPAC to meet them, Kai Nishiki pushed back on the idea of having to meet the target need. What if the community did not want to create space for more people? Bugga questioned the figure's validity, saying the projections seemed like an overestimate. Maydan responded that the number they landed on was about 10,000 fewer people than what was projected in the Maui County 2014 Socioeconomic Forecast Report, and factored in new data from 2018, which predicted less growth.

> Based on new numbers that they came out with in 2018, [the figures] were ratcheted down. And we haven't seen the growth that was predicted during the time of the Maui Island Plan. But you have 33,000—that's quite a lower growth rate than we previously had. But you have to think about, as I mentioned, 60 percent of the population growth is from babies being born. It's not from people moving here. That's significant. There are a lot of people, as I'm sure you all know, who would like to live in West Maui, who work in West Maui, but can't afford to live here, can't find a home. And there's also many families that are doubled and tripled; there's quite a bit of crowding. Even if the growth rate has slowed, there could be many reasons for that

slowing. It could be because there's not the housing. There's not the opportunity for people to live in West Maui. And like I said, we do not have a crystal ball to know what the growth is going to be. But we would be very negligent if we did not plan for growth, if we did not try to accommodate land and potential uses to address the workforce housing shortage that we have and the crowding that we have.

On the other hand, Dylan Payne speculated whether the projected number of units created by the growth maps would actually get built. "What I'm driving at is, I think when we create this plan, and we say, 'Okay, here's where we're going to put housing,' [that] doesn't necessarily mean that's ever going to get built." He wondered whether planners could produce data showing how many homes were projected to be built in the 1996 plan and how many were actually built. Maydan said such data could be produced, but asked whether it would change the decisions of committee members. "Yes, there are many inhibitors to building housing, to initiating and completing projects. I think we know a lot of what those barriers are. So let's address them. Honestly, I think doing that research might take an incredible amount of staff time that would be directed much better in other places."

Of the five growth alternative maps presented to the CPAC, options one and two would allow for the least and the most growth. Option one would restrict growth to about 3,000 units, or about half of the projected need, while option two would allow the development of about 12,000 units. The remaining options would offer variations of the two options.

The Planning Department recommended the fifth map, which Maydan described as most closely reflecting the public input they received at community open houses in 2019. This growth alternative focuses growth close to existing infrastructure and services, as well as in and north of Lahaina Town. It was also the alternative that was the closest match to the housing need, providing a surplus of 800 units.

\* \* \*

In previous meetings, the CPAC had engaged in lengthy debate about how to reduce the number of short-term rentals in West Maui with the hopes of creating more long-term housing inventory. Central to this conversation was a review of the Minatoya list, which is a list of non-hotel apartments, condos and developments that can legally operate as short-term or vacation rentals. Some committee members were concerned that small, hotel-like properties currently designated as residential would no longer be allowed to operate. To address this concern, planning staff reviewed and recommended "hotel" designation for several properties on its preferred map.

*     *     *

In the Maui Island Plan, the subdivisions of Launiupoko, Plantation Estates and Kapalua were given rural growth boundaries even though they were located on agriculturally zoned lands. This implied they were more rural than agricultural in nature. The subdivisions could seek a rural residential community plan designation, and eventually a zoning change, within these boundaries. But those who participated in the planning process did not support this idea. They were concerned that making such changes would perpetuate the loss of farmland to "gentleman's estates." Commented Maydan:

> The overall community feedback was to keep these ag subdivisions as ag. Basically, the only feedback we got in support of changing these areas to rural residential was from the landowners within those subdivisions. Given this feedback, in the Planning Department alternative, we've kept these areas as ag. In addition to the strong community sentiment, we did this for a number of reasons. Changing the areas to rural residential isn't necessary to accommodate future growth. There's also a concern the increased density that rural zoning would permit in these areas that are removed from jobs and services would be inappropriate. And we did not see any overall community benefit to changing these ag subdivisions to rural residential.

Payne questioned the logic behind the department's decision. "When Jen [Maydan] was explaining it, she said, 'Oh, the people that live there, the landowners wanted it to be rural. But that's not what the community wanted.' That seems strange to me." He pointed out that the Planning Department designated some areas, such as the area above Ironwood Ranch, as rural residential when they seemed more agricultural in nature. Maydan responded,

> We've had a lot of discussion amongst our team as far as what to do with these rural growth boundaries that are around existing ag subdivisions. We understood the conversations and the intent at the time of the Maui Island Plan. We had discussions both ways. We had concerns. Hearing from the community definitely weighed in on the decision to leave these as ag. The pattern in these areas perhaps seems more rural, but these areas were developed with ag state land use, ag community plan, and ag zoning. Everyone

who developed those lands [and] bought those parcels understood that this
is ag; they knew what they had.

Planning Director Michele McLean, who took a more moderate approach
to addressing the topic, added:

[The development in those areas] wasn't planned the way that rural growth
is typically planned, as a buffer between urban and agriculture. It just happened we had a two-acre minimum lot size in ag that got used wherever
it could, and that has more of a rural feel to it. It's a failure of county agricultural zoning that allowed that pattern of development in the ag district
without promoting agriculture, and without getting benefits of agriculture,
with the residential use of those lands. No use crying over spilled milk. What
do we do about it now? I can see arguments on either side, and I don't think
one is much stronger than the other. It does have more of a rural feel. That
is what the Maui Island Plan calls it. But on the other hand, we don't want
to exacerbate something that in retrospect a lot of people aren't happy with.
We make our recommendation, but you guys have to make yours. It's not
an easy call. And it's a discussion that's been going on for a very long time.

## "Not Everything the Community
## Wants is Bad for the Deal"

### *January 21, 2020*

For the first time in the West Maui CPAC process, committee members would
hear directly from the area's large land developers. A panel on culture and the
environment would immediately follow, offering their perspectives on the
development projects. In brief public testimony at the start of the meeting,
Planning Commissioner P. Denise La Costa and Mark Deakos, owner of 3-P
Consulting, spoke about development. "I'm a planning commissioner. But this
is from my personal point of view. I would like the developers that are present
and all of those who want to build projects in Maui to stop buying credits and
start building homes that are required for those permits," said La Costa. Deakos
aired concerns about the county's 201H fast-track process, which can exempt
development projects that meet certain thresholds for affordable housing.

201H developers will tell you everything you're doing here through this
process is critical and very important...of course, unless they file a 201H
plan, right? Then [they] just have to win over five council members, get

an exemption to the community plan, maybe an exemption to zoning. So keep that in mind. That's a big concern. Makila Kai is a big example. West Maui wasn't a big fan of it. Certain people were, but that passed 201H. I think every other project in West Maui is coming down the 201H avenue.

*    *    *

Most of the development projects had been discussed or on the docket for more than a decade. What stalled their progress became the subject of debate throughout the CPAC proceedings. Dylan Payne asked the representatives why their projects have taken so long and what about the current environment would allow them to progress. The biggest reason cited was financial feasibility, though some projects also contended with litigation challenges. Tom Schnell, a consultant with PBR Hawai'i representing Maui Land & Pineapple Company and its Kapalua projects, said their progress was stalled by the 2008 recession, company downsizing and changes in leadership. "Now Maui Land & Pine is getting into a position where they can move forward on their development projects," he said.

Regardless of the reasons, the lack of progress frustrated policymakers who sought to create more affordable inventory. In public testimony months prior, Maui County Councilwoman Tamara Paltin suggested the CPAC consider language in support of "sunsetting" or expiring project entitlements after a defined period of time.

Each development representative was given three minutes to talk about their project, and the majority did so in a straightforward way. They described the number of units, zoning and location relative to growth boundaries.

The first presenter was Paul Cheng, who represented Maui Oceanview LLP and its Pulelehua project. The project had gained widespread community support for its affordable housing components. Committee member Joseph Pluta described the "unprecedented" support he witnessed for the project at a recent Land Use Commission meeting. "I love to see how things are possible. And I'm hoping that some of that can spread over, across the panel to everybody else," he said. Others lauded Cheng's efforts during the meeting and asked him to explain how he garnered support for the project. He responded,

> I really liked [that] the community told me what they needed. And I really tried to help every which way I can. And, you know, I believe in sharing. You can't win it all; you shouldn't win it all. To the extent I can afford to help, I want to help. And then when you listen to folks, you learn a lot, and

then you adapt it to the plan. It works. That's my story. Not everything the community wants is bad for the deal.

After Cheng came Schnell, Maui Land & Pineapple Company's representative. He spoke about two projects, Kapalua (Lahaina Project District 1) and Kapalua Mauka (West Maui Project District 2), both of which had been granted entitlements and "project district" designations. Decades later, neither of the projects were complete. "Maui Land & Pine plans to develop the rest of the Kapalua Project District Two within the next 20 years," Schnell said. He said his client wanted to keep both project districts and questioned the county's decision to do away with them.

> I understand the planning department and maybe the CPAC wants to eliminate project districts within Maui Island. But the recently approved Lānaʻi Community Plan and Molokai Island Plan do allow project districts, and they allow the possibility of additional project districts on those islands. [I'm] questioning why you want to eliminate it on Maui Island. And if that's the desire, it would be preferable if the existing project districts could remain if there were no more project districts approved. That's a policy decision. But these project districts have already been established. And there's been representations and commitments made.

Josh Dean, the brother of CPAC member Jeri Dean, represented four of Peter Martin's projects: Makila Rural East, Polanui Residential Project, Waineʻe Residential Project and Puʻunoa Project. He briefly referenced the projects' fact sheets and mentioned that two of the projects were in the rural growth boundaries and two were in the urban growth boundaries.

The final presentation came from Lawrence Carnicelli, then-Planning Commission chairman and the representative of Olowalu Elua Associates. Unlike the presenters who came before him, Carnicell did not delve into the details of the projects and instead talked about the concept of community. Back in 2010, the Hawaiʻi State Land Use Commission (LUC) deemed the project's Environmental Impact State unacceptable, in part because of the absence of archaeological studies and insufficient responses related to water supplies. In an attempt to revive the project, Carnicelli sought the committee's support.

> The fabric of Maui, the essence of Maui is small towns and rural communities. At some point in time, we stopped building communities, and

we started building housing. But if I look at my handout, the values and principles that guide Olowalu Town is it's a community for Maui families.

Committee member Dawn Hegger-Nordblom asked Carnicelli where the project stood with the LUC. He responded:

> As you know, it did not pass the Land Use Commission in about 2010. Right now, I would have to say the next hurdle is this. Does the CPAC, and ultimately the County Council, does the community want to have a community in Olowalu?

After Carnicelli's presentation, CPAC member Ravi Bugga criticized him for retaining his position as Planning Commission chairperson while also representing a proposed development project. "I have to confess I'm surprised to see you sitting there. I mean, isn't there perceived to be a conflict of interest if you're head of the Planning Commission, and you're also pushing a real estate development in Olowalu?" Despite Carnicelli's assertion that he sought clearance from the Ethics Commission when he joined the Commission, Bugga continued to express his dismay.

* * *

CPAC member Karen Comcowich challenged the developers to consider more than profit. She asked them to consider how their projects could benefit the community.

> How are you supporting the greater community, helping the residents of Maui, not your own pocketbooks and not the developers' pocketbooks? We want to help the residents of Maui to have fair and equitable lives, and also to protect the integrity of our environment. So I'd like to see how your plans are addressing that.

The questions that Comcowich raised were not just a matter of smart business or decency—they were a matter of law, as Keʻeaumoku Kapu, CEO of Aha Moku o Maui, Inc., would later point out in the same meeting. Hawaiʻi state law required the Department of Land and Natural Resources and the Planning Department to ensure Native Hawaiians had unobstructed access to cultural and environmental resources from the mountain to the sea. State laws also protected heirs' rights to kuleana lands: lands awarded by the Hawaiian Kingdom to families who were originally farming those lands. Despite the existence of these laws governing land and water use, Kapu said they were often missing from conversations like these.

> We should be at the table with the developers; we should be at the table with the Planning Commission; we should be at the table. We should be the first priority ones at the table to make sure that everything is transparent. Everything has to work in unity. If not, further complications come and all of a sudden.... [If] there's no transparency with the general public well enough [with] the Native Hawaiian community, then you have an uprising. There's issues of concern that haven't been addressed. There are kūpuna from that area; that hasn't been addressed.

Kapu and his fellow panelists, 'Ekolu Lindsay, president of Maui Cultural Lands, and Kaipo Kekona, a local farmer, Aha Moku representative and member of the Maui GPAC, appealed directly to the developers and decision makers in the room. Lindsay offered a definition of community to start discussion: "Those who have lived in the area long enough to develop an attachment to the land and ocean strong enough to take action." In his comments, Lindsay referenced Schnell's response to Hans Michel's request that Maui Land & Pineapple lands address the runoff from their properties. Schnell said he hadn't "been on the ground during the rain recently, so I'm not fully aware of the issue." Lindsay later responded to Schnell's comments with criticism:

> If you're a developer and you're going to tell me, "I don't know the impacts on the ocean, because I didn't see the last big rain," shame on you. Shame on you. You should know. We are relying on you to develop projects that are responsible, [that] take care of all of our cultural resources. That includes everything in the ocean, everything on land and air. You should know every single impact. You do a grubbing and grading permit during the wet season? I don't think so. "But the county gave it to me. It made it legal." But it doesn't make sense. You need somebody in your organization that has common sense. We are not just a bottom line, spreadsheet line item that you can adjust appropriately to save some money, so you can increase your bottom line. Do not sell into economics, understanding development is economics. But there is a morality side to it as well.

He later mentioned his father, the late Ed Lindsay, a community leader who foresaw the coming wave of development on Maui. " 'Every single one of these valleys,' he told me, 'They're going to be developed. I don't think we can stop them. But we can make them responsible for the developments.' Him and Peter Martin got into some big scraps. But at the end of his life, in 2010, they were good friends. He made Peter into a more responsible developer. A lot of the people may not appreciate him, but I think his heart's there; just got to steer him."

For their closing remarks, Kapu spoke about the desecration of burial sites and Kekona spoke about agriculture. Kapu asked the development representatives to move forward cautiously, to consider the County's forthcoming overlay and the archaeological inventory assessment.

> Many things to consider when you start looking at one build up. When you start talking about concreting this whole area, I must definitely tell you guys, [burials are] going to come up. They've been coming up. And we've been responsible for putting them to rest again. Every time you wake them up, we got to put them to rest. That's my job. Maybe we can all come together; maybe I get a chance to be good friends with Peter Martin. No ways. I doubt it. Because he doesn't share the same values we do. None of them do. I just hoping they start to realize, maybe the next two, three burials that they dig up, it's not them calling me. It's the state that has to call me, because I'm responsible for all burials, and I put myself in that position. Why? Because they cannot speak for themselves.

Kekona advised the CPAC to keep Launiupoko in agriculture, and said that allowing development in Olowalu would encourage sprawl, which should be discouraged in light of climate change.

> When projects of sprawl come up, and you thinking about rezoning just Launiupoko, trust me, lo and behold, everything will be up for grabs for try and rezone everything else. I mean, they're going to have every single angle and reason why. [ . . . ] This place was the Venice of the Pacific. That was not written by our kūpuna. The people who came on the missionary ships and the whaling ships, this was their *mana'o* [thought, idea, opinion]. Food from Lahaina had sustained villages that was established on Lāna'i. For centuries, people, the people of Lāna'i, came to Lahaina and grabbed food in times of famine. So that tells you alone this place was more than capable of providing food for hundreds of thousands. Can we get back to that point? It'll take us quite a while. We've taken some abuse over here. But I not gonna give up and I'm gonna keep pushing forward on that.

As the meeting came to a close, Payne asked panelists for their advice on balancing the needs of the community. Lindsay offered a simple answer: focus on the few things that matter, such as 'ohana, health and environment, and let your decisions be guided by how those things might be impacted.

## "What's Really Going on Here?"

### *January 23, 2020*

The CPAC began its deliberations on the growth alternative map for West Maui. Committee members would need to decide whether they wanted to adopt the Planning Department's designations for the Kapalua projects represented by Tom Schnell and the agricultural designation for Plantation Estates. Prior to making those decisions, however, they listened to testimony from landowners in the subdivision.

Brad Paulson, a resident and board member of Plantation Estates Homeowners Association, came before the CPAC again to appeal to change his subdivision's zoning from agriculture to rural. In his testimony, Paulson said the rural residential designation better matched the character of the neighborhood.

Unconvinced by Paulson's rationale, committee member Ravi Bugga pressed him to share the "real reason" for their push to redesignate: "You've submitted two or three written testimonies, attended all these meetings, including community meetings for the last year plus, that's a lot. Just to ask for pictures to match words. To my mind, I'm still struggling to find what's really going on." Finally, Paulson explained the state's agricultural law prohibits any provisions that interfere with agricultural activities. Paulson was referring to the Hawai'i Right to Farm Act, which was passed by the Hawai'i State Legislature in 2001. The law states:

> No law, ordinance, or resolution of any unit of local government shall be enacted that abridges the right of farmers and ranchers to employ agricultural technology, modern livestock production, and ranching practices not prohibited by federal or state law, rules, or regulations.

This made creating uniformity in standard design rules—which would add value to the homes—difficult to obtain. Subdivision owners often threaten legal action because they do not have the flexibility to do what they want, said Paulson. "There's just innumerable fights in our neighborhood about somebody wants a fence a certain way, instead of another."

Few were sympathetic to the owners' desire to change the zoning. Even Hans Michel, who is a farmer and took a pro-development view, said he wasn't sure he could sympathize with the Plantation Estates owners. "To me, agriculture is agriculture, then leave it be. And [the] association you don't need because there's too many guys poke their nose all over the place. [ . . . ] I don't know if I can sympathize with you because you like to change it to rural residential, which puts a lot of more cars on the road, where we don't even have the road for all of you."

As Bugga, Jennifer Maydan and others would point out throughout the process, the people who bought lots in the Plantation Estates Subdivision knew they were purchasing agriculture lots and they purchased them anyway. Paulson himself acknowledged that developers capitalized on the agricultural zoning. "Developers, when they came through, could develop land more quickly and without rezoning. And they did. But it leaves us with a set of laws that is a mismatch." About half of the subdivision already has homes on it, and of those 53 existing homes, Paulson guessed that about 10–15 of them were occupied full time.

Rather than changing the community plan designation, Karen Comcowich suggested the lot owners collaborate with farmers.

> The vision from people who lived on the west side was that they were going to subdivide this land, and people who wanted to live on the farm and farm the land they were living on would be able to have that little piece of farmland—not a huge piece, not an industrial commercial site, but a little piece of farmland to actually be able to farm. What happened, obviously, is people with more money and less interest in farming came in and took that property. To me, I would prefer to see it stay in agriculture, and to see communities such as yours, who have the resources, to pay farmers to farm their land rather than landscapers to landscape.

Paulson, who said he does farm his property and tries to sell the fruit he produces, called Comcowich's idea an interesting one. He supported the idea of community farming parks, which could provide free access to the land: "That seems like an interesting experiment that we should be doing."

John Kindred, who also represents Plantation Estates, took a different approach to Paulson's testimony when his time came up. He accused the Planning Department of endorsing gentleman's estates by allowing the subdivision to remain in agricultural zoning. Kindred said at the time the county made an agreement with the neighborhood to accept "agriculture land conservation," or the planting of grasses and trees to stabilize the soil, as an acceptable form of agricultural activity. He said a better approach would be for the county to abolish agricultural subdivisions, after the redesignation of Plantation Estates as rural residential.

> I thought it was ironic after all the discussion about gentleman estates and ag land that the Planning Department came out with a recommended map which shows our neighborhood is ag land, when in fact we're composed of gentleman estates. This recommendation effectively endorses and perpetuates gentleman estates in ag land.

Kindred went on to share anecdotes of how, by putting up barbed wire fences or allowing people to sleep in vans on their property, some of his neighbors were using the agricultural zone to violate the association's covenants, conditions and restrictions (CC&Rs), and then use the agricultural zoning rules to "evade compliance."

> We had an incident where one of our owners was doing farming and had a farm employee; that employee actually was living in a truck on the property, and that, in our view, is undesirable. That owner suggested that was absolutely essential for his conduct of his farming activities. Furthermore, it came to our attention because that individual, that farm employee, committed a breaking and entering on an adjoining property to effectively utilize the laundry and shower facilities of the adjoining neighbor who was not present for a period of a few weeks.

The more Kindred's rationale for a zoning change became clear, the more annoyed some of the CPAC members became. Karen Comcowich:

> I'm really sorry that your neighborhood has had to deal with some of the struggling people on Maui who can't find a place that they can afford to live. That sounds very difficult. But one of the things about your community is that after they decided that [they wanted] a rural designation, the West Maui community came out very strongly saying not only do we not want future gentleman estates...the West Maui community would like to enforce what was already established, and what the community desired, which is houses with farms around them.

Kindred called Comcowich's comments a mischaracterization. He said the association did an extensive analysis of the general community sentiment about the rural residential designation, and the feedback on Plantation Estates was positive. He acknowledged the comments about other gentleman's estates in West Maui were negative.

Immediately following the exchange between Kindred and Comcowich, testifier Lee Aaron Yap, a Lahaina resident, summed up the community's frustration.

I understand you guys' plight, but you guys bought into something that you guys want to just hold your money value on that house. You guys are worried about fences that are barbed wire fences that bring your property value down. That's what we're talking about here—bringing your property value down. I live right down in Napili. We grew up in your area. Nobody's farming up there.... If you guys throw a bunch of palm trees out there and call it farming, that's not farming; you're not feeding anybody. You have a bunch of tangerines and a bunch of homeless places that can take that food and people will be very thankful for you. You might not get money out of it, but you might have a happy face. You might make some friends out there. But that's where you guys should start. Take care of the community, maybe the things will change what people view of what your land is. The gentleman estates property part? We already are comfortable with it. I know it ain't gonna change. I've been watching you guys do that for 20 years. I watching Launiupoko, I watching Kapalua, I watching Olowalu turned into that. What you're saying is already happening, sir. It happened at Macnuts in Waiehu. It happens all over this place. We've come to accept it. But what you guys don't accept is that when somebody like us buys the land there and we decided to throw up a barbed wire fence and have our pack of dogs and our pigs run wild, that's when you people lose your mind. That's the only reason that you guys are up here is that somebody is probably running through your guys' grass with their boats and their pigs and it drives you nuts, and you guys can't do anything about it. Sorry to say like Hans and all these people have told you, you bought into a place where you should have known the rules. Don't come here and change the rules. Come here to live—when you go to Hawai'i, live like a Hawaiian. When we go to Indiana we live like Indianans. Don't try to come here and change what's already there. Maybe it's not the best. But what we have as agricultural [zoning], it holds us some sort of rules. If you guys take away that stuff and let it be rural, all we are doing is letting the wolf run the pack. Take care of the sheep because all us local people, we're the sheep on this island. We just watching all this money come in and change what we have here, and it's not changing for the better.

The Planning Department recommended keeping Plantation Estates in agricultural designation rather than changing it to a rural residential designation as requested by lot owners. But the CPAC members could not come to agreement on a designation.

Comcowich made a motion to accept the Planning Department's recommendation. Yvette Celiz seconded the motion. Pluta and Payne argued in support of changing Plantation Estates from agriculture to rural residential zoning. Pluta:

> I was very impressed with the fact that the testimony we received regarding the logic for making this what it is, instead of what it isn't, was very persuasive to me. Especially the resort association, which is the whole area. When asked for the people's input, the entire association of the area wants this to happen. Then we're going against that with this motion.

Bugga, in response to Pluta, said, "I'm concerned that we're using a sledgehammer to kill a fly. In fact, we've been asked to change the designation to help with enforcing CC&Rs and so forth without knowing the implications for other developments on the rest of Maui."

Comcowich's motion to adopt the county's recommendation to keep Plantation Estates in agriculture failed in a 5–5 vote. Vice Chair Jeri Dean and members Bugga, Celiz, Comcowich, and Angela Lucero voted in favor of the motion, while members Donald Robert Gerbig, Dawn Hegger-Nordblom, Michel, Payne, and Pluta opposed.

\* \* \*

Both Leilani Pulmano and Kai Nishiki were absent from the meeting. Pulmano emailed her testimony to the rest of the committee when they arrived at the meeting. Payne and Comcowich asked to review this testimony, but Deputy Corporation Counsel Michael Hopper advised against doing so because it could potentially violate the Sunshine Law. He advised the committee to submit future testimony in person at the meeting if they wished to do so.

\* \* \*

As Tom Schnell mentioned in a previous meeting, Maui Land & Pineapple wanted to keep its Kapalua Project District One. However, the county sought to phase out "project districts" due to the difficulty of administering them. In place of the "project district" designation, the county reviewed the Kapalua projects and assigned matching community plan designations to the project.

If the CPAC adopted community plan designations for Kapalua Mauka, explained planning administrator Ann Cua, the landowner would be required to follow those designated uses. If they keep the "project district designation," they could make changes and seek approval for their plans later down the line. But if they wanted to make changes under the county's proposal, they would need to seek a community plan amendment, which would trigger an environmental assessment.

> I think the question is if [Maui Land & Pineapple] did not get phase two
> project district approval for the rest of Kapalua Mauka, what would happen?
> If the community plan goes through, with whatever designations, that
> would kind of dictate where land uses would occur. If their development
> is consistent with that, and they come in for Phase Three approvals, then
> there's no problem. But if they decide that they want to do something dif-
> ferent, they don't have that flexibility—they would have to seek a Commu-
> nity Plan Amendment. And a Community Plan Amendment is a trigger
> for Chapter 343. So they'd have to do an environmental assessment or an
> environmental impact statement.

Payne said the county's approach seemed logical and asked Schnell if the landowner had any proposed alternatives other than keeping its "project districts." Schnell responded they would be open to continuing to discuss the issue with the county. Michel then questioned Schnell about the affordable housing promises made by Maui Land & Pineapple when the project districts were created.

> [Kapalua Mauka] got built out and they promised the people they will make
> affordable houses in Pulelehua, and during the regime with Macnut the
> whole thing fell apart because the company did not have enough funding
> anymore. What happened to that promise for affordable houses while the
> high-end guys got their houses on the hill?

Schnell said the commitment to build 125 affordable homes through Pule-lehua was still in place; the responsibility was transferred to the new owners.

Eventually, Bugga made a motion to accept the Planning Department's recommendation for Kapalua Mauka (Project District Two), with a request that staff meet with the developer to discuss creating a cultural center within the project. Celiz seconded the motion. Payne asked if the county could create a project district designation that could stay in place for several years: "Basically leave it as is, but then have that project district sunset to this recommendation if the landowner doesn't do anything within, say, 10 years or something. That would give them the opportunity and the time to develop their preferred plan for the project district."

Payne's fellow committee members pushed back against his suggestion, with Dean saying the landowner had ample opportunity to work with the county. Gerbig asked if the landowner still had options in the process to propose an alternative. Planning Director Michele McLean replied that yes, the landowner could appeal to the CPAC later in the process, or the Planning Commission or the County Council. Bugga's motion passed by a 9–1 vote with Payne dissenting.

The approval for Kapalua Project District One moved much more swiftly. Bugga introduced a motion to accept the Planning Department's recommendation. Payne seconded it, and the CPAC voted unanimously in favor of the motion.

* * *

The final action taken by the committee was to accept the county's recommendation to grant hotel designation to two Minatoya list properties in the Kapalua sub-area. The list was created by the Minatoya Opinion, a legal memorandum allowing certain apartment-zoned properties to operate as vacation rentals.

Planners chose a threshold of 85 percent or higher of units operating as short-term rentals to determine which properties operated more like hotels. However, Pluta argued that 65 percent, a type of supermajority, seemed like a more appropriate benchmark. But Comcowich wanted to see fewer on the list.

> A lot of [the vacation rentals], when I moved here 15 years ago, were actually apartments and where people lived. Since Airbnb and VRBO took over, those apartments have gone off the market for people who live here. That's exacerbating the problem we have with affordable housing. The reason we want to kind of sunset some of this is so we can have more access to housing without necessarily needing to wait for it to be built. Just going with what the owners are currently doing as their use is not necessarily the best thing for our community.

However, McLean pointed out that county staff and councilmembers were discussing the "phasing out" of the Minatoya entitlement. She viewed such an action as unlikely, and said a more realistic scenario was the entitlements would be scaled back. That's when a change in designation could factor into which properties could stay on the list.

> At some point in the future, I've heard talk among councilmembers, and even among some of my own staff, of phasing out the Minatoya entitlement. And if that were to be done, that could be done for all of these properties across the board, no matter what you designate them. However, I don't think that would happen. To that extent, I think it's more likely that some properties would be retained. And one of the ways to make the distinction between who gets to keep the short-term rental entitlement versus who doesn't could be the Community Plan designation.

Councilmember Tamara Paltin said she was supportive of the county's recommendation. She spoke about the council's near-term efforts to limit the number of short-term rental permits to their existing levels in South and West Maui. She also said they were interested in scaling back the list based on which properties were paying taxes at the short-term rental rate. Bugga made a motion to accept the county's recommendation, and Gerbig seconded. The motion passed by a vote of 7–3 with Michel, Payne and Pluta objecting.

## "The Community is Really Against this Part of Development"
### *February 4, 2020*

Next, the CPAC reviewed the growth map for Kāʻanapali sub-area, including two long-proposed developments with affordable housing components. One was Pulelehua, which gained rare and broad community endorsement because of its responsiveness to residents' input. The other was a cluster of subdivisions known collectively as Kaʻanapali 2020. Developers for the project convened a community advisory group in 1999 after encountering strong opposition over its original plans. The group's participants included the late Ed Lindsay and two CPAC members, Joseph Pluta and Hans Michel. Two members of the Lindsay family, Ekolu and Puanani, who replaced her husband Ed in the group, asked the CPAC to approve the project in its entirety.

The 917-acre Kaʻanapali 2020 project consisted of three main parts: Puʻukoli'i Village Mauka, Kā'anapali Town North, and Kā'anapali Town South—a property bordering Hanaka'o'o Beach Park, a favorite among locals. Even though Kā'anapali Town North and Pu'ukoli'i Village Mauka were already fully entitled projects, meaning their development plans had already been approved by the county decades prior, the Planning Department's recommendation diverged from these plans. Their proposed growth map would designate Pu'ukoli'i as Agricultural versus Small Town Center—the designation preferred by the project's developers and advisory group. Planner Jennifer Maydan explained why the county recommended keeping the land in agriculture:

> We did this based on a lot of the feedback we got from the community as far as the massiveness of the development, and especially concerns of the Kā'anapali Town South area—the reality of how far mauka the Pu'ukoli'i Village area is, the necessity of the bypass extension north. But based on feedback from the community, we scaled down the project to what you see on the Planning Department recommended right now.

However, some CPAC members pointed out the northern portion of the project was already fully entitled, negating any recommendations the county or the community plan had. Leilani Pulmano made a motion to grant Pu'ukoli'i a designation of Small Town Center. But before they could take a vote, chairperson Kai Nishiki proposed an amendment to approve the redesignation while also keeping the southern portion of Kā'anapali in agriculture: "So we're taking a vote on the amendment to include a condition that upon approval of adding Pu'ukoli'i that Kā'anapali Town South would remain ag." The motion failed. A subsequent vote to change the designation of Pu'ukoli'i from Agriculture to Small Town Center passed. They also voted unanimously to adopt the county's recommended designation of Small Town Center for Kā'anapali Town North.

\* \* \*

With the northern portion of Kā'anapali largely approved as envisioned, the committee moved on to designations for the southern portion, which was a much bigger concern for CPAC members, residents and planners. Karen Comcowich commented:

> I understand this plan has been in the works for 20 years, and I really appreciate all the work that's been put into it. But the community is really against this part of development. It is right above Hanaka'o'o Beach. It's where the

community has a beach that's in town. It's the only beach left the community has in town. The community is very against this particular section of development. And maybe that's more recent, as everybody's gotten pushed out more. Maybe the community was more in favor of it 20 years ago.

Though Pluta pointed out project plans included a park area above Hanaka'o'o Beach, Comcowich referred to it as "more of a pocket park." County planners cited overwhelming community support for keeping this southern portion designated as agriculture. Comcowich invited the Ahu Moku Council, an advisory body of native Hawaiians with ancestral ties to the areas they represented, to provide their input on the matter. They spoke in support of keeping the area undeveloped, particularly because all of the surrounding areas were approved for development. Chairperson Kai Nishiki then asked Ahu Moku councilmembers whether they would prefer a designation of Agriculture or Park/Open Space—the former would allow some residential development. U'ilani Kapu responded, "We want it open space, because what's going to happen in Kahoma? They are going to develop it. That's going to have a big, drastic, adverse effect down below and with the waterways coming from up there that blows out Hanaka'o'o when it does pour—that's a huge thing. We're looking at it from top to bottom."

In contrast to the county's recommendation that Kā'anapali Town South stay in Agriculture, the developers sought a mix of Urban, Resort Hotel and Small Town Center for the area. When Pulmano asked why the Resort Hotel designation did not appear on the master plan for Ka'anapali 2020, project representative Chad Fukunaga responded, "The Ka'anapali 2020 map is an evolving thing. It hasn't been updated in a little while, although the vision has changed. The map itself may be a little dated, so it does not reflect the limited-service hotel. But it was discussed in a Ka'anapali 2020 meeting, voted on and approved by the group." Although Pulmano introduced a motion to adopt the county's recommendation for Kā'anapali Town, she later withdrew it. Nishiki then introduced a new motion to designate Kā'anapali Town South as Park and Open Space, Comcowich seconded. The motion failed in a 5–4 vote with Nishiki, Ravi Bugga, Angela Lucero, Comcowich and Pulmano voting in favor, and Dylan Payne, Michel, Pluta and Don Gerbig opposed. By default, the county's recommendation remained. The development of Kā'anapali Town South would stay limited for the time being.

*        *        *

At the request of the landowner, the CPAC unanimously voted to grant a Neighborhood Center designation to a single small parcel known as the China Boat Restaurant Property. Lastly, in a 7–2 vote, the committee adopted the county's recommendation to grant Resort Hotel designation to two Minatoya-list properties: the Kahana Outrigger and Papakea. Bugga, who voted against the recommendation, expressed concern the designation would allow the properties to become redeveloped as larger, more resource-intensive hotels in the future.

## "Project Districts are Antiquated"
### *February 6, 2020*

With decisions on Kāʻanapali 2020 behind them, the CPAC began its discussions about Pulelehua. Several projects, including this one, had been granted Special Project District designations in the 1996 West Maui Community Plan. Because of the cumbersome nature of administering the designation, the county's Planning Department was taking steps to phase them out. Some committee members argued to keep them, particularly for developments already granted the entitlement. Leilani Pulmano:

> Pulelehua received Community Plan Project District. With that designation the entitlements allow flexibility. And that's the purpose of actually going through a Project District entitlement process. Now I take a look at this, what was designated, and it seems to me that we're sort of walking backwards on that, because now we're deciding where it is that Residential is going to be and where it is that some of the Commercial is going to be, as opposed to they have the ability to designate where that is. I'd like to, frankly, allow them to continue that flexibility.

Responding to Pulmano's comments, planning program administrator Pam Eaton said one of the main reasons why the county updated the community plan designations was because "Project Districts are antiquated." While the intent of creating Project Districts was to allow flexibility, planning administrator Ann Cua said the whole process has become cumbersome. "The whole process hasn't worked completely how I think it was envisioned to [by] the department. As it is now, the existing Project Districts have encouraged people not to go through that process, and we're not recommending any new Project Districts," she said.

The developers of Pulelehua were agreeable to lifting the Project District designation and worked with planners to align their plans with the new designations being proposed by the county. However, project representative Paul Cheng submitted testimony at the Feb. 6, 2020, meeting to request 23 acres of the plan be changed from Open Space to Rural Residential to allow the construction of one home. "We noticed the map shown on your official record indicates an area on the far north end of Pulelehua is designated as Open Space/Park. In fact, our plan as approved by SLUC for that area is an Estate Lot designated for one house within the 23 acres." That home, as Kai Nishiki later clarified, was to be Cheng's family home.

Joseph Pluta introduced a motion to approve Cheng's request. Hans Michel said he was concerned the luxury homes would be built before the affordable housing piece. "Now this is the new contractor which spins all the wheel; they get everything going, which we're glad we have affordable housing, but I would like to see the 125 houses get built first because that is something never when happen while the high-end guys have all their nice houses on the hill." Nishiki interjected to say his comments were not related to the motion. The CPAC passed with nine members in support of the change. Michel opposed.

Following the vote, Pulmano introduced a motion to designate all of Pulelehua a "Special Purpose District."

> I think we're walking back [Pulelehua's] entitlements. And although I think that the developer is agreeable to it, I just think from a matter of principle, that we're walking back their entitlements. They're fully entitled Project District on community plan, and fully entitled Project District on change in zoning. It's consistent with their standard; the developer is fine with that. But I think that in 20 years from now, it still allows flexibility. My second point is if you take a look at your map, and you look at Pulelehua versus you look at Kāʻanapali Town North, that is not fully entitled. But yet their whole development is fully flexible with the Small Town Center designation.

However, Eaton explained the Special Purpose District designation was created for a particular type of development that was so unique it could not be covered in any other plan designation. Her examples included an airport or a harbor. Pulmano asked whether another plan designation aligned with the "intent" of her motion. Eaton responded, "I'm not sure what your intent is—is your intent that you just don't want developers to have to say where they're going to put what where? Is that what is meant by flexibility? That's what I'm trying to understand." As a matter of principle, Pulmano said she wanted Pulelehua to be afforded the flexibility it was originally granted. "I know this developer has his plans, and he certainly wants to move forward with it. I just see the disparities in the level of flexibility between Pulelehua and Kāʻanapali town in terms of the designations for Community Plan." Pulmano's motion failed by a 2–8 vote. Yvette Celiz abstained from voting, which counted as a second vote in favor of the motion. A subsequent vote to adopt the county's designations for Pulelehua passed unanimously.

\*     \*     \*

The next development up for consideration was the Villages of Lealiʻi, affordable housing projects all on ceded lands[11]. The northern portion is overseen by the Department of Hawaiian Home Lands, while the southern area is managed by the Hawaiʻi Housing and Finance Development Corporation (HHFDC). Pulmano disclosed that she currently served as chairman of the HHFDC board. She said the Board of Ethics reviewed her role and concluded she could participate and vote on matters related to the project. The committee's decisions focused on the HHFDC portion of the project. Although the developer sought a Residential designation for the entire project to maximize development, the Planning Department recommended a more restrained approach. Ravi Bugga introduced a motion to accept the county's recommendations. The CPAC passed the motion in an 8–2 vote, with Payne and Celiz opposed.

\*     \*     \*

While the CPAC did not have the authority to make zoning decisions, what it decided to do about land use designations would affect what zoning requests could be made within those designations. That is why projects like Plantation Estates appealed to the CPAC to change their area from an Agricultural

---

11. "In 1898, when the United States annexed the Hawaiian Islands and transformed them into a territory of the United States, the self-proclaimed 'Republic of Hawaii' 'ceded' about 1.8 million acres of land to the United States. This transfer remains surrounded by controversy, because the participation of U.S. military and diplomatic officials in the 1893 overthrow of the Kingdom of Hawaii has been recognized to be 'illegal' and a violation of international law by the U.S. Congress in the 1993 Apology Resolution, which also says that the transfer of the lands in 1898 was 'without the consent of or compensation to the Native Hawaiian people of Hawaii or their sovereign government.'" (https://www.civilbeat.org/2010/10/5914-what-are-the-ceded-lands-of-hawaii/)

designation to a Rural Residential designation. With a rural designation, Plantation Estates owners could later request their lots be rezoned Rural Residential.

Planner Kate Blystone explained the close relationships between the two in the early spring meetings when the CPAC was making land use designation decisions. "You can't separate community plan designations and zoning," explained Blystone. "Some of the reasons why someone would want a Community Plan designation that's Rural Residential over Agriculture is just for what Ann said—that you can then get the zoning of Rural and subdivide your property. So that's one [reason]. So those two go together, that's really important."

Neither Maui County nor the County Council can grant a zoning change that is inconsistent with the Community Plan, planning administrator Ann Cua explained. "That's why your designations are so very important—because we can't approve a change in zoning that is inconsistent with your Community Plan designation. One of the questions that you had about why, why are people coming to me, you know, wanting a Rural Residential? Well, one of the reasons is maybe they want to do half-acre lots in the future."

## Conflicts of Interest

### February 18, 2020

Albert Perez from Maui Tomorrow testified again in reference to a 1992 capacity study, which concluded that West Maui is beyond its wastewater and transportation capacity.

> We're still beyond capacity. Now we're pushing up against freshwater capacity. There are other types of infrastructure, like the space on our beaches— how many people can we squeeze onto beaches that are disappearing because of sea level rise and erosion? I would just like to ask this committee to please prioritize all of our remaining infrastructure for truly affordable housing, not for visitor accommodations, and not for anything more than a limited amount of Commercial to service the affordable housing.

Perez went on to express his concerns over the vagueness of the land use designation definitions, and how they could be used to exploit the system for the sake of development.

> When you have the wrong person in charge of the mayor's office and the Planning Department, they're going to interpret things broadly to allow

development, and that's what has happened in the past. That's what will continue to happen. The language as it is right now is vague, and it will be exploited by developers and needs to be tightened up and made more specific.

\*   \*   \*

At the previous meeting, Leilani Pulmano disclosed her position on the board of the HHFDC. Other CPAC members would also come to disclose, or be accused of, conflicts of interest. In his public testimony, Darren McDaniel mentioned two examples of committee members' bias. Both examples referenced the misuse of kuleana lands in Kahoma. The first mentioned Hans Michel's farm animals running loose in the area, and the second example was a house built in Kahoma owned by Jeri Dean's family. Several minutes after McDaniel's testimony, Keʻeaumoku Kapu singled out Dylan Payne for his conflict of interest as an employee of West Maui Land Company. Kapu's scathing testimony was met at one point by someone yelling, "Who talks like that?" from the audience.

> Another one, Kahoma Village, that one I take very seriously because my kūpuna is from that valley and I don't like the way these guys, hoodlums, West Maui Land Company as well as Kahoma Land Company, cutting off our access and allowing the so-called person who claims he bought prop-/ erty with one warranty title, he put an additional gate up there [with] permission of Hawaii Housing & Financial Development Corp. under your supervision. Mr. [Peter] Martin, I'm here to give everybody fair warning. [...] Whatever you guys do I have a conflict with you. And if I have to file a contested case hearing against you, Mr. Dylan, the so-called person that is responsible for selling all these property with a warranty title deed or quitclaim, I will be on you every step of the way.

Developer Peter Martin spoke immediately following Kapu. A person could be heard in the background talking over Martin's testimony.

> My goal is to build homes for our local people in Olowalu [on] land I have, or my partners and I own. And in Makila. After six or seven years, on the general plan, [the committee] voted very strongly in favor of it. They spent many, many years analyzing it, and we planned for that. And now, the CPAC. I'm not sure exactly why—I wanted to ask that question—why is it not on the Community Plan, and my Makila lands are not on it either now?

Chairperson Kai Nishiki called for a recess due to the disruptions: "I realize there's a lot of emotions, and I'm just asking everyone to respect our community, and our ability to hear the voice of everyone in our community. I understand you may have disagreements, and those will have to be handled outside of this arena."

Payne, who sought an opinion from the Maui County Ethics Board based on his employment, said he would follow the advice of the board. It advised him to disclose his position as realtor with the West Maui Land Company and refrain from voting on projects on lands owned by the company. In the same meeting, Payne also shared his connection to the Church of Jesus Christ of Latter-day Saints, and refrained from voting on matters related to Church-owned property.

\*  \*  \*

A major topic in the community planning process was how to handle non-agricultural subdivisions built on agricultural land. The Ala Hoku subdivision within the Lahaina area was one such area. County planners recommended designating the land Rural Residential, a decision Payne supported but questioned: "I was curious as to the department's rationale for that change, given that there have been other areas that have sought to do the same thing."

Planner Jennifer Maydan acknowledged the challenge of designating these types of subdivisions. The County considered taking the same approach for all but realized that each project needed a case-by-case process. Maydan justified the county's recommendation to designate Ala Hoku as Rural Residential given its proximity to urban areas and the smaller lot sizes:

> In your community plan area, you have several areas that are existing ag subdivisions that have a rural growth boundary around them from the Maui Island plan. And this is something the Maui Island community is going to be talking about for a long time as we go through and update all of the community plans. When we first came to the task of putting community plan designations on these areas, one thought was, okay, we're going to have one methodology that we're going to go forward with. But as we started looking at the individual subdivisions, they are all unique from each other. It really is going to be done on a case-by-case basis, and there is not a one-size-fits-all solution for all of these existing subdivisions within the Rural Growth boundary. With this one, our recommendation is to make it Rural Residential.

Whether the owners at Ala Hoku wanted an Agricultural or Rural Residential designation became the subject of debate. Payne said the owners he spoke to were supportive of changing the designation from Agricultural to Rural Residential. "They're functioning as an ag community because of what zoning requires, but it lives more like rural," he said. But according to Nishiki, all of the owners of Kahana Nui, the name of the subdivision on Ala Hoku, viewed their area as an agricultural community and wanted to retain their existing Agricultural designation.

> I would support leaving this as ag because of the desire of the existing community; they did say they're an ag community. I believe we should leave it as ag. They had sought to intervene at the Land Use Commission for Pulelehua because they didn't want Pulelehua to get their designation to increase density, and wanted the community to be cognizant that they were an ag community. I just believe we should leave the designation as is.

A motion introduced by Karen Comcowich to keep the Ala Hoku subdivision under Agricultural designation failed in a 5–6 vote. Nishiki, Comcowich, Bugga, Lucero and Celiz voted in support of the motion, while Payne, Gerbig, Pulmano, Michel, Hegger-Nordblom and Pluta opposed.

\* \* \*

Several committee members expressed concerns over the need to prepare for the impacts of climate change—namely, shoreline retreat and its management. The county seemed to have a strong policy on managed retreat but no tools for implementing the policy, Pulmano said.

> If we don't provide some sort of implementation action for what we have in our written policies, I think the people, residents as well as hotel owners, are going to fight tooth and nail to try to do seawalls. I don't want to fearmonger, but it's quite a large asset for them. And if there's no policy to encourage them moving to managed retreat, then I think that they will stay as long as they can until it's no longer viable.

A majority of members agreed that managed retreat, rather than taking other measures such as sea wall construction, should be encouraged for properties on the coast. What they struggled with was whether the CPAC should designate specific areas for relocation should a property need to move inland. Pulmano made a motion to highlight golf courses makai of the highway in Kāʻanapali as a potential shoreline managed retreat area for the Kāʻanapali resorts in the "areas of change" section. The CPAC voted unanimously in support of the motion.

*   *   *

Hanakaʻōʻō Beach Park, also known as Canoe Beach, is often referred to as one of the few "local" beaches left in West Maui. However, the land mauka of the park is privately owned. In a previous meeting, Chairperson Kai Nishiki made a motion to designate 200 acres above the park as open space. But that motion failed. In this meeting, describing her proposal as a compromise, Nishiki brought forward a motion to designate 100 acres of the area as open space.

> Many in our community have voiced that they do not want development across the street. And this area potentially could have, and there's been several proposals for there to be, projects directly mauka of the highway. I would like to propose the first 100 acres be park and open space so that there isn't development. Development is allowed in the mauka portion only of that parcel, even though I really don't support any development in that area. But I feel like I am compromising.

In contrast to Nishiki's proposals, the developers of Kaʻanapali 2020 sought to build on most of the 200 acres. However, Pluta, who sat on the Kāʻanapali 2020 Community Advisory Council, said some members of the group strongly advocated to keep the area open space. But they had not worked out the details.

> Ed [Lindsay] was our cultural advisor towards the cultural significance of that area—actually all of Kāʻanapali 2020. He was very much concerned that we kept that as a park area, the area closest to Canoe Beach. And I wish he was still here with us so I could ask him for more research. [...] For 20 years we talked about this area. What we didn't talk about specifically was all the little infill circles of what would be there except for that park.

Most of the CPAC members appeared supportive of the motion, which could potentially create more park space, parking and a cultural center. The committee adopted the motion in a 10–1 vote, with Payne opposed.

## THE COMMUNITY'S OLOWALU

*February 20, 2020*

The final area considered for growth in the community process was an area south of Puamana all the way to the turn at Honoapiʻilani Highway, when the road veers mauka toward the center of Maui. This largely undeveloped expanse comprised Makila, Launiupoko, Olowalu and Ukumehame. Developer Peter Martin sought to develop two projects within the area: one in Makila and the other in Olowalu. To maximize the density of development allowed in these areas, Martin sought a Rural Residential designation for them. But county planners citing community opposition to development recommended the CPAC support an Agricultural designation to limit growth.

> The meeting to hear public testimony and to deliberate over this area generated one of the largest turnouts of any CPAC meeting. Nearly 30 people—among them residents who claimed lineal ties to the area, developers, construction workers, and other community members—were split over whether to allow more intensive development. At one point, chairperson Kai Nishiki needed to stop the meeting to regain decorum. The Olowalu area in particular was the subject of considerable testimony.

\* \* \*

Olowalu was the site of a Native Hawaiian village until 1790, when American Captain Simon Metcalf ordered an attack on the people after hearing some villagers stole a small boat. The massacre killed 100 Native Hawaiians. Many testifiers spoke of the cultural significance of Olowalu because of the burials and heiau located there.

> Olowalu Town and Olowalu Ekolu, affiliates of West Maui Land Company owned in part by developer Peter Martin, attempted to build in the area starting back in the early 2000s. But in 2015, the Hawaiʻi Land Use Commission denied acceptance of their final environmental impact statement for the project, in part because it lacked sufficient archaeological surveys.

> Beyond cultural concerns, many opposed Olowalu's development for other reasons. Marine scientists and environmentalists testified against the project because it would harm Olowalu's "mother" coral reef, which was already struggling to survive runoff and warming ocean temperatures. Worsening traffic was

another concern. Drivers sat for hours on the congested two-lane highway that connected West Maui to the rest of the island. Parts of the road, which runs parallel to the ocean—so close it is practically on the beach—become submerged during floods and high surf. Residents also voiced concerns over the area's lack of water and susceptibility to fires. The land around Olowalu looks bone-dry and flammable, the outward manifestations of a multi-year drought.

On the other hand, some acknowledged these concerns and still supported development for Olowalu. Some area descendants were among those who advocated for the construction of homes, especially if a portion were "affordable" and made available to local families. They reasoned that the lots would be sold one by one to wealthy foreigners if the county did not allow Martin to proceed with his plans. Their emotional pleas spoke mostly of residents' desire to stay in West Maui, where their families have been for generations.

Adeline Rodrigues, a 90-year-old Native Hawaiian resident with ancestral ties to Ukumehame and Olowalu, described the CPAC meetings as one of the last opportunities to determine the fate of the area and the people who were of the place. She expressed a desire to see Olowalu restored as a town and community.

> I love my place of birth. My mom and dad were born in Ukumehame. My great-grandparents were also born in Ukumehame, so you can see I can claim lineage in the ahupua'a of Ukumehame and Olowalu. All these lands you see here will be sold lot by lot to people from the mainland with lots of money, and no community will be created. [ . . . ] So this is our one opportunity, our only opportunity to participate in planning the future. If we don't make use of the chance right now, the lands will be sold and we won't have this chance again at any time to design the area in an overall way. I want to see the ahupua'a of Olowalu restored to its full potential of a functional town and sustainable community. Let's not forget the planners are here to help us plan, help people live in a community and not tell us or dictate to us a final decision—especially one that is in opposition to our traditions, our culture and our way of life.

Rodrigues's son, Hinano, who previously opposed development in Olowalu, also testified in support.

> If we permitted workforce housing in Olowalu, at least 45 families will be able to live there. Initially I was against this project, because making the left

turn to go to Wailuku was impossible in the mornings and evenings. Even more difficult was when they installed that blinking light to tell people to slow down. It now creates a parade in front of my left turn. But I've since changed my mind. If 45 families are going to be able to live in Olowalu, then I suppose I can put up with the traffic.

Others with ancestral ties to Olowalu and Ukumehame challenged the developers' claims to the land. Linda Magalianes said she supported the construction of workforce housing but opposed the proposed location for the Olowalu project. She said the developers did not rightly own the land because all of it was designated kuleana lands.

> Every part of the mahele in Olowalu is kuleana lands. How these guys come? That's what I like know. You know, they don't own those lands. Those are kuleana lands by law. You don't own it. It's cloudy. It's still cloudy today. I did a lot of research [and it's] still showing cloudy. So I don't know how you guys can develop there.

One testifier, Jen Mather, criticized developers for pitting community members against each other. Those like Mather, who testified against West Maui Land Company's proposal to build more homes in Olowalu, emphasized they were not against development. Rather, they challenged irresponsible development that would worsen water shortages and fire hazards, and disrespect the area's culture and history.

> Obviously, we're dealing with a housing inventory challenge, but we have to be really smart about where we provide those answers and those homes. If we were to do it there in Olowalu, like the landowners are lobbying, that's sprawl, not smart growth. It's also just more predatory housing development that is pitting desperate community members against one another. I think it'll be important to listen to the traditional voices—people in this room, of this 'āina, rather than the foreigners who come looking for their piece of paradise. They feel privileged thinking they should get a house because they moved here two, five or 10 years ago. I'm a kanaka. I'm not from Lahaina, but I call this place my home because my home is concrete and pavement now on O'ahu. And our family land here on Maui, in Haneo'o, in Hamoa and Hana, was sold to foreign investors generations ago. It's not a new thing. And before I see Maui become a concrete jungle, I'll leave to lessen

the burden on this ʻāina. The people who just moved here are clamoring for more housing, sending in testimony that any affordable housing is good and saying how much they love this place. It's not love; that's abuse. Developers who are saying they just want to build housing out of love? That's not love; that's still abuse.

Kamauna Kahaialiʻi, who identified himself as a longtime resident of West Maui, agreed that affordable housing is needed but noted that rightful ownership to the land should be determined first. At the time, some area descendants and developers were in lawsuits to determine who held legal claim to kuleana lands.

When Martin, president of West Maui Land Company, testified before the CPAC he painted a different picture of community sentiment—one overwhelmingly supportive of his plans.

> I had an idea yesterday to try to get a feeling for what the community wants. I'm not sure exactly how you can find the community, but I sent out an email to a bunch of people on my list. And I got 160 replies, and I shared them with county, and they're beautiful to read. I was surprised at the strong support. One hundred and sixty—I didn't read them all yet, but I don't believe there's more than one or two against development. I asked the question: "Would you like to see homes in the Olowalu area and Makila?" And I sent a map, and the responses are beautiful.

Immediately following Martin's testimony, CPAC member Ravi Bugga questioned the legitimacy of Martin's claims.

> I haven't had time to Google every single person on that list, [but] a significant number of them are from your associates, customers, suppliers, contractors, real estate agents and developers, right? Mr. [Stanford] Carr is on there, a real estate guy on there. A number of them are interested parties. You didn't pick these names out of a phone book, so thank you for that. But frankly, from my point of view, these are hardly objective and impartial. I just wanted to put that on the record here.

Though roughly half of Martin's proposed project would include "affordable homes," he said they needed to be priced at 120 or 140 percent of area median income to make them accessible to working professionals. Bugga asked how Martin could prevent buyers from reselling the homes for profit or turning them into short-term rentals. Martin said he could personally select the buyers and use deed restrictions to require owner occupancy and prohibit short-term rentals.

> Ones I control, I can sell to anybody as long as I don't discriminate people by race and by religion. If a guy comes to me and he's from Lahaina, I sell it to him. I get to sell to the people I like. It's a free market.

One of the last people to testify on plan designations, which would impact proposed developments for Olowalu Town, was Lawrence Carnicelli, the project's representative and the chairman of the Planning Commission.

> In Olowalu we want to build a town. We want to build a community. At the top of my thing right here it says, "Olowalu's focus is to build a community for residents of Maui" as opposed to just constructing houses. In Pam's presentation, she had 10 principles for smart growth. Olowalu might be the only place on the island that's possible.

Some committee members sided with those who wanted to see more homes in Olowalu. They cited the area's existing Urban designation under the Maui Island Plan and the need for affordable housing as main reasons for why they supported a change in plan designation to Rural Residential.

The CPAC would not make a designation decision for Olowalu Town until the next meeting. But for an open space area between Launiupoko and Olowalu, they voted to change the area's designation from Agricultural to Park and Open Space. Kai Nishiki introduced the motion, and it passed by a 7–3 vote. Leilani Pulmano, Hans Michel and Joseph Pluta opposed. Dylan Payne recused himself from voting after disclosing his employment with West Maui Land Company.

* * *

For the northernmost portion of this sub-area—Puamana to Launiupoko—both Payne and Pulmano recused themselves from discussing or voting on the area due to conflicts of interest. Pulmano said her company owned three lots in Makila Ranches Phase Two, and Payne worked for West Maui Land Company. Citing concerns over sea-level rise and climate change, Nishiki made a motion to change the area's designation from Agricultural to Park and Open Space.

Part of my intent in looking at this entire coastline and putting things into
Park and Open Space and Conservation is to give a voice to the voiceless. We
really need to be planning for sea-level rise and climate change and protect
our coastlines from development—and also the wetland areas.

Nishiki's motion failed in a 6–3 vote with Dawn Hegger-Nordblom,
Angela Lucero, Karen Comcowich and Yvette Joyce Celiz voting in favor,
and Hans Michel, Joseph Pluta and Donald Gerbig opposing. Ravi Bugga
did not vote.

*            *            *

Immediately following the failed motion for the coastal area between Puamana
and Launiupoko, Nishiki proposed the same designation for 40 acres on the
makai side between Launiupoko and Olowalu. Here she cited concerns over
culturally significant sites, potential impacts of runoff and sedimentation on the
coral reef, sea-level rise, and protecting recreational areas for future generations.
    Nishiki and Carnicelli entered into a heated exchange when she asked
him, as the representative of Olowalu Elua Associates, to comment on her proposal for the 40 acres. He spoke about the proposed Olowalu Town project as
a whole and said it was surrounded by 600 acres of state-owned land, of which
200 acres are designated as "park open space and those types of things." He said
there were plans to build a police station and fire station in the proposed area,
directly across from the Olowalu surf break. Nishiki responded by asking, "In
your discussions with the department for a fire station and a police station, how
do they feel about being underwater?" Sections of the proposed area were within
the projected sea-level rise zone, and one of the plan's policies prohibited the
siting of public utilities in this zone, Hegger-Nordblom pointed out. Prior to
calling for a vote, Nishiki commented:

Olowalu is very dangerous when there's a lot of people in this area. People
are running across the road to use the bathroom; they're running across the
road to park, and this area right here is a prime location for a park and a
cultural center. I ask your support for [the] community and for the future
generations to really think ahead in this area. How amazing would it be
for our community to know the area won't have any development and
we'll be able to let our kids go surfing over there without being in danger
of being run over because they got to run across the street to try and use
the bathroom?

The motion to designate this area as Park and Open Space passed in a 7–3 vote, with Michel, Pluta and Pulmano opposed and Payne recused from voting. The motion passed to the sound of applause from the audience.

\*   \*   \*

The final portion of the sub-area up for discussion was Makila. Three affordable housing projects, using the 201H fast-track process, were proposed for Makila. The County Council approved one project but denied the two other projects proposed by Martin's companies: Kipa Centennial, LLC and Hope Builders. The original plans for these sites called for 50 homes. However, in the process of re-evaluating the projects, Ginoza said they were now considering building up to 100 homes, each on a 5,000-square-foot lot, if they could tap into the County's wastewater treatment system. To do so, the community plan designation needed to be changed from Agricultural to Rural Residential.

CPAC member Pluta asked Ginoza if there were "questions about the title." Ginoza replied no, but someone in the audience could be heard shouting, "Yes, there is!" However, when Nishiki invited the individual to speak as a resource person, she declined. After Ginoza confirmed his clients held clear title to both properties, Pluta introduced a motion to designate both parcels as Rural Residential instead of Agricultural, as recommended by the County's Planning Department. This opened the floor for discussion.

Pulmano asked Martin if he would still need to pursue the 201H process given his current plans for the property. But as he took a circuitous route to replying, Nishiki cut him off because she said he wasn't answering the question. "You'll never learn if you don't listen," Martin said in response.

County Councilmember Tamara Paltin explained that changing the designation to Rural Residential would allow developers to use the 2.96 process, which only requires 25 percent affordable housing. Leaving the Agricultural designation in place and requiring Martin to do the 201H process would require at least 50 percent affordable housing.

In the last 10 minutes of the meeting, the person who declined an earlier invitation to testify as a resource person asked if she could now speak. After Nishiki denied her request, the person continued to interrupt the meeting. Nishiki was then forced to take a recess to regain decorum. When the meeting resumed, Nishiki gave the person, named in the public record as Miss Kinimaka, the opportunity to speak. Kinimaka read from an August 1995 article that quoted Title Guaranty Escrow Services President David Pietsch as saying, "We're the only state in the nation where the state's title is no good."

Pluta's motion to change portions of the Makila area from Agricultural to Rural Residential failed in a 2–8 vote. Hans stood with Pluta while everyone else opposed. Payne recused himself from voting.

## "This is Not a Vote Against Affordable Housing"
### *February 25, 2020*

The committee continued its review of the southernmost portion of West Maui. CPAC chairperson Kai Nishiki introduced a motion to adopt the county's recommendation to keep the Launiupoko growth area under Agricultural. Planner Jennifer Maydan said the larger lot sizes, distance from services, and community feedback were what led to the county's decision. Not everyone agreed with the county's characterization of the area, however. Dylan Payne said it seemed relatively dense and conveniently located near town, which made a Rural Residential designation a better fit.

When Nishiki kept referencing the "community's" desires in her remarks, Hans Michel asked who she was referring to. She replied:

> The Planning Department has spent almost two years, I believe, reaching out to our community and going through the maps very carefully. And if you look at the infill maps as well as the Planning Department recommendation, those maps really reflect what the community wanted. So, yes, I do think that our community has been educated, [and] they have given very valuable input.

Although engaging an entire community is difficult, the county did reach out as much as it could, Maydan added. "The feedback we got was, overwhelmingly, the community did not want to see a lot of development south of Lahaina Town, and in particular for Launiupoko people wanted to leave it as ag."

In some way, the CPAC's designation for Launiupoko did not matter because most of it was already developed, argued Payne. "But it could signal the intent of the community to say, 'Hey, this area should evolve to something that is more of a rural nature,' because that's what it already is. And that would speak to better stewardship of resources. That's my opinion of how reclassifying this area from ag to rural could benefit the community," he said.

Jeri Dean, who spoke for the first time in a month, commented at length about her desire to give developers a chance to provide affordable homes. She expressed particular concern for the "gap group": those who earned too much to qualify for lower-AMI affordable housing but not enough to purchase market-rate homes. She and Aina Kohler had been absent from the past four meetings.

> If you have two teachers, the income they bring in, they can't qualify for affordable. They can't even qualify for workforce. That's that gap group. And so, in my mind, I'm thinking we've been having these conversations since I've been here at the CPAC. [...] In Olowalu you have a developer there that actually has land designated for a fire station, but we're not even allowing that conversation to happen. We're not a deciding board. But we are a board that gives the opportunity to at least give it a chance. Let the conversation happen at another level, because we're just recommending. It doesn't start here. It doesn't end here. In my opinion, I'd like to see my children be able to build a home or buy a home that's not clustered in the Lahaina area, that is either out north, or even like in this ideal area. I'm proposing we also support the designation the [Maui] Island Plan recommends, not only because of the island plan, but because of the discussions that many of us have had. And I know you're going to hear from both sides—the community doesn't want development there. At the same time, there's a lot of people in the community that does want it there. But by shutting it down here, it just makes it even harder. I mean, it takes years and years and years for something to go, for something to get passed, whether it's affordable or workforce housing.

In response to Dean's comment, Karen Comcowich said she, too, wanted her children to have a chance to have a home in West Maui. But she also wanted to give them more green space and the opportunity to decide how they want to build, in a way that does not harm the environment.

> Maybe give it a few years so we can see how things pan out before we are just allowing more development and allowing the runoff and the problems to continue to occur. Give our children the chance to have the greenery and the open space to develop if they want to. We can't remove [development] once it's there. But they can put it there if they want it in the future.

The committee took a vote immediately following Comcowich's remarks. In their closest vote yet, the CPAC voted 7–6 to adopt the county's recommendation for Launiupoko.

\* \* \*

Next up for discussion was Olowalu Town, which was represented by Lawrence Carnicelli, the Planning Commission Chairman and representative for Olowalu Elua Associates. Angela Lucero opened up discussion by making a motion to adopt the county's recommendation to keep the area under Agricultural designation. The designation would not prevent the developers from constructing homes in Olowalu; rather, it would limit the density allowed. The need for affordable housing was often used as justification for allowing all proposed developments to move forward, and those who voted to limit development in certain areas were accused of being anti-development. Lucero addressed this false dichotomy in her remarks.

> I'm not anti-development or anti-density. I'm [for] density in the correct areas. And I think that's what planning should be. And I think that's what smart growth is supposed to be. That's great they want to do the small town, but I would like to place our homes near our jobs. And there's not going to be jobs out there. [...] People may paint this as anti-development or anti-density or anti-growth, or I'm not a supporter of affordable housing. But I fear that us just designating areas for Residential or Rural Residential isn't going to give us our desired outcome. If our desired outcome is affordable housing, that is going to require a mix of housing types. That's the whole reason [the Planning Department] is doing this. That's the whole reason they redid all our designations. That's the reason that the county is working on different tax structures. I just want us to be cautious, because just designating an area for homes hasn't gotten us very far, has it? We have a whole bunch of luxury homes all around us. And I know there's a lot of factors that play into that. But I just want that to be clear: this is not a vote against density. This is not a vote against affordable housing.

At the invitation of CPAC member Dawn Hegger-Nordblom, a representative for the Aha Moku Council named Linda Magalianes shared the reasons behind her opposition to higher-density development.

> First of all, there's a lot of cemeteries within Olowalu. One of the main reasons why they were shut down in that meeting was because we found iwi kūpuna in Olowalu and they didn't bring that forth in the EIS. [...] Like I said in the last meeting, I'm for affordable housing. No doubt about

that. But not in Olowalu. Olowalu is too sacred to a lot of the local people here. I don't envy what you guys going through right now, but again, not in Olowalu. You guys really got to read the report of that last shutdown. There was a lot of things they never provided that we had found. And 'til today, we still finding things more about Olowalu. Does people know that Olowalu was a massacre? Do you guys know that 175 of my family members died in that massacre? I have them buried in the Nahina cemetery that we own in Napili.

All but two of the written testimonies—only Peter Martin and Carnicelli wrote in support of the project—opposed Olowalu Town. These letters came from current area residents who spoke about their struggles with the developer and his unfulfilled commitments to them and the county. Prior to taking the vote on a designation for Olowalu Town, Comcowich referenced the written testimony in her closing comments.

The reason we supported the other developments is because they're close to jobs and infill. It's also because while this developer may mean well now—I don't like to vilify anybody; people generally are the heroes of their own story—he may mean well, but he has historically not done well. And this is evidenced by the responses from the people who bought land from him. These aren't people who didn't want to like him. These are people who wanted to like him, and he didn't follow through on promises he made to them. So how can we as a community trust a developer to follow through on the promises he's making that don't really have any legal requirements? He's saying it's going to be affordable, but how can we be sure unless there's a legal requirement?

The remarks from committee and community members proved enough to advance Lucero's motion. In a vote of 7–5, the CPAC opted to keep the Agricultural designation for Olowalu Town, effectively taking a step toward limiting its development. In a related action, the committee unanimously voted in favor of designating a small makai portion of Olowalu as Park and Open Space.

* * *

In the previous meeting, a motion by Joseph Pluta to designate the Makila area as Rural Residential failed by a 2–8 vote. Without enough votes to change the designation, the county's recommendation for the area stood by default.

Committee member Aina Kohler, who was absent for that vote and discussion, said she wanted to revisit the topic. Her request called into question whether the CPAC could bring back topics from previous meetings, and whether not the same motion could be made in subsequent meetings. Planner Jennifer Maydan said the committee's rules did not preclude them from introducing the same motions. In an attempt to bring closure to the discussion surrounding Makila, Nishiki motioned to adopt the county's recommendation. County Councilwoman Tamara Paltin and marine biologist Donna Brown spoke about the area prior to the committee's vote. Paltin testified that keeping Makila in agriculture would require the developer to use the expedited 201H process to subdivide. Theoretically the process would create more affordable housing because to use 201H, developers needed to commit to at least 50 percent affordable housing. Brown, a professor of marine biology and oceanography at the University of Hawai'i Maui College and longtime research diver, urged the CPAC not to allow higher-density development given the impact of runoff on coral reef health.

> I think this whole area between Lahaina and the Pali should be left as open. Everywhere we've developed on the island, the reefs have died. And the reefs are really in trouble. And you might have heard the reefs all over the world are dying because of global warming. What we need to do is to try to preserve whatever we can and keep the things as healthy as we can, where we can. And just keeping this area undeveloped will help a lot. And also, because our main income on this island is tourism, we're just going to kill the golden goose if we continue to develop every inch of land. We're going to be like O'ahu and nobody's going to want to come here.

After hearing from both Paltin and Brown, the CPAC voted 11–1 to keep Makila in agriculture. Pluta opposed and Payne abstained.

## "THIS SUBDIVISION DOESN'T LOOK LIKE AGRICULTURE"
### *February 27, 2020*

The question of what to do with existing gentleman's estates—luxury homes built on agriculturally designated and zoned land—continued to plague the CPAC into the new year. The Planning Department decided to take a case-by-case approach to the issue, further complicating the matter. For the area where the Plantation Estates subdivision was located, the county recommended an Agricultural plan designation. But both a motion to adopt the county's recommendation and a motion to change the designation to Rural Residential failed to garner enough votes.

With the issue unresolved, Brad Paulson and former planning director Will Spence testified again in support of changing the plan designation for Plantation Estates. Spence called for a new approach to recognize subdivisions like these.

> To me, as a planner, I have watched for nearly three decades now the sub-division of ag land only to be growing really beautiful luxury homes. And personally, I find that kind of offensive. Call them fake farms, gentleman's estates, whatever you want to call them—to me, they're not agriculture. To me, they are a Rural Residential kind of land use, and they should be recog-nized as such. When we started down the path and the Maui Island Plan, we started showing some of these subdivisions as Rural Residential, recognizing them for what they really are—not pretending that they're farms, not pre-tending that they're real agriculture, but going, "Hey, these are residential subdivisions." We've had this land use pattern since I can remember, and it's been criticized for as long as I can remember, including myself as a critic. What we started doing with the Maui Island Plan was to start a different path. [ ... ] We could start saying, "Hey, this subdivision doesn't look like agriculture. This subdivision looks like Residential; you should come in for a change in zoning." Start a different pattern. Let's quit calling these things agriculture when they're not. I know for Plantation Estates, I just glanced at the MLS the other day—there's a home in there going for $8.7 million. If we just continue to designate these subdivisions as agriculture, it's not going to make that $8 million home into a farm. It's not going to make the landowner a farmer. It's not going to make them produce food.

Ravi Bugga asked Spence what he thought the implications of changing the designation would have on similar subdivisions across Maui. Spence did not have an answer to the question. "It's illegitimate to be calling these—sorry, Peter—these kinds of subdivisions 'agriculture.' I'd like to start down a new path," Spence said. "Really, what you would be doing if these subdivisions eventually got zoning to two-acre rural, you're calling them what they already are." Dawn Hegger-Nordblom questioned why Plantation Estates Lot Owners Association did not seek rezoning through the State Land Use Commission, and opted instead to dedicate their time to attending CPAC meetings. John Kindred, Association president, said they were told they needed to secure a Rural Residential designation first.

We were advised 10 years ago that we needed to be designated [Rural Residential] within the community plan in order to ultimately pursue a possible rezoning, where we will most likely go before the Land Use Commission at some point. Our first step was the Maui Island Plan. We're in the rural growth boundary. This is our next step. We were told 10 years ago that this would happen three years after the Maui Island Plan. Well, here we are, eight years later. But we're spending a lot of time because we really care about addressing this basic question. [ ... ] Whether or not a community was illegitimate originally has nothing to do with us as residents. That has to do with what the county decided to do with a developer at some point in time. Get rid of all that. Don't let those kinds of developments happen. Let's go to public hearings. And let's have the issue addressed in that fashion.

When asked whether 100 percent of the lot owners supported the change in designation, Kindred said most did, though no survey had been conducted. His response also revealed that Plantation Estates lot owners had always planned to pursue rezoning of their properties.

The majority support the designation. We haven't taken a survey of that. But we've certainly polled all of our owners in annual meetings over the course of these many years that we've been thinking about this. [ ... ] Every landowner has given a covenant to the developer to ultimately rezone to Rural. That's quite unique. I think when we look at some of these other communities, property deeds don't have those things. Ours do. And it also says that it gave the declarant of our community the right themselves to pursue this designation change in the community plan hearing processes.

Bugga affirmed his belief that changing the designation would legitimize what were illegitimate developments to begin with. Albert Perez of Maui Tomorrow shared Bugga's perspective and asked the committee to maintain all existing agricultural designations.

I don't think that we should be rewarding any kind of abuse of our agricultural lands. I think that is, in essence, what is being asked for. And we're at this point asking to go to Rural Residential when they bought there and it was Agricultural; it should stay Agricultural. Our farmers are not able to farm and make a profit. Depending on the year, more than half the property gets sold to outside investors from outside Hawai'i. They're driving up the prices of housing for local people, and ag land for farmers. And so there's nowhere to actually be a farmer [and] make a profit. This is a big problem. I would like to thank you for sticking with it, keeping the ag land.

\* \* \*

A parcel historically designated as Industrial became the subject of debate among committee members who questioned whether heavy industrial uses should be allowed in Lahaina Town. Some CPAC members supported allowing the parcel to keep its existing designation. Donald Gerbig suggested the parcel likely received its zoning based on its historic use as a sugar factory. He argued that changing the designation would have unintended consequences. Others were concerned about allowing uses that could potentially impact the community's health. They wanted the designation changed to allow only light industrial use, which was permitted through the Urban Corridor designation recommended by the county. A motion to change the parcel's designation to Industrial failed in a 4–8 vote, with Michel, Gerbig, Payne and Hegger-Nordblom voting in favor. A subsequent motion to adopt the county's recommendation to designate the area Urban Center Corridor passed by a 10–2 vote, with Payne and Leilani Pulmano opposed.

\* \* \*

According to the Maui County General Plan, West Maui lacks enough inland park space for its current and projected population. The committee entertained the idea of creating a large park in Lahaina Town, south of Lahainaluna Road. Kai Nishiki, who introduced the idea, cited the General Plan's findings and the community's desire for more open space in her proposal.

> While there isn't development in this area, I think it's very important to protect those areas. I actually envisioned a central park running from Lahainaluna Road, actually all the way to Launiupoko. And to expand the Launiupoko area so that we could have one, continuous greenway, two, open space and park area, and to offer a buffer between proposed neighborhoods mauka of my proposed park area. So I believe this strip right here would provide a nice continuous park area. We will be able to help service the needs of those on Lahainaluna Road, which a lot of residents in that area have said, "We don't have any parks." There's . . . how many schools up there? But no real park.

The land proposed for the parks was owned by Peter Martin's companies, Hope Builders and Waine'e Land and Homes, affiliates of West Maui Land Company. Kyle Ginoza, the companies' representative, said the developers opposed designating the area as Park and Open Space because they had other plans.

Both Nishiki's motion to designate the 40-acre parcel as park and open space and Dawn Hegger-Nordblom's motion to designate the parcel as Public/ Quasi-public failed to get enough votes to pass. Several CPAC members said they supported the creation of a park but did not like the location Nishiki proposed. Payne, Comcowich and Celiz said a better location for the park would be north of Lahainaluna Road. However, none of the committee members introduced a new motion for another location.

In a rare moment of agreement with developers, Comcowich introduced a motion to adopt the Waine'e plans from Hope Builders. This motion would remove an Industrial designation and add an Urban Center Corridor designation to the 40-acre parcel. Celiz seconded the motion, which passed in a 10–1 vote with Payne abstaining from voting.

## The CPAC Finds Common Ground

### *March 3, 2020*

With work on the growth map largely behind them, the committee took a second look at previously discussed policies and actions. The Planning Department was tasked with revising these items based on the CPAC's input and bringing them back for resolution. Members found common ground on most of the items and voted unanimously to advance many.

Their actions included amending the county code to prohibit development within gulches, to require low impact development, and to prohibit the backwashing of pool water outside property boundaries.

In another unanimous decision, the committee adopted a policy to require developers to consult—and provide evidence of their consultation—with the Aha Moku Councils representing proposed project areas. CPAC members heard extensively from kanaka maoli leaders about the lack of consultation despite several laws requiring input from Native Hawaiians regarding impacts to the cultural and natural resources, and kuleana land rights and access. Commented Ke'eaumoku Kapu, an Aha Moku Council representative:

> This is really good news for us. We always have been trying to be at the
> forefront any time any development project came up to try to provide some

kind of consultation with a lot of the local components or people, and it's all about generational knowledge.

\* \* \*

In terms of transportation, they unanimously supported a policy from Hans Michel to prevent development within the future transportation corridor identified for Kapalua to Central Maui. Michel, a farmer and longtime resident of Lahaina, spoke of the need to act preemptively to plan for future transportation solutions.

> As a small interpretation, Kelawea mauka had to remove 18 houses for they could make the bypass going north. And that corridor we're talking here, we do not like people go build houses or apartments or whatever have you. Make a corridor up the mountain and then in 50, 60, maybe 100 years from now—we don't not know what Maui gonna do in the future, but we have to leave that opportunity open for people have a corridor for mass transit.

They also voted to develop trails and greenways, to protect existing government trails, and to protect public access to these trails as part of a larger integrated recreation and transportation network.

\* \* \*

Other policies and actions, though they did not garner unanimous support, advanced through majority vote. This included a climate-change-related policy to address the need for shoreline retreat. The original proposed policy sought to "reserve" golf courses as the potential new site for properties needing to move inland because of sea level rise. CPAC members expressed concerns over private property rights and whether the county had the authority to designate land for this purpose.

Ultimately the committee voted 7–4 in favor of a policy to allow community plan amendments for the purpose of managed retreat:

> Proposed Community Plan Amendments for new development on existing golf course land in Kāʻanapali makai of Honoapiʻilani Highway should be approved only for existing shoreline development that is retreating inland because of impacts from sea level rise or other coastal hazards.

They also advanced a related policy to require new construction to be located mauka of the 3.2 feet of projected sea level rise. This one moved forward with little discussion. To address concerns over taking landowners' economically viable use, the county added an exception at the end of the policy: "except a minimum buildable area shall be provided to allow for reasonable development."

The committee also retained a policy to require new developments to install charging stations for electric vehicles in West Maui despite an attempt to delete it. A motion to get rid of the policy was introduced by Leilani Pulmano and supported by Michel, Joseph Pluta, Dylan Payne and Donald Gerbig.

\* \* \*

Some committee members attempted to strike another policy aimed at preserving agricultural lands. A decision on the policy was put on hold until after the CPAC finished its review of the growth maps. Pulmano, who moved to delete the policy, said it was redundant given the CPAC's plan designations. The policy stated,

> Prohibit conversion of agricultural lands outside of the Maui Island Plan's growth boundaries, and limit conversion of agricultural lands within the growth boundaries to urban and rural designations in West Maui unless it can be demonstrated that: a. conversion is required to accommodate the population or employment projections for the region, or; b. conversion will facilitate shoreline retreat by directly replacing an existing development of similar size and character. Public facilities developed under this policy do not need to be of comparable size to the public facilities that they are replacing.

Several members said they wanted to keep the policy in place as added protection for agriculture and open space. Lucero said the committee did not have an obligation to develop all of the lands within the urban growth boundary, and she referenced similar sentiments expressed by Planning Director Michele McLean. The motion to remove the policy failed in a 5–6 vote with Michel, Pluta, Payne, Gerbig and Pulmano voting in favor, and Nishiki, Hegger-Nordblom, Bugga, Lucero, Comcowich and Celiz opposed.

\* \* \*

After completing its review of the county's recommended policies and actions, the committee pushed for creative solutions to address the housing shortage. Nishiki and Pulmano successfully advanced a new suite of actions for this purpose. Nishiki proposed an action to direct the county to identify legal and procedural barriers to constructing safe and affordable housing, including modular housing, for farm workers. She also sought a new legal designation for modular housing, but it was tabled for future discussion. Nishiki's other proposed and adopted action directed the county to study the repurposing of commercial/industrial buildings for residential use. Pulmano proposed an action to amend the zoning code to increase density for infill development outside of shoreline setback areas and historic districts. All members, except for Nishiki, voted in favor of the motion.

Ravi Bugga introduced a motion to require credits or units used to meet workforce housing requirements for projects in West Maui to be located within West Maui. This proposal generated much discussion between members. Pulmano said credits are commodities and that limiting their use to a specific area would make them less attractive to developers, which would result in fewer affordable homes being built. Bugga was unmoved by this argument, saying developers of multimillion-dollar projects could afford to construct affordable homes where needed. Pluta agreed with Bugga, and also took issue with the lack of deadlines for developers to fulfill their credits. Housing and Human Concerns Director Linda Munsell corrected Pluta's statement, pointing out that developers must build a workforce unit to earn a credit. The motion failed in a 6–5 vote, with members Pluta, Bugga, Lucero, Celiz and Comcowich voting in favor, and Michel, Payne, Hegger-Nordblom, Gerbig and Pulmano opposing.

## "This is the First Time We've Heard Anybody Oppose It"
### *March 4, 2020*

Throughout the community planning process, as they sought to change the land designation of their community from Agricultural to Rural Residential, John Kindred and Brad Paulson maintained they were not aware of any objections from fellow landowners. However, for the first time since the beginning of the West Maui planning process, written testimony opposing the designation change surfaced. These concerns called into question whether those who had represented the subdivision were being transparent.

One testifier was Adam Quinn, a farmer who manages land for an off-site owner in Plantation Estates. While the Rural Residential designation would not prohibit agricultural activities, it would uphold the CC&Rs that Kindred and Paulson sought to enforce. Those CC&Rs limited certain agricultural activities in favor of the association's desired neighborhood characteristics— characteristics that increased the property value of Plantation Estates lots but harmed existing ag operations like Quinn's.

As I understand, the current CC&Rs prohibit labor from entering the community prior to 7 a.m. And in ag, if anybody's ever been a farmer to any degree, you know that plants don't really pay attention to a chronograph. Not unlike the army, we start well before 7 a.m. This morning, for instance, we were on site by 4:30. We didn't finish it up until about 11:30 p.m. The CC&Rs with regard to labor stipulate that it's 7 [a.m.] to 4 [p.m.] or 5 [p.m.], and that simply doesn't work for ag. In our case, we grow microgreens in a greenhouse. We're also in the soil with romaine lettuce and other general head lettuce, I think I mentioned in the report. Weekends and holidays, laborers not allowed to work. Clearly, we would still completely continue to be able to do that—the use of tractors so on and so forth. Generator use, we use a generator in order to power our refrigeration unit, which runs 24/7. If we were asked to shut that down for as little as eight hours, we would lose the complete harvest. If this CC&R style of management for our particular operation were to be mandated, I think we'd probably be closed and out of business inside a week.

According to Quinn, there were other neighbors located below the farm that also were practicing agricultural activities and who said they opposed the land designation change. Though Quinn did not own the property on which he farmed, he said the landowner was notified about the potential change and voiced his opposition.

Quinn's testimony caused at least two CPAC members to soften their positions. Leilani Pulmano, who consistently voted to keep the West Maui Plan in line with the Maui Island Plan, said the disagreement among neighbors caused her to reconsider whether to support a change in land designation. And Hans Michel, a farmer, suggested the CPAC visit the area to get a better sense of the character of the area before voting.

Following Quinn's testimony, the committee invited Paulson to come forward to answer questions. Chairperson Kai Nishiki asked why Paulson and others stated there was no opposition to the project when there appeared to be. "I specifically asked you if anyone was doing ag in this area, and did they oppose [the rural designation]." Paulson replied, "This is the first time we've heard anybody oppose it." He then asked Quinn, "How did you find out about this meeting tonight? Who contacted you?"

Nishiki was not alone in her questioning of Paulson's earlier testimony. Angela Lucero weighed in. "I'm having a hard time reconciling the fact that there's things that are happening that are agricultural-related that you said outright that you did not appreciate," she said. "And now you're just saying, 'Oh, well, we're not trying to restrict any type of agriculture.'"

In defense of his previous testimony, Paulson said, "We have a community association in our neighborhood. And the purpose of a community association is to regulate the behavior of a neighborhood look, design, feel. And we want to be able to do that. The problem with an Agricultural zoning provision is that the second anybody raises agriculture as a concern, there's a lawsuit threatened and you're not even able to have a reasonable discussion as neighbors about the community design rules." Nishiki said she was shocked by Paulson's response. "You guys have not been honest since the very beginning, and I don't think our members appreciate that," she commented.

Bugga, consistent in his opposition to the designation change, viewed the association's request as heavy-handed and unnecessary. "Are we using a hammer to kill a fly here? Why should we change the land use designation from ag—which we're all trying to encourage—to help you talk to your neighbors?" Dawn Hegger-Nordblom encouraged Paulson to resolve the issues between landowners in the subdivision before proceeding any further in the process. "When you do go for a boundary amendment from Land Use Commission, any neighbor can ask for a contested case. Anybody who has an issue with ag to rural can intervene. It's one of those things where I think you want to figure it out now, preferably before another meeting."

Dylan Payne and Joe Pluta didn't budge from their support of the land designation change. Pluta maintained his belief that the change would not impact landowners' ability to do agriculture. Payne criticized Nishiki for the way she spoke to Paulson.

Chair, I do remember the question that you posed. You asked if everybody supported ag in the area. And the response was everybody that they have spoken to supports rural residential. I'm sorry. I don't appreciate you going off on a member of the public like that. [It] was a bit disrespectful.

Pluta offered a motion to change the land designation and include language to allow existing farms to continue operations, although planners and other members pointed out the county cannot regulate CC&Rs. The motion failed with members Payne, Gerbig and Pluta voting in favor, and Nishiki, Pulmano, Hegger-Nordblom, Celiz, Comcowich, Bugga, Lucero and Michel opposed. Immediately following Pluta's failed motion, Bugga moved to accept the agriculture designation. That motion, too, failed.

* * *

In some cases, despite disagreement among committee members, the CPAC voted to adopt redundant language used to emphasize important issues. For example, in the Waineʻe growth area of Lahaina, relating to a development already approved through the 201H fast-track process, the committee voted unanimously to include a policy reiterating the developers' responsibilities to protect kuleana access, conduct archaeological surveys and provide affordable housing.

* * *

The committee unanimously supported the designation of Park/Open Space, barring golf course development, across from Napili Bay and the Hanakaʻōʻō area in Olowalu, and at Honokeana Bay/Cove. "I think our residents have felt pushed out for many years, but they are really feeling the pinch right now due to over-tourism. I think that we really need to put a high priority on providing for the needs of our residents for our future generations, for the keiki," said Nishiki. Another motion by Karen Comcowich to designate a park area along Lahainaluna Road passed by majority.

## "If Everything's a Priority, Then Nothing's a Priority"
### *March 10, 2020*

The CPAC adopted a long list of action items to direct Maui County's funding and work. But they struggled to evenly rank the workload, giving the bulk of action items medium priority. County staff and some committee members urged the CPAC to refrain from adding to the list, which would make the plan more difficult to implement.

Unwieldy as it might have appeared, though, the list of action items was an improvement from the previous two community plans, which almost doubled the amount of action items, said Kathleen Aoki from the county's Implementation Division. Still, she encouraged the committee to keep the list manageable. "There's 1,213 action items in all of our plans," she said. "The more we keep putting on there, the higher that number goes, the less focus there is to get things done. Going back to what Dylan is saying, [if] everything's a priority, then nothing's a priority." Whether the committee heeded this advice remained unclear as they moved ahead with adding more action items and proposing higher priorities for existing items.

Joseph Pluta successfully advocated for making the identification of a multimodal transportation corridor from West Maui to Central Maui a high priority. "That definitely needs to be done to protect us from having to deal with issues where you have to move people, places, things out of a corner—and that can be very expensive and sometimes life-changing," said Pluta.

Leilani Pulmano pushed to increase the rank of several action items related to culture. Among these actions was the installation of pedestrian and bicycle wayfinding and cultural signage.

Committee members proposed, ranked and adopted several new actions. Pluta added an action to fund and implement a shelter and housing program. Citing input from an agricultural panel, Pulmano introduced a new action to assist the community in developing a food hub to be used by farmers to process and market their products. Nishiki advanced a new action to encourage the development of more affordable senior care homes. Hans Michel gained support for a veterans' and memorial park.

### *May 12, 2020*

In early March, the state of Hawai'i shut its borders to tourism to prevent the spread of COVID-19. The last two meetings of the West Maui CPAC were held online. The first of these meetings, on May 12, 2020, was a training on how to use BlueJeans, a new online meeting platform. No public testimony was received.

## A VOTE WITH RESERVATIONS

### *May 19, 2020*

All but one of the people who gave public testimony at the final CPAC meeting supported the committee's version of the West Maui Community Plan. Jen Mather, Albert Perez and Hawai'i House Representative Tina Wildberger were among those who voiced their support. Perez spoke about the plan in the context of the COVID-19 pandemic. For many residents, the decline in tourism strengthened the case for diversifying the economy, better managing the visitor industry and taking steps toward food security for Hawai'i.

> I support your decision to keep Makila, Olowalu and Plantation Estates in agriculture. Maui, and particularly West Maui, is going to be seeing less tourism in the so-called "new normal." And the tourists that do come—once they figure out how to let people come without infecting the rest of us—

they're going to have to be paying more for airline tickets. They're going to have to be catering more to them. We need to focus on a higher quality of tourist. And the higher-end tourists don't want to come and see suburbia. We need tourism to be on our own terms.

Developer Peter Martin was the only person who objected to the plan, taking issue with the committee's decision to keep the Olowalu and Makila areas designated as Agricultural. While the designation would not prevent houses from being built, it would limit the density allowed.

I just don't understand how you've been able to deny people that want to live in Olowalu and Makila. [...] I know I love living in Olowalu. I know my daughter does. Dylan does. [...] It's just amazing that most of the planners aren't from Maui. Nothing against people not from Maui. I love people not from Maui. I'm not originally from here, but it's just interesting how the more local folks are very supportive of it. I sent [my email] out and got 160 responses. And the one commissioner is just wrong if they think these people are being forced by me or they work for me. They're just friends. I've been in the community a long time. I know a lot of people, sent it out to a wide swath of people. They answered from their heart. No arms were twisted.

For the final meeting, the Planning Department directed the CPAC members to submit no more than three proposed amendments to the final plan. Planner Jennifer Maydan said they received amendments from four committee members: Karen Comcowich, Kai Nishiki, Leilani Pulmano, and Angela Lucero ahead of the meeting. One new policy to "promote and encourage knowledge creation" in coordination with cultural practitioners was proposed by Lucero and adopted through consensus by the CPAC. Other amendments passed were changes in wording. In the last sentence of the vision statement, Nishiki proposed to replace "visitors are welcomed with aloha" to "quality of life for residents is a priority."

*       *       *

A majority of the committee voted to transmit the draft West Maui Community Plan to the Planning Commission, with several members—Leilani Pulmano, Joseph Pluta, Dylan Payne, Dawn Hegger-Nordblom, and Donald Gerbig—agreeing to do so with reservations. Some, like Payne, pointed out that while they supported the transmittal of the plan, they still had reservations about its content. Pulmano reiterated her concerns over the lack of alignment between the draft plan and the Maui Island Plan. Gerbig questioned the validity of sea-level rise data. Hegger-Nordblom said she was concerned about how the COVID-19 pandemic would impact the plan. Developers would later use the final vote results, along with a letter signed by committee members who voted with reservations, to persuade the Planning Commission to change the content of the plan. Kai Nishiki and Karen Comcowich, who voted to move the plan forward without reservations, expressed a belief the plan reflected the community's wishes.

# PART 2

# MAUI PLANNING COMMISSION

## A CHANGE OF PLANS

The West Maui Community Plan was transmitted to the Maui Planning Commission in the summer of 2020, as the impacts of the COVID-19 pandemic began to ripple around the world. Hawai'i closed its borders to tourism. Meetings migrated online, where people could interact from a distance. Hawai'i's forced isolation shed a different light on tourism, agriculture and the long-term health of communities. These concerns featured prominently at the Planning Commission meetings. But the added pressure of operating during a pandemic wasn't the only difference between the CPAC and the Commission. Unlike committee members, all commissioners were appointed by the mayor. They also hailed from different areas in Maui, and their responsibilities were much broader than the West Maui Community Plan. The Planning Commission was tasked with advising the mayor, the Planning Department and the county on the island's planning matters. Over the course of 10 meetings—one-third of the meetings held by the CPAC—the Planning Commission changed the West Maui Community Plan in key ways. The voting majority of the Planning Commission favored removing barriers for developers promising affordable housing. On the controversial issue of Plantation Estates, commissioners voted to change the plan designation from Agriculture to Rural Residential. And in their final hour with the West Maui Community Plan, they made a slew of consequential changes. In a policy that would "prohibit" fast-track processes for the "Areas of Stability," they replaced "prohibit" with "discourage." They deleted language to phase out short-term rentals in Lahaina, to allow the use of modular housing to house farm workers, and to require the construction of one workforce housing unit for every permitted visitor unit.

## Maui Planning Commission

### *July 28, 2020*

The West Maui Community Plan was now in the hands of the Maui Planning Commission. Lawrence Carnicelli, who at the time represented the embattled Olowalu development project, would lead this next phase of the process as the Commission's chairperson. Some, including West Maui CPAC member Ravi Bugga, questioned whether Carnicelli should stay in his role while employed by a company financially invested in the plan's outcomes.

Dick Mayer, the first person who testified at the first Maui Planning Commission meeting on July 28, asked Carnicelli to recuse himself from the chairmanship and the Commission. "I know it's a legal issue and an ethics question, but I'm going to ask that he (Carnicelli) withdraw from this," Mayer said. "Come back and testify as many times as you want at the meetings as a public citizen, which you have every right to do. But I think to be chairing the Planning Commission in this very important role is not appropriate."

Carnicelli, in defending his decision to stay on the Commission, said the opinion he sought from Maui County's Board of Ethics suggested he need only recuse himself from matters involving his employer: Olowalu Elua Associates, a subsidiary of Peter Martin's West Maui Land Company. "So, when it comes to the West Maui Community Plan, when it comes to Olowalu and anything that has to do with Olowalu, not only am I not going to vote, but I'm not going to participate in conversation. As a matter of fact, I'm not even going to chair at that particular time." Carnicelli went on to criticize the CPAC itself for lacking integrity in its process. "I think that there [were] many things that happened in CPAC that lacked a tremendous amount of integrity, but that's just my opinion."

\*　　\*　　\*

CPAC chairperson Kai Nishiki, and members Karen Comcowich and Joseph Pluta, all testified at the first Commission meeting. Nishiki and Comcowich both urged the Commission to approve the plan without significant amendments, while Pluta advocated for reversing some decisions made despite staff and community objections. "There was quite a number of issues where I don't believe the staff planner's recommendations and the community . . . the overall community meetings were representative of what the CPAC decided upon instead," Pluta said.

In its proceedings the CPAC extensively debated whether they should use words like "shall" and "require" that carried the force of law. In some instances, the CPAC's majority passed language to require rather than encourage action. The Planning Commission, at Carnicelli's request, began to reverse these decisions. One of his first requests was to change "require" to "encourage" in Policy 2.1.9 related to water development.

> This, again, was my change, and the reason why is when you look at public and private water systems, there are systems that are regulated heavily by the PUC, right? I mean there's all kinds of federal and state regulations over the top of public and private water systems. And for the community plan to make this a requirement, it could potentially be contradictory to what the PUC actually wants, and so that's why I just put "encourage" rather than "require."

## "It's Basically a Money-making Scheme"
### *August 25, 2020*

One difference between the CPAC and the Planning Commission hearings was the people who showed up to testify. Perhaps the accessibility of online meetings or the perceived receptiveness of the Planning Commission played a role in this increased participation. Among those who first testified before the Commission was Howard Hanzawa, a proponent of Kaʻanapali 2020 and former employee of Kaanapali Land Management Corp. Hanzawa, ʻEkolu Lindsay and Tom Blackburn-Rodriguez asked commissioners to reverse the changes adopted by the CPAC, the largest of which was the designation of 200 acres of open space and agriculture above Hanakaʻōʻō Beach in Kāʻanapali Town South. By contrast, an early iteration of Kaʻanapali 2020's plans for the same area included a "limited-service" hotel and more residential development. Kaanapali Land Management Corp. representative Chad Fukunaga asked commissioners to designate according to the project's master plan: "We request these areas be designated consistent with the Kaʻanapali 2020 plan to include a mix of Small-town Center and Urban Center Corridor, or at a very minimum, to place the southern area that would be left as is to align with the agricultural uses."

\* \* \*

The debate over changing the land designation of Plantation Estates continued well after the West Maui CPAC proceedings. Those in support of the change advocated for a Rural Residential designation, which they believed more accurately described the subdivision. If adopted, the new designation would allow lot owners to fully enforce their homeowners' association rules, which could impact agricultural activities but increase property values. Those against the change supported the protection of West Maui's remaining agricultural lands, and expressed concern over the implications of endorsing the misuse of these lands by wealthy landowners and developers.

Gary Grube, the owner of Hua Momona Farms in Plantation Estates, testified in support of the designation change. He claimed commercial farming was not viable for the vast majority of Plantation Estates because of poor soil quality and a lack of water.

> Many times a year, we and the rest of the community are asked to curtail water use based on supply levels. I just can't imagine how anyone else could justify starting a farming operation in Plantation Estates. In conclusion, I feel strongly the proposed change to Rural Residential designation for Plantation Estates is appropriate in light of the primarily residential aspect of the neighborhood and the fact that commercial farming is essentially untenable.

William Spence, and lot owners John Kindred and Brad Paulson, also testified again in support of the change. CPAC member Ravi Bugga, who responded incredulously to their testimonies, continued to oppose the designation change for what he viewed as its true intent.

> Many people told me, including realtor friends of mine, that the real reason was probably property price increases. I didn't quite take it seriously. But after the CPAC vote on this, Mr. Brad Paulson from Plantation Estates was heard outside the meeting room [being asked], "Why do you want this change, anyway?" And his reply was, "It's to increase our property prices." So thank you, Mr. Paulson, I have the answer to my question that I've asked for six months. It's basically a money-making scheme and confirmed by every realtor I've spoken to and lots of hits on Google as well, with an average home price of five million in Plantation Estates, plus or minus. As an example, a 10 percent increase would give half a million in profit to each owner there. A 20 percent increase would give a million dollars in profits. . . . So, certainly special interest groups like homeowners, certainly real estate agents and developers, benefit from this. But, you know, we talk a lot about ag here—how does the broader West Maui community gain if developers buy ag land relatively cheap, build gentleman's estates, reclassify, rezone it and just rake in the profits?

When asked pointedly by Carnicelli whether financial gain was the real reason behind the campaign for a designation change, Kindred answered that it was not the primary reason. "But to come back to the primary reason, we, our owners, want the right to farm, but they don't want the obligation to farm," he said.

\* \* \*

Other CPAC members testified before the commission, too. Joseph Pluta and Leilani Pulmano urged commissioners to "align" the community plan with the Maui Island Plan. In other words, allow more development within growth boundaries. "Most of the rural growth areas that are reflected in the Maui Island Plan are not included in the community plan," Pulmano said. She also asked the Commission to add existing project districts to the newly created "Special Purpose District" designation. She had previously attempted to accomplish this in CPAC, but her motion lacked enough votes to pass. Tom Schnell, a representative for Maui Land & Pineapple, also sought to keep existing project districts—especially those granted to his clients.

> If the Commission and the Council and the Planning Department feel that additional project districts are not warranted, I can understand the reasoning behind that. But the existing project districts, especially Project District 1 and 2, are actually not only community plan designations, but they are zoning designations. So the land is actually zoned Project District 1 and Project District 2, and those are part of the Maui County Code, which can only be changed by the Council.

Carnicelli opined after Schnell's testimony that adopting a plan that conflicted with existing zoning did not make sense. "I appreciate you bringing it up, because I think this is something that we don't want to create a plan that has conflicts just right as soon as it becomes law, right? I mean, it just doesn't make sense."

## WHAT'S THE PLAN?

### *September 8, 2020*

Testimony in favor of adopting designations that matched the master plan for Kāʻanapali 2020 continued to come in, as did testimony from Plantation Estates lot owners seeking a plan designation change for their subdivision.

Bob Pure, a longtime participant in Kāʻanapali 2020's community advisory council, which the project's developers convened in 1999, spoke on the importance of tying in major transportation networks in the area. He referenced surveys conducted by the group showing that 40 percent of those who work in West Maui do not live there, and of those who worked there, 80 percent said they would move there if given the opportunity. He used this figure to advocate for developing the maximum number of affordable homes, as envisioned in the Kaʻanapali 2020 master plan.

Part of the difficulty in discussing the Kaʻanapali 2020 project, as Planning Commission Chairman Lawrence Carnicelli later pointed out, is that the map presented by Representative Chad Fukunaga did not match the master plan. The most notable omission on the map was an area designated Resort-Hotel. Commented Fukunaga,

> Aside from the Resort-Hotel designation, the designation[s] on this map are not different from what we show on our Kaʻanapali 2020 master plan. It just depends how you interpret them. We would like this plan to be approved as shown. However, I'm trying to present a plan with a minimal amount of... [inaudible] ... from the current proposed draft plan. I'm being cautious not to overstep or ask for too much.

*       *       *

Former Maui County Planning Director Will Spence, who previously spoke in favor of changing Plantation Estates to Rural Residential, returned to the Commission to ask that all of West Maui's existing luxury subdivisions be designated Rural Residential. He reasoned community plans describe what is already there, and mislabeling such subdivisions "hurts our planning efforts" by allowing developers to claim their luxury projects as agriculture.

> We don't call residential as Open Space or hotels as Industrial, because that just wouldn't make any sense. I think the same thing is true with the luxury housing projects, but for some reason we continue to pretend that these are farms in our planning documents. All the while we complain about mansions and speculation sprawl, and I agree I think these are really the worst kinds of sprawl.

Plantation Estates lot owners Sharon Saunders and Michael Gronemeyer testified for the first time before the Planning Commission, reiterating the points made in Grube's earlier remarks about why the subdivision was not suited for farming. Gronemeyer insisted Plantation Estates was mischaracterized and its proponents unfairly treated during the CPAC process.

> I observed during the CPAC process that there were some misstatements made during the meetings, and they appear biased or not consistent with the law or the facts. Even today that happened. The Planning Department often stated that a Rural designation would mean increased density, which we do not want, and we think that intelligent zoning would make sure that didn't happen.

\*    \*    \*

Developer Peter Martin was the last to testify. He wanted to remove language from the "Areas of Stability" section that would prevent the approval of gentleman's estates or the use of fast-track permitting processes. Martin also reiterated points made in previous meetings about the community's desire to live in Olowalu and Makila, where his companies were proposing to build residential subdivisions. Prior to Martin's testimony, Planning Commission Chairperson Lawrence Carnicelli recused himself from the meeting due to his conflict of interest as Martin's employee. He handed the chairmanship to Stephen Castro. "As I've said before, Mr. Martin is one of the partners in the company I work for. I just don't want to preside over the meeting during his testimony," Carnicelli said.

\*    \*    \*

As the CPAC had, the Planning Commission would hear from all of the major land developers whose projects would be impacted by the West Maui Community Plan. Pulelehua, an affordable housing project that gained support for its responsiveness to the community's requests, was among them. Half of the development would consist of affordable for-sale and for-rent homes, a portion of which would be offered at 60 percent below the annual median income.

An urban growth boundary surrounded the area proposed for Pulelehua, with other specific mixed-use designations within the project itself. One lot designated Rural Residential was to be the future home of Paul Cheng, the project's representative and president of Maui Oceanview LP. Carnicelli and Commissioner Kellie Pali questioned why Cheng's lot was given a Rural Residential designation while the Plantation Estates owners struggled to change their designation.

"But then there's a piece to the north, right behind Kahana Ridge, that's Rural Residential. Is that part of your land?" Carnicelli asked. "Okay, that's the estate lot that I was talking about," Cheng replied. "That's yours?" Carnicelli replied. "Yeah. That's…hopefully, will be my retirement home." Carnicelli then asked Cheng if he encountered any pushback on the designation change, since several CPAC members said they were against Rural Residential for Plantation Estates. "Within our project district zoning, there's a category called large estate lots. So we're just—this is one estate lot that we have designated within the project district subdistricts," Cheng responded.

Pali went on to question the zoning designation around Cheng's lot: "There is a white box, and I think you've mentioned your potential future retirement home, which I giggle about. I think on this map it's suggested Rural Residential. What is the current zoning? Is it Rural Residential now? Or is this the proposed change—to be Rural Residential?"

Cheng responded, "I think because the project district was passed 15 years ago, in 2006, I think the whole area within Pulelehua is in Urban now, if I'm not mistaken. It is not in ag, and hasn't been in ag since the original project district was passed. Now, I'm not a full expert on all the legalities, and the proper title, and names of it. But as I said, within Pulelehua's original project district approval, they had done a very usual thing. When MLP did it, they went—and the Planning tells me that all the time—they went to extreme detail, which is not typical with other project districts."

Pali's line of questioning sought to weigh whether Pulelehua and Plantation Estates were treated differently in terms of their zoning. Both her and Carnicelli's questions would later be used to justify their decision to support a land designation change for Plantation Estates.

Planning Director Michele McLean confirmed the area around Cheng's lot was designated Rural Residential. However, unlike Plantation Estates, the entire project area for Pulelehua had a variety of community plan designations, not just one.

*       *       *

Unlike the detailed plans put forth by the developers of Pulelehua, Maui Land & Pine represented by Tom Schnell did not have plans to show the Planning Commission. The company no longer had a development division; it was in "a survival mode at this point with paying pensioner benefits and maintaining the preserved areas…trying to turn the company around."

County planners had reached out numerous times to help the company develop its plans to no avail. In the absence of input from Maui Land & Pine, county planners used their own criteria to propose designations that aligned with the Project Districts. But Schnell said the company did not want the county's plans; it wanted its own plans.

> What the problem for Maui Land & Pine now is that they need to redesign their plans for Kapalua Mauka because market conditions have changed. And they're not in a position right now to redesign plans. So with the Planning Department designations of, for example, residential areas here, they based it off of topography or different criteria that the Planning Department laid out. And you know, logically, it made sense with the topo or the land uses or the . . . [inaudible] . . . of the land. But these areas may not be where Maui Land & Pine ultimately wants to build the residential.

Carnicelli pushed back against Schnell's explanations. "It's a little bit frustrating right now to go, 'Okay, we want CPA, just Project District so we can do whatever we want,' right? 'We don't know what we want to do, so just give us that so we can do whatever we want.' It just seems counterintuitive to what we're trying, which is a plan." Schnell responded, "We don't want to do whatever we want. We want to do what's allowed under the current project district zoning and ordinance, which allows so many areas of Residential, so many areas of Commercial."

With Schnell doubling down on retaining Project Districts, and the Planning Commission and Planning Department emphasizing the improbability of this option, the parties were stuck. The case of Kapalua Mauka highlighted a larger issue with developers hanging on to decades-old entitlements with no immediate plans to build. This created a gridlock that did nothing to ease the need for affordable housing and rentals. Director Michele McLean commented,

> Sticking with Project District, that's not something we want to entertain. And the Council, I'm sure most of you are aware of this, from time to time the Council starts talking about "use it or lose it" entitlements. These entitlements have been there since 2006, I think. So you've had them for that long, and you still don't have a plan enough to use four different community plan designations. [. . .] Put some pen to paper and work with us on figuring out where you want these designations to be.

## "The Infamous Plantation Estates"

*September 22, 2020*

After prodding by the county, Tom Schnell finally brought forward plans for Maui Land & Pine's Kapalua projects. Those plans attempted to match the county's new designations against the company's current plans for the area. Moreover, Schnell asked for the ability to adjust designation boundaries.

> We would prefer to not have the hard lines and have the parameters to say within this area we can develop a maximum of 260 acres for Residential, five acres Commercial, and that could be within this area, the entire Project District 2 area, which is defined by the Rural Growth or Urban Growth Boundary.

Carnicelli wondered out loud whether the community plan could include language that would support such adjustments for existing project districts but without overriding the County Council's final say in the matter. Under the existing processes, such adjustments would require a community plan amendment. "Of course, you're making a recommendation to the Council. So it would ultimately be up to them whether they want to relinquish their authority for community plan amendments, but I think that's a reasonable approach for former Project Districts, because it is a notable change from the way community plans have been established before," said Planning Director Michele McLean. Carnicelli clarified he was not suggesting a change in authority or even allowing the boundaries to be "malleable." Rather, he questioned whether the community plan should include context language about existing project districts. McLean said they could go a step further and include language allowing flexibility for former Project Districts:

> For lands formerly designated as Project District, the boundaries between designations can be adjusted, provided the total acreage of each designation remains the same. Such adjustments may be proposed by the landowner and must be approved by the planning director.

Commissioners approved the added language and the new designations for Kapalua and Kapalua Mauka by consensus.

\*     \*     \*

The CPAC passed much of the Kaʻanapali 2020 project as proposed by its developers and community advisory group. But a major change from what was submitted by the project team was CPAC's decision to designate almost all of Kāʻanapali Town South as Open Space and Agricultural. As planner Jennifer Maydan explained to the Planning Commission in September 2020:

> In CPAC's decision to designate Kāʻanapali South [as] a combination of ag and park/open space, their rationale was to keep visual separation between Lahaina and Kāʻanapali, as well as protect Hanakaʻōʻō Beach and the near-shore waters as far from development runoff and to also provide significant park space for the community.

By contrast, the Kaʻanapali 2020 group's plan called for 10 acres of park and open space, and to develop the rest into single- and multi-family homes, and commercial and mixed uses. Fukunaga argued their plan would protect the view plane above the beach park. "Now I stood at Hanakaʻōʻō Beach Park, and I looked up, and I only could see to where the train tracks used to run," he said. "I couldn't see anything further mauka than that. But then I realized that our 2020 group had already planned for that area to be Parks and Open Space, and then the area just above that to be Single-Family. I think the plan is well thought out; it already protects the views. It allows for a good traffic movement."

Commissioners openly struggled with how to proceed—should they respect the wishes of the Kaʻanapali 2020 group, which had been working on their plan for decades? Or should they preserve 200 acres mauka of the "only local beach left"? Commissioner Kellie Pali, who was born and raised in Napili, remarked on the complicated decision before them:

> I think it's amazing what the CPAC has done in the few years that they did it, but like you mentioned, we've had people working on this maybe a couple of decades. And we can't really weigh one over the other, although I think it's much easier to try to spend other people's money or decide how other people want to use their land when it's not yours. And so I'm trying to be super cautious of that and respectful. And then how does that fit into our whole community as a neighborhood and island? And it's difficult. I'm struggling.

Commissioner Kawika Freitas said when the Kaʻanapali 2020 plan was developed some of the proposed housing projects did not exist, which may have led the group to seek more residential development than needed. He supported the CPAC's designations for the area. "I remember clearly a few, very, very passionate and adamant that that area above Hanakaʻōʻō stay open and have an area the locals can enjoy—the beach and the view all the way up to the mountain—and seeing open plan versus development," Freitas said.

Although Carnicelli would only vote to break a tie, he said he would not support the motion. "It's interesting the weight that we give to CPAC, right, when you got Kaʻanapali 2020, and you got this group that has looked at this thing for 20 years," he commented.

Commissioner La Costa introduced a motion to adopt the CPAC's version for Kāʻanapali. The motion passed with six votes in support. Thompson and Pali abstained.

*     *     *

Plantation Estates owners found a less hostile, more supportive audience in the Planning Commission. The testimonies of lot owners and a desire for consistency ultimately swayed the commissioners to adopt a designation change for the subdivision.

"We get to start right up to the infamous Plantation Estates," Carnicelli remarked as he opened up discussion. According to county planners, the greater West Maui community overwhelmingly opposed changing the designation of Plantation Estates to Rural Residential. This sentiment led them to recommend keeping the subdivision of luxury gentleman's estates under Agricultural. Discussion over the change was so emotionally charged and divisive that after more than 30 meetings, the CPAC could neither pass a motion to keep the designation or to change it.

The Planning Commission found themselves torn on the issue, too. What decision would make the most sense in terms of zoning? What decision would be best for West Maui? Could the community afford to lose more agricultural land to luxury home development?

Addressing comments made earlier about farming being untenable due to a lack of water, Commissioner Mel Hipolito, who once farmed the area as an employee of Maui Land & Pine, countered:

I worked for Maui Land & Pine; we farmed that area. I drove trucks, I drove tractors, irrigation up in that area, so I know that area can be farmed. I heard some of the testimony that because of the black plastic, nothing can be farmed. But again, chair, if you look islandwide, there's a lot of areas that used to be pineapple. It is being farmed. [...] Puʻu Kukui was, at one year, [the] world's wettest spot. There is water up there. When you get the warm ocean air at that steep and you get the cool mountain air, you get blessed rain almost every day.

Some believed Plantation Estates lot owners simply sought financial gain from the designation, which unnecessarily fueled opposition to their request, said Commissioner La Costa. Speaking as a real estate broker, she said she did not believe property values would change. "I don't know from where the concept or the misnomer came that it would increase property values if it were Rural Residential, because I don't think it will, and I've been selling real estate for 28 years."

Another point made by commissioners was the fact that the Rural Residential designation did not exist at the time of development. Had it existed, owners and developers might have sought that designation. Commissioner Pali said, "It's not that we're stealing from ag lands per se. But when they didn't have a designation, then it just all got thrown into ag, and so it is appropriate to identify the uses, in my opinion, and label it appropriately."

Commissioner Freitas said he took issue with lot owners who benefited from the cost savings and ease of building on ag land. But now, after having taken advantage of the benefits, they were seeking a designation change. "The question is, are we here to fix a mistake from earlier, or are we fixing something that provided a benefit in the beginning of the development?" Commissioner Tackett agreed with Freitas. "I feel they're very fortunate to have what they have, and they're very fortunate to be able to [do] what they do on ag land. [...] And I believe that is ag land and that it should stay ag land."

Although he did not find the case for changing the designation particularly compelling, Carnicelli objected to the reasons for keeping Plantation Estates under Agricultural. "All of the arguments that I've heard against the Plantation Estates being ag and not Rural have all been punitive. They've all been, 'You were ag, you bought ag, you should stay ag; oh, you're going to make more money.' Who cares if they make more money? I don't care."

McLean offered her perspective when Carnicelli asked her to comment on the change.

We do like calling things what they are and then also planning for future growth. There definitely are benefits to calling ducks, ducks. There are various residential zoning districts going to five acres, or maybe even up to 10 acres, to allow gentleman's estates. But the idea is for those entitlements to happen before the fact and not after the fact. Commissioner Pali is correct when she said earlier on the ag was the default zoning district, and the changes that happened to the ag district, which were in 1998, were meant to limit the number of gentleman's estates. But that hasn't been administered well. It hasn't been regulated well. It's been abused. But the idea was to keep land available for ag use if that will happen at some point in the future. Now, do I think Plantation Estates is going to convert to a big ag-producing region? Probably not. But we're in unprecedented times right now. You never know when that might change. And designating these Rural would be the first step in that direction, and not having that opportunity down the road. [ . . . ] And I agree that the opposition to this did seem to be punitive, but nonetheless, it did seem that the community felt very strongly about keeping these areas in ag along with the CPAC vote. So, I'm not giving you any direction at all. I'm giving you arguments on both sides, because this isn't an easy one. It's not an easy one for me.

Tackett shared his concerns about how the Planning Commission's decision would impact the soaring cost of homes. "If you continue to enable these things to go that way, you're going to continue to get things that are more expensive. And if you can stop things from going that way, you might not get affordable housing back, but at least you'll stop the runaway train, which I think is important for Lahaina."

Freitas introduced a motion to keep the area in agriculture, which failed in a 4–5 vote. He, Tackett, Castro and Hipolito voted for the motion. Commissioners Edlao, Pali, La Costa, Thompson and Carnicelli opposed. Immediately following that, commissioners voted 6–2 to change Plantation Estates' designation to Rural Residential. Freitas and Tackett opposed, and Hipolito abstained.

In a follow-up action in response to concerns of increasing density through the land designation change, the Planning Commission added language by consensus to require a two-acre minimum lot size and to prevent further subdivision should the Plantation Estates lot owners pursue a zoning change to Rural.

## COMMUNITY PLANS ARE GUIDES AND LAW

### *October 13, 2020*

Those involved in updating the West Maui Community Plan criticized the county for allowing so much time to pass before updating the plan. In response, county planners proposed additional language to prevent such delays in the future:

> In the past few decades, the county has not kept pace with the community plan updates, which are supposed to be adopted every 10 years, with each plan having a 20-year vision. However, there is a renewed commitment to this effort, and it is expected that this plan will be updated 10 years after its adoption.

Planning Commission Chairman Lawrence Carnicelli questioned whether this time period was realistic given what had happened historically. He asked his fellow commissioners whether the plan should be approached as a 30-year plan versus a 10-year plan. However, Planning Director Michele McLean observed that the West Maui Community Plan has taken more time to develop because it is a complete rewrite of the plan rather than an update. Future updates would not take as long.

Commissioner Kellie Pali used the proposed wording as an example of how the language in the plan leaned more toward control versus guidance. Her comments illustrated a broader ongoing struggle over whether the plan should carry the force of law.

> My understanding is that the plan is a guide. The plan is an idea. And I just feel like I keep seeing language that reflects the opposite of a guide. I see language as, or even hear words like pressure, or in this beautifully organized book, "require, shall, must." And those just aren't words of guidance; they seem like words of control. I'm starting to get lost with what is the purpose of the plan. Now I'm sort of [a] little confused.

The fact is, the community plan is both guide and law, a point that Carnicelli and county planners made. Planner Jennifer Maydan elaborated:

> Yes, community plans are absolutely a guide for the future. They are also adopted by the County Council by ordinance and they are law. Community plans play many roles. In our county, they provide guidance to the community landowners, developers, of how the county wants to grow over the next few decades. They are law when other ordinances point to them and say, "You shall comply with the community plan." Some examples are a change in zoning, special-use permits when you're in the SMA. Those laws point to

the community plan, and they shall be in compliance with the community plan. There are times where the community plan is more of a guide. It's a vision. It's aspirational. It's a guiding light of how our communities in our county want to grow. It does become a little confusing.

\* \* \*

The CPAC had identified the Pioneer Mill site and the Lahaina Gateway Center for redesignation as Urban Center Corridor (UCC), which would allow higher density development and existing light industrial uses. Committee members ultimately decided against designating the areas as Industrial within Lahaina Town, even though such areas already existed. Comcowich, a Lahaina resident, said she and her colleagues were concerned over how heavy industrial use might affect community health.

The other area identified for heavy industrial use within the community plan area was a four-acre site near the wastewater treatment plant in Kāʻanapali. Beyond this site, the CPAC never identified any other sites for heavy industrial use. Now the Planning Commission had the opportunity to decide whether to allow future industrial uses somewhere else in West Maui.

Developers earlier testified on the need to designate such sites. Chad Fukunaga, representing developers of the Pioneer Mill site and the adjacent Lahaina train station, said his clients currently conduct a number of both heavy and industrial uses at Pioneer Mill. Therefore, he asked commissioners to approve an Industrial designation for the site. Kyle Ginoza, representing the Lahaina Town South Project, sought a reversal on a CPAC decision to designate his company's property as Urban Center, a mixed-use designation that would allow for light industry uses but not heavy ones.

But as both Maydan and McLean pointed out, industrial uses are governed by zoning. Changing the community plan designations for the aforementioned projects would not impact industrial uses. "That's an existing entitlement. The only way that can be changed is by council action to change it, and I'm not aware of any effort at this point to change that," McLean said. Ginoza pushed back on this rationale, saying he was still concerned about creating inconsistencies between the plan designation and the zoning. He said his company was targeting the parcel for propane storage, which would require heavy industrial zoning. "That's why we're quite adamant to retain the industrial zoning—because that is one of our chief downstream uses for this parcel," Ginoza said. "My concern is if there's inconsistent land use designations, that may hinder our process going forward."

Pali, who said her father lived in one of the industrially zoned areas, made a case for allowing existing industrial uses to continue where they are rather than identify a new site. "I personally feel like we do need to have some sort of industrial area on the west side. We don't know what the future holds. [...] And instead of trying to see where it would fit best, the people in this neighborhood, including my dad guys, they've already been living with it; they've already accepted it in their backyard."

The commission debated the issue exhaustively before passing a motion to designate the project area north of Lahainaluna Road as Urban and the area south as Industrial with no special-use permits allowed. Commissioner La Costa dissented, and Carnicelli recused himself.

*      *      *

Both CPAC members Dylan Payne and Kai Nishiki spoke before the Planning Commission in October about the areas in and around Lahaina. While Nishiki urged commissioners to support CPAC's recommendations to designate large areas as Open Space, Payne appealed to them to revisit those decisions in light of the need for affordable housing. "While all aspects of the community plan are important, the areas of change and areas of stability really lay out in detail the community's desires and intentions. Everything mentioned in these sections was discussed extensively, and we all voted to adopt. Perhaps member Payne was absent from those meetings. I can't really explain his comment. Please support these sections and approve as presented," Nishiki said.

Though the CPAC's decisions identified areas that could accommodate growth to meet the projected number of units needed in West Maui, Payne argued only a small percentage of what is planned actually gets built.

> Just because something goes in the plan doesn't mean that it actually ever happens. I think the only evidence you need of that is to look at the '96 plan and see what was approved and put in that plan that has not ever happened. I would encourage you to take a look at those areas, specifically in the urban growth boundaries, and say, "Okay, where do we want to allow for housing to potentially happen?"

According to Nishiki, the estimated housing units possible with the scenario presented by CPAC for review was 7,950—over a thousand more units than the 6,923 units needed by 2040. Rather than identify more areas for growth, Nishiki suggested Maui County consider a "use it or lose it"-type policy that would place an expiration date on approved development plans.

It was our job to make sure that within the growth boundaries there was adequate housing that they could build, if they so choose. The challenges in getting housing built could possibly be pushed off on developers. And maybe this body could consider putting in sunset clauses on entitlements, which would put pressure on developers to either use the entitlements or lose the entitlements, and let somebody else move forward on building housing for our people.

\*   \*   \*

Host Hotels, represented by Kekoa McClellan, did not submit any projects to the CPAC. However, McClellan appeared before the commission to discuss two "potential" development projects. The first was the construction of a new oceanfront tower on their Hyatt property. The second was a "limited-service room hotel" in a parking lot area located between the current Hyatt driveway and Honoapiʻilani Highway. He said a proposed policy to prohibit the construction of new visitor units unless an equal number of workforce housing units were built was problematic for Hyatt's future plans.

\*   \*   \*

In public testimony, Peter Martin said he would like to see more areas designated Residential. When asked by Commissioner Tackett what he thought the biggest hurdle was to completing affordable housing projects, Martin responded:

> I would say it's the political will. If [the County Council] would just let these 201H's get through—and that's for 100 percent owner-occupant homes— and if we just start voting "yes" so you didn't risk three or $400,000 to get a "no." We're not giving up. I'm not selling the land. Eventually, even my children will hopefully get to build homes for other people.

\*   \*   \*

Ginoza also appeared before the commission to request they reverse a CPAC decision to designate a portion of the Lahaina Town South or Waineʻe project as Open Space. Ginoza's client, Hope Builders, one of Martin's companies, wanted the parcel to remain in agriculture to allow for some development. But Commissioners La Costa and Pali argued to keep the Open Space designation given the need for more parks in Lahaina and the parcel's proximity to an industrial area. Pali introduced a motion to keep the Open Space designation and to support the CPAC's recommendations for the rest of the area. The motion passed by majority with Freitas and Tackett dissenting.

## "Zombie Development"

### *October 27, 2020*

At the end of October, the Planning Commission dove into plans for the subarea between Puamana and the Pali, including Launiupoko, Olowalu and Ukumehame. Back in 2006, Peter Martin's proposed developments for these areas made their way inside of the Maui Island Plan's growth boundaries despite pushback from the community. Those opposed to development in Olowalu and Ukumehame cited unresolved concerns over the area's disputed land titles, cultural sites including numerous known burials, coral reef degradation and traffic. Even Dean Frampton, who represented the Olowalu Town project in the absence of Chairman Lawrence Carnicelli, acknowledged the conflict.

> Olowalu town was a controversial project, if not the most controversial, but one that ultimately got on the Maui Island Plan with the rural growth boundaries and the urban growth boundaries that you see in the map I'm sharing. The project got on the map in large part [due] to a consistent message that resonated with the community. That message was: Maui has historically been an island of small towns and small communities.

When the Olowalu Town project came through the West Maui Community Planning process, it encountered the same opposition as it had during the Maui Island Plan. This time, however, the Planning Department and the CPAC responded to the public outcry by designating most of the area as Agricultural and Open Space. These recommendations carried forward to the Planning Commission, who would now need to decide where they stood.

All but two of the 33 people who testified at the October 27, 2020 meeting of the Planning Commission opposed residential development for Olowalu. Martin and Dylan Payne, a West Maui CPAC member and employee of Martin's West Maui Land Company, both testified in support of the projects. This showing was the latest demonstration of public opposition against the project over its long history. West Maui CPAC member Karen Comcowich described Olowalu as the "zombie development." "No matter how many times the community tries to bury it, it keeps rising from the grave," she said in her opening testimony to the Commission.

About four years prior to this meeting, the State Land Use Commission turned down Martin's bid to secure entitlements for Olowalu Town. Dick Mayer, a member of the Maui General Plan Advisory Committee, commented:

One of the main reasons for why they turned it down was the excellent testimony of the previous Planning Director, Will Spence, when he stated that what we don't need is an isolated community along the highway from Central Maui to West Maui that will add more traffic congestion and problems in that area, far from public facilities, schools, school buses, wastewater, et cetera. There is a background for having turned down development in Olowalu.

Beyond the fact that allowing development in Olowalu and the surrounding areas would be antithetical to the principles of smart growth, there were other reasons for striking the idea down. For one, Olowalu is known to be an archaeological hotspot. Testifier Noelani Ahia remarked,

> Olowalu is a highly sensitive area. I've spoken with multiple archaeologists who've done work in that area and say that just about anywhere you go there's going to be iwi kūpuna, not to mention heiau and petroglyphs, cultural layers. This is not an area to put housing. You make it sound like you're doing us a favor by putting, you know, multiple subdivisions instead of 18 gentleman's estates. There's gentleman's estates all over the west side that are for sale right now that are not selling. We don't need that and we don't need these subdivisions either. Not in these sensitive areas.

A week prior to the Planning Commission's meeting, several people were arrested on another one of Martin's properties for attempting to prevent the desecration of iwi kūpuna. Ahia commented,

> These women put their bodies in front of a gigantic machine with a four-foot bucket with huge blades that was digging through the ʻaina in a very, very sensitive area known to contain burials. They were arrested. These are wahine that have kuleana to this ʻāina, and kuleana to protect iwi kūpuna. That they were taken...and criminalized by MPD [Maui Police Department]. They were arrested under the premise of being citizen's arrest on behalf of the landowner and the construction company. Highly illegal. Several days later, iwi kūpuna was hit on the same project further down the line. That was our "I told you so" moment.

Later, when Planning Commissioner Freitas questioned Martin about the incident, he stated that he believed bones were actually brought in as infill from another site. Martin remarked,

We didn't even have to have a monitor. I voluntarily paid for one. It wasn't a requirement. And we had a monitor there. And we're almost finished with the job. And so some people jumped in the trench, and we stopped, and they did get arrested. But they're just confused about whether we're doing something right or wrong [...] we're not going anywhere close to known burials. We did find a portion of a skull. I didn't see it, but it looks like it was infill. No, excuse me, it was almost certainly infill.

Martin's testimony conflicted with the other testimonies, including Maui County Councilmember Tamara Paltin, who confirmed the sites discussed were known burial sites.

The second point that I wanted to make is that those were known burial areas. And because there was no permit for the Waineʻe property, it didn't trigger SHPD (State Historical Preservation Division) review. The concerns brought to me from the community, I wrote a letter to Maui Lānaʻi Island Burial Council. There is records in the CRC minutes of known burials from Hinano Rodriguez. The Maui Lānaʻi Island Burial Council recommended a stop work order that was ignored. And it was 'til the SHPD, the county archaeologist, and the Maui Lānaʻi Burial Council could make a visit to the place and determine the situation before they stop work. Then a human skull was found. So, you know, that's the type of developer we're dealing with.

Several marine biologists also spoke against the proposed development in Olowalu. Donna Brown, a professor at the University of Hawaiʻi and a 40-year resident of West Maui, said:

As a marine biologist, I've spent a lot of time doing surveys of the coral reefs around Maui, and I can tell you the reef out in front of Olowalu is one of our healthiest reefs we have. And even so, it's not doing very well, as all of our reefs are not doing very well. We really cannot afford to lose this one— or any of them, really—but especially this one.

Similarly, John Starmer, chief scientist at the Maui Nui Marine Resource Council, testified that the Olowalu reefs were special and worth protecting.

The reefs in Olowalu are really, really amazing, but they have been impacted. [...] And they are still on the road to recovery. They've had issues like the unpermitted management of erosion along the highway. All of this stuff has turned a reef that is still spectacular but is impacted into something that is vulnerable.

Proponents of Olowalu Town contended that if the county did not allow affordable housing, the lots would be sold off to wealthy landowners who would build gentleman's estates. In their minds, development was inevitable. Commented Commissioner Christian Tackett:

> So that's what all nine of us is struggling with right now. In my opinion, not the other nine, but in my opinion, it's like either we let them do the 18 or no affordable come from it … or they do some of the 18 and we get some affordable. And according to what everybody has said so far, nothing should be built over there. But that's not what's on the table right now, because those 18 lots are already approved.

Testifiers criticized this kind of reasoning. One said she believed the developer was pushing the either/or narrative to cause fear. Said testifier Tiare Lawrence:

> I think they're using the 18 lots as a scare tactic. I think it's total, complete *shibai*. The reality is the state and the county still need to work together in identifying where the proposed realignment is going to go. And perhaps portions of that realignment would have to be bought from Peter Martin or West Maui Land Company themselves. So there still is the potential for them landowners to still make money off of those lands with the proposed realignment route. […] So, you know, we hear, like, "Oh, we want affordable housing." Well, you know what? We have several projects that are on the books about to be built in locations where there is walkability and access to work and schools, medical facilities. That is where we should be building. That is smart growth. A proposed town in Olowalu to me is irresponsible development.

## Homes For the Wealthy or Local Families?
### *November 10, 2020*

Earlier in the month, the Planning Commission listened to about 30 in-person testimonies and received well over 100 written testimonies against proposed residential developments between south Lahaina and Olowalu. The proposed projects—Puʻunoa, Polanui, Makila Rural East and Olowalu Town—would be located on land owned in part by Peter Martin, who sought a change from Agricultural to Rural Residential to allow for higher-density development along the southern end of West Maui.

While people voiced their concern for all of the projects, they were especially against developing Olowalu Town. Commissioners needed to decide whether to approve or deny a plan designation change for each individual project. They also needed to change or accept Policy 3.7.2, which read: "Gentleman's estate projects and projects following the State 201H or County 2.97 process shall not be approved within this area of stability." State 201H or County 2.97 were expedited processes available to projects with at least 50 percent affordable housing. They exempted such projects from certain zoning and regulations. Testifiers often criticized these processes, which they viewed as problematic loopholes. Two specific areas would be affected by the policy, north of Makapuapua Point and south of Puamana.

Commissioners questioned the weight of this policy because developers could still request a waiver from it. Planning Department Director Michele McLean explained the policy's potential role in future decision making.

> The reason that I think it still has value is because in asking for an exemption, that developer would have to call to the council's attention that this policy exists in the first place. And so, the council would have to consider that in the context of the whole development: "Okay, we're going to let you have sidewalks on one side. We're going to let you build two residential standards even though you're on ag land." But while the community plan says they don't want these affordable housing projects in these regions, are we going to give an exemption from that? So while they have the authority to do that, it does call to their attention that this policy is in there. So they would have to consider that before granting an exemption. So it does still have value. It doesn't prohibit it, but it does still have value.

Commissioners were split on whether to keep or remove the policy. Commissioners Jerry Edlao, Kawika Freitas and P. Denise La Costa voted to keep it, and Commissioners Mel Hipolito, Kellie Pali and Dale Thompson voted to remove it. Without a majority to remove the policy, it remained in place.

\* \* \*

Commissioners who supported Martin's request viewed development as inevitable. They described their decision as one that would either benefit wealthy outside investors or local, full-time residents. In other words, if they did not support Martin's projects, he would be forced to sell the large agricultural lots to the highest bidders, who would inevitably build gentleman's estates. That land would then be lost forever to local families. But if they did support Martin's proposals, he could take steps to build homes that would be affordable to a wide range of income levels. This scenario was described as a scare tactic by some and a reality by others.

Martin opted to speak on his own behalf before commissioners took their votes. He started off by questioning the validity of the CPAC vote count, and ended with an emotional plea to give residents the opportunity to live on the land—a plea that surprised some given his strained relationship with kanaka maoli, who disputed some of his land titles and who had fought with him over his lack of respect for burial sites on his land.

> Seven out of the thirteen CPAC members—Don Gerbig, Aina Kohler, Leilani [Reyes Pulmano], Joe Pluta, Jeri Dean, Hans Michel and Dylan Payne—all wrote in saying they want to see housing for local families. So to say the people in the community do not want housing there, it's just not true. It's not a vote. And I hope you get to the bottom of it and respect the process and that it was stolen, and I hope you also read my letter to you folks. I wrote it this morning. I've written every time. And I just want to end with, from the days of Big Five, the sugar companies, since the Great Māhele, the land has not been available for us, the citizens. The Big Five kept it away, and you guys are keeping it away. It's just criminal.

Martin, who choked up during his remarks, continued past his time as commissioners tried to cut him off. "That nobody gets to live on the darn land—you should all be ashamed of yourselves... I hope you read this, yeah—you want to destroy families," he said.

Freitas immediately called a vote to keep the CPAC's recommendations in place. But Commissioner Tackett asked Freitas to pause to allow for discussion, and then asked Long Range Division Planning Director Pam Eaton whether Martin's testimony had any validity.

> No, Chair. I can tell you the facts are that there was a developer panel [that] presented to CPAC on Puunoa, and Kyle Ginoza did deliver a presentation,

but there was no specific discussion about the Puunoa project, and I believe there's an issue with regard [to] Urban Growth boundaries, but with regard to the seven of the 13 [CPAC members], that's not accurate.

Unsatisfied by Eaton's response, Pali pressed the Planning Department to clarify the CPAC's action on the Areas of Stability. She referenced notes from the May 19th CPAC meeting in which Dylan Payne asked county planners whether the committee could discuss the proposed Areas of Stability. Eaton clarified the section had not been discussed in the meetings. However, she said her staff emailed the committee, instructing them to review the draft and propose any amendments or changes. Payne had not requested any changes.

The Commissioners voted on the change in land designation for each project individually. For Puunoa, the majority voted to keep the project under Agricultural versus changing it to Small Town Center, as passed by CPAC and recommended by the Planning Department. But motions to do the same for Polanui and Makila Rural East failed by an evenly split vote. The projects were right next to each other and fell within the rural growth boundary in the Maui Island Plan. Immediately after these votes, Commissioner Pali called for a motion to designate the projects as Rural Residential. These, too, failed by a split vote: Pali, Thompson and Hipolito voted for the change, and La Costa, Freitas, and Edlao voted against it.

*   *   *

After all the testimony that highlighted the cultural significance of the area proposed for Olowalu Town, the need to protect one of Maui's most important coral reefs and the lack of infrastructure, all those things seemed secondary to the need for affordable housing. Commissioner Pali commented:

> If the area itself is lacking infrastructure or dangerous to our coastlines or, you know, maybe the iwi kūpuna could not be protected, I would say that they're going to have to go through their natural process and SMAs and all that to make sure that the project is sound. But to do a blanket kapu—no can—we're going to kill it right now and we're going to discriminate on the families that are making a little bit more money but still qualify for affordable homes. Saying that they'll never get that kind of opportunity to experience other parts of the island and they have to go Central [Maui] because we're helping them, I disagree with that.

Leading up to a motion to change the designation of Olowalu Town to allow for proposed housing, Commissioners Tackett and Hipolito also alluded to their support for the change.

> I personally don't know the guy (Peter Martin) at all. Never, never, never, never talked to him, seen him, you know what I mean? Never spoke to him, but I can tell you this—that it doesn't cost anything for him to get his $19 million. That's the easiest thing for him to do. So the fact that he's willing to even go through any of this to try to make something affordable tells me that he's putting forth an effort.

Hipolito, who voted to keep the other proposed projects in agriculture, voiced a change regarding Olowalu Town. He would later introduce a motion to change the area's land use designation to allow for affordable housing.

> Listening to Mr. Frampton, you know what they're willing to do and I don't really want to shut the door on them at this point. I really...I want to give them the opportunity to show us that they really mean what they say— that they can pencil out for it to be affordable, to take all of the concerns that was brought up by all these testifiers which I highlighted—from the no water, sewer, protection of reef, sea rise, the burial sites, water shortage, road relocation, and especially this one word that I wrote that was highly, highly voiced at the last hearing. Respect. That there was enough respect for the developer towards the local community.

Freitas expressed disappointment at his fellow commissioners' comments. "It's kind of sad, because we went through each individual development, and it was pretty clear by the majority of the testifiers two weeks ago that right across this entire subsection, subarea, it was to remain agriculture," he said.

Commissioner La Costa appealed to fellow commissioners to take into account the sacredness of the site and the public testimony against development.

> I'm going to read from page 94. "Olowalu is the site of a large pre-contact Hawaiian settlement, which is evident [given] the number of archaeological sites found in the area, including petroglyphs, burials, heiau, trails, rock shelters, agriculture and fishing shrines, house sites, boundary and navigational markers, loʻi and awai." Yes, we need affordable housing. Yes, we need workforce housing. There are thousands of units that are being

proposed north. I was absolutely appalled by the way that the kūpuna were treated in this area. This is an incredibly sacred area. If you spend any time up there going past the petroglyphs with someone from the area, of course feel what is going on there... I think there are projects that do not have the sensitivity, do not have the propensity of the people who live in the area to say, no, you can't do that here because this is where our ancestors are. We have iwi kūpuna, we have burial sites, we have... this is pre-contact Hawai'i. So I have a major problem [with] anything being done in Olowalu, regardless of whether it's multi-million on the ocean or affordable at 399. It just hurts my heart to think that Hawaiians have one last place to call their own.

In the end, no one budged from their positions. A motion to change the designation of Olowalu Town from Agricultural to Residential, Small Town Center and Public/Quasi-Public failed in a vote of three to three. Hipolito, Edlao and Pali voted in support of the measure, while La Costa, Thompson and Freitas voted against it. Without a majority vote to change the recommended land designation for Olowalu Town, it would remain in place.

## "It is the County's Responsibility to Build Housing"
### *November 24, 2020*

With one meeting remaining for their review of the West Maui Community Plan, commissioners shifted their focus toward steps Maui County would take to implement the plan. Agency heads provided written suggestions about the "Implementing Actions" and some of the policies. Most shared their concerns over staff capacity and limited funding.

Comments were provided by the Department of Water Supply, Department of Fire and Public Safety, Maui Metropolitan Planning Organization, Department of Parks and Recreation, Department of Housing and Human Concerns (DHHC), and the Mayor's Office. Some agencies remarked on actions and policies they viewed as problematic. DHHC's Linda Munsell wrote:

Page 62 Policy 2.5.11 limiting the location of 201H and 2.97 projects and requiring them to include sidewalks, parks, bus stops, etc, goes against the intent of the 201H and 2.97 laws, which allows these projects to request exemptions from these kinds of requirements. We may be able to limit 2.97 because it's a County ordinance, but it is my understanding that we cannot preempt state law. The project will have the right to ask, and final passage or denial of a project contrary to this policy would be up to the Council. Again, additional requirements [equal] increase in cost.

Most of the changes proposed by the Maui County Planning Department and other agencies added specificity without changing the actions' intent. Without further discussion, commissioners voted by consensus to adopt the changes proposed by Maui County.

\* \* \*

Only one commissioner, P. Denise La Costa, suggested a change to an action item. The action stated, "Propose legislation to amortize the short-term occupancy list and phase out short-term rental use to make more housing units available for long-term occupancy."

> If somebody buys a property, it's always been used for short term rental, and they're told, "Gee, sorry; you're not going to be able to use it now because the county has changed their mind," I think that infringes on people's property rights. And I think if that were the case, then the county would be looking at class-action lawsuits left and right. It is the county's responsibility to build housing and provide housing, not individual owners who have owned a property and used it for a particular use for years and years.

Her motion failed by a 4–1 vote with Mel Hipolito abstaining. However, on the same action item, the Planning Department recommended limiting the scope of the action by adding that it would apply to "properties with low percentage of short-term rental use" and not all short-term rental properties.

## Closing the Door Completely
### *December 8, 2020*

At the Planning Commission's final hearing on the West Maui Community Plan, industry groups and individual homeowners pushed back on two proposed policies that they said would inadvertently worsen the area's affordable housing challenges. One would halt permitting for additional visitor units unless an equal number of workforce housing units were developed in the same subarea. The other sought to phase out short-term vacation rentals in the Lahaina Historic District in a multi-pronged approach to retaining the area's residential character.

The Hawai'i Construction Alliance, the Hawai'i Building and Construction Trades Council, Host Hotels and Resorts, and the Pacific Resource Partnership (PRP) voiced their opposition to the proposed policy. The groups shared the same language in their written testimonies. They argued the policy "will reduce the number of affordable housing units constructed in West Maui while at the same time taking jobs away from local people and making home ownership for those families impossible."

Real estate groups and vacation-homeowners testified against a proposed policy to phase out legal, short-term vacation rentals in West Maui. The Realtors Association of Maui, Inc. submitted a letter on behalf of its association and the more than 1,700 Realtors they represent, saying the policy action would violate owners' vested property rights.

Homeowners who operated legal short-term vacation rentals warned that the policy, which they called misguided, would harm the island's economy while doing nothing to ease the affordable housing shortage. Several of them cited the significant tax revenue generated by their units and questioned how Maui County might make up the shortfall should they decide to move forward with their plans. Kathleen Gildred commented,

> I also understand that there's not enough affordable housing on the island, but is eliminating high-end, short-term rentals [going to] solve the actual housing problem? If, for example, my house were a long-term rental, it would rent for around $6,000 a month, which would hardly help solve the problem of affordable housing. If short-term rentals were discontinued, it would mean less jobs for cleaning and maintenance people who need to keep the house in top shape all the time for our renters. Plus there would be a substantial loss to the county revenue without short-term rental property tax. A phaseout of short-term rentals in West Maui could create a tax revenue shortfall of up to $60 million. If that were offset to Maui homeowners, that could be around $2,200 increase to everyone's real property tax.

Other homeowners who ran legal short-term rentals encouraged the Planning Commission to accept the changes that had come to West Maui rather than fighting them. Russell Evans stated,

> I think the horse is out of the barn. You're not going to stop Airbnb. Exactly what Chairman Carnicelli said—we've got to come together and learn to live with it. This is the way of the world. This is the way of Paris. This is the

way of Hong Kong. This is the way of New York City. This is the way of
Los Angeles. Everywhere in the world, people are renting their homes out.

Evans suggested Maui County encourage the creation of call centers as
a way to generate jobs and inspire businesses to help build housing for their
employees. "People will come move to the island; there will be people who can
afford the rents. The businesses will build the apartments for them to live in.
And you'll get what you want, but you don't need to put the short-term rental
homeowners out of business."

On the other side of the issue, resident Delaney De La Barra spoke in
support of the policy to phase out vacation rentals.

> On a personal level, the lack of long-term housing has affected myself and
> my family [...] when a place that I was staying at was sold to be a vacation
> rental. [...] Since 2015, [I] had to move six times living on the west side. I
> have a seven-year-old daughter. So I am calling in to support policy 2.5.16
> by increasing the long-term residential housing inventory by any ways that
> we can, including phasing out and converting existing vacation rentals.

The final version of the West Maui Community Plan retained language
to phase out existing vacation rentals and offered two pathways to get there:
"Propose amendments to the County Historic District Ordinances to allow
existing hotels, prohibit new vacation rentals, and phase out existing vacation
rentals that are not hotels or inns. Phasing out could be accomplished by count-
ing vacation rentals toward short-term rental home permit caps or by attrition."

\*    \*    \*

On a policy to promote sustainable building practices, Commissioner P. Denise
La Costa suggested strengthening the language by using "require" in place of
"promote," and adding solar panels to the list of requirements. Carnicelli said
he wouldn't support the change. His comments touched on the ongoing struggle between those who viewed the plan more as a guide and those who viewed
it more as law:

> We're trying to legislate through the Community Plan process. That's
> riddled through this entire plan. Great idea, wrong place, in my opinion.
> You don't put this in a community plan. If it's "promote," let's leave it. If
> it's "required," I can't vote in favor of that, because now what we're doing

is we're using the community plan to supersede ordinance and what's actually law.

*     *     *

After hearing testimony from industry groups, Commissioner Christian Tackett moved to change a policy that would halt the creation of new visitor units in West Maui unless an "an equal number of workforce housing units are concurrently developed in the same subarea." He expressed concern over the impact such a policy would have on new construction and the local workers who depended on it. "When they change the number to one-for-one, I don't believe we're going to get any housing units out of it," he said. A former carpenter and educator, Tackett said hundreds of local students participated in the carpenters' training programs and will need employment in their trade when they graduate. "This is where the local kids are going; this is where they're working. I would really like to see that verbiage change, so that some affordable [housing] can still be made." His motion passed by consensus.

Kellie Pali suggested deleting or rewording a policy to phase out legal short-term rentals in the Lahaina Historic District. "But I am compelled to agree with many testifiers," she said. "Just because I handle financing and I see the type of homes people are buying, I'm compelled to say that that policy will not actually result in affordable housing. I fear that we would have more of a ghost town."

In response to Commissioner Pali's comments, Planning Director Michele McLean suggested adding language to determine whether phasing out short-term rentals would increase long-term housing or not. Pali responded that she was leaning toward just taking out the "phasing out" piece altogether. She made a motion to amend the policy by deleting the last portion. Her motion passed by consensus.

*     *     *

Pali then moved to change a policy that would prohibit gentleman's estates and affordable housing projects using the county's fast-track processes in the "Areas of Stability" section. She went back to a position she had held throughout the meetings—that she did not want to close the door completely on future projects.

> We don't know that just because we have 7,000 projected projects that would fulfill the need of West Maui that one or two projects may get stopped, or developer funds might run out, or something might change

and now we don't meet the need. To shut down other options, I think, would be dangerous. I don't want to mess with the integrity of what was meant here. I don't want to completely delete it. But I think maybe adding language that...we desire that it doesn't happen...just something a little bit more open. That would be my recommendation.

At this point, Carnicelli recused himself from discussion because of his conflict of interest as a representative for Peter Martin's proposed Olowalu development. This particular policy had significant ramifications for Martin's project. Should the policy remain in place, he would need to go through much lengthier processes to have his projects approved. Without it, he could take a shorter route to approvals, and if approved, would be exempted from many other restrictions.

Pali continued the discussion on the proposed policy by saying she wanted to retain the integrity of the intention but not take a "hard line." She suggested replacing the word "prohibit" with "discourage."

The reason why they want to say they don't want the State 201H or [the] County's 2.9 is because it's sometimes...in all policies that are created, there are the abusers that will take a good policy meant for good people, and then they'll abuse them. [I'm] not saying someone is or isn't abusing them specifically, but in general. I think the goal, I believe the intent of this, was to make sure certain developers don't use it as a way to slide their projects in under the cover of affordable housing.

Aligning with Pali, Commissioner Jerry Edlao suggested weakening the language further. Some commissioners wanted to retain the authority to review projects on a case–by-case basis. "Saying 'discourage' is kind of keeping the door half-closed in my mind. Maybe we should just say 'may be considered.' You know, this way [we are not] saying yes [or] saying no, and we still have the opportunity."

Commissioner Kawika Freitas spoke against changing or removing the policy based on testimony overwhelmingly against development in the Areas of Stability, alluding to testimony against development in Olowalu.

I wanted to remind the commissioners in that last meeting that we did take the vote, of those that passionately spoke out, including the ladies that jumped in a ditch to stop the machine. You know, I feel this is another opportunity to continue to try to get this passed ... by going through this again and again until it finally passes. I'm going to vote and remind everybody that it was overwhelmingly for leaving [the land designation as is].... And so I'm not going to change my mind on what I voted the last time, which was to leave it as is.

Following Freitas' remarks, Pali responded to clarify her position before making a motion to amend the proposed policy to replace the word "prohibit" with "discourage."

What I'm saying is that if and when we ever needed to build here, that there would be a vetting process, which would take place: they have to come to the commission, and they have to go to the public again, and they have to go to council to even attempt to get it built. And all I'm saying is we don't know what the future holds. We don't know how the shapes of our island and the communities will start to form or what might happen. And I'm not comfortable with closing the door completely.

Pali's motion passed with Commissioners Freitas and La Costa dissenting.

\*    \*    \*

The Planning Commission adopted language that prevents further subdivision of Plantation Estates lots should the owners collectively or individually seek rezoning to Rural. Changing the land use designation of the Plantation Estates subdivision was a hot-button issue, stirring years of testimony and discussion.

\*    \*    \*

For a second time, La Costa moved to take out action item 5.08, which directs the county to propose legislation to make use of short-term rentals with low occupancy percentages available for long-term housing. She expressed her concern that the policy infringes on personal property rights and could open the county up to lawsuits.

I think that any time you try to take away people's property rights, and what has been done for years and years and years, I don't know if the county can afford to defend itself for 12,000 property units, which is how many rentals there are on the island. There are about 8,000 in West Maui, and if you start taking away those property rights from the people who have Airbnb, short-term rental . . . it's not going to substitute with housing—they can't afford to rent those. And I just think that this is asking for tons of lawsuits.

Carnicelli advocated for leaving in this policy because of community sentiment toward the need for long-term housing. Pali wanted to retain it but remove language that could infringe on personal property rights. "I don't like the word 'phasing out' too, because that's an infringement on property rights," said Pali. "But the reality is we would have limitations there. But I don't want to miss the purpose. The purpose is to look at our vacation rental inventory, and let's look at what we can do and how we can do it. And then the ultimate goal is long-term units, apartments, homes."

La Costa proposed amending the policy to focus on creating long-term housing without prescribing how to get there. Her proposed language stated: "Propose legislation to make more housing units available for long-term occupancy." Her motion passed with Freitas as the sole dissenter.

\*   \*   \*

Tackett proposed amending an action item that would give special consideration to modular housing to address housing needs for temporary and seasonal farm workers. He expressed concern the policy might attract a flood of modular units that would be discarded or misused.

> I understand what they're saying what [the policy is] here for. But I'm saying if you bring those [modular housing units] here, you're going to find those problems, because as they get old, they're going to get let back into the general public. And as farms go out of business, and then some might even be stolen and put into the bushes. And none of these modular systems that you're talking about will ever have any labor from anybody on Maui go into it. All the money to purchase these things will all go out of state.

His motion to strike the policy's reference to modular housing passed by consensus.

# PART 3

# MAUI COUNTY COUNCIL

## "The Paradigm Has Certainly Shifted"

The Maui County Council, led by a progressive majority, began its review of the West Maui Community Plan in early February 2021. In the coming years, the council majority would be described by local news reports as one that pushed the status quo. Under the leadership of West Maui Councilmember Tamara Paltin, the Council's Planning and Sustainable Land Use Committee took on the task of reviewing the plan. They adopted designations to create more green space, to buffer against climate change, and to stem the loss of agricultural lands to luxury development. On key decisions where the Planning Commission and the CPAC diverged on these issues, the council almost always sided with the CPAC, restoring language that reflected its priorities. Through the vast majority of its actions, the committee endorsed a future for Maui County that prioritized full-time residents' quality of life, agricultural lands, environmental health and cultural preservation. As *Honolulu Civil Beat* reporter Marina Starleaf Riker wrote in 2022: "They put forth a number of bold policies that bucked Maui's long standing political establishment, like enacting a temporary moratorium on the construction of new hotels in hopes of curbing overtourism, raising taxes on second homes to pay for affordable housing and pushing for the county to take back control of water long managed by plantations."

## Maui County Council Planning and Sustainable Land Use Committee

### *February 4, 2021*

The first day of public hearings lasted more than four hours and covered a wide range of topics. Representatives of the Aha Moku Council, a network of kūpuna and Native Hawaiian cultural practitioners who advise the state on natural resource management, were among the first to testify. Keʻeaumoku Kapu and others were concerned over the development of culturally and historically significant lands. Maui County had recently hired archaeologist Janet Six to complete a credible archaeological survey identifying sensitive areas warranting protection in West Maui, and Kapu expressed hope that Six's work would inform decision making.

Testifier Fay McFarlane of the Aha Moku Council asked the Council Committee to change the definition of wetlands from the one used in the Clean Water Act because not doing so would exclude historical wetlands. In its place, she suggested using the fisheries definition of wetlands so that historical wetlands also might be included in the interpretation. She also asked the Council Committee to change the terms "endangered" and "threatened" to "native" and "endemic" to help ensure protections for native species even if their populations increased.

*　*　*

One of the major decisions made by the Planning Commission—a decision that reversed the CPAC's recommendation—was to adopt a new land designation for the Plantation Estates subdivision. Lot owner and board member Sharon Saunders testified before the County Committee in support of the change. But she also pointed out what she viewed as a discrepancy: the Rural Residential designation granted to Plantation Estates should have included neighboring Honolua Ridge. She referred to the two areas as "actually one community."

*　*　*

Throughout the process of developing the West Maui Community Plan, those charged with reviewing, amending and adopting the plan's policies and actions questioned whether the plan was legally binding or advisory. In an attempt to address the misconceptions, Planning Director Michele McLean said, "There's a section from 2.80B that clearly says there are provisions that are meant to be guidelines, and provisions that are intended to have the force and effect of law."

She cited several examples of how community plans had the force and effect of law. Under all of these conditions, actions were required by law to comply with community plans. These examples included changes in zoning and the administration of Special Management Area permits, County Special Use permits, subdivisions, the Capital Improvement Program and the county budgets. McLean went on to explain that community plans are advisory in the cases of Ministerial permits, including building permits, grading permits, plumbing permits, and electrical permits. Beyond these permits, she said county staff use community plans as a guide in many other ways. "The policy guidelines are still very important on a day-to-day basis."

\* \* \*

The owners of HC&D, LLC, a longtime concrete batching plant located in Lahaina, voiced their concerns about plan designation changes that could affect their ability to continue what are called "light industrial" operations. Roberto Andrion, a representative for the local chapter of the International Longshore & Warehouse Union (ILWU), spoke in support of keeping the current land designation for the areas in which the batching plants are located.

> We believe the land should remain as industrial to ensure cement operations can continue on the Island of Maui. HC&D provides a number of good-paying jobs on Maui, and this is more important than ever with our current economic conditions. Maui County has been the hardest hit county in the State of Hawai'i from the COVID-19 pandemic. Thousands of workers have lost their jobs; many are still unemployed today.

\* \* \*

Several Plantation Estates landowners appeared before the County Council Committee in support of the Planning Commission's recommendation to designate their subdivision as Rural Residential. Gary Grube, owner of Hua Momona Farms in Plantation Estates, testified to the difficulty of farming due to the rough terrain and plastic debris left over from the sugar cane plantation days. Though he managed to make the conditions work, he didn't believe his neighbors should be forced to farm. Paltin asked Grube if he was concerned about how the change in designation would limit his operations:

> Mr. Grube, currently the CC&Rs don't have any restrictions on ag activities, and my understanding is because state law doesn't allow restrictions on ag activities on ag lands, ag subdivisions. So my question is, knowing that the two previous iterations of your subdivision CC&Rs had severe limitations on ag activities—limiting it to the farming of Norfolk pines, limiting the types of animals that were allowed, even dogs and cats and whatnot—you have no concern that relinquishing this ag subdivision status could cause CC&Rs to change in such a way that would affect your operations?

Grube's answer spoke to the legal protections afforded to agricultural land in Hawai'i, somewhat contradicting his testimony that the change in designation would be beneficial to his farm and others. Confused, Paltin countered, "Oh, I guess I'm not clear with your answer. I thought the protection was only available if the land was designated ag, and if it changes to rural, then you don't have the same sorts of protections as when it is in ag." Grube said he wasn't an expert on the subject, but understood the designation in and of itself would not impact his farm. A subsequent change in zoning, however, would.

*       *       *

The ongoing debate about whose opinion should shape the Community Plan persisted with the County Council. "When we're going over this, it is important to remember that this is the West Maui Community Plan. It is not intended to be a developer's plan, or an off-island owner's plan, or a Realtor's plan," said CPAC member Karen Comcowich, testifying before the Council.

Conversely, Kyle Ginoza, who represented the proposed developments for Waine'e and projects south of Lahaina, said some who participated in the process tried to stifle other people's voices.

> There was a bent toward accepting some people's opinions as the voice of the community, and trying to stifle other people's voices as the voice of the community. And I experienced that during one of the CPAC meetings, during the map discussions. What I would suggest to you, and I would hope that you . . . really hope that you would do, is to not just listen to or not take the CPAC plan and the Maui Planning Commission plans as if you should just agree and rubber-stamp.

Ginoza said those who attended the CPAC meetings were "intimidated by" or "just being bullied" by those in charge of the process. The hostile environment he described kept regular people from becoming more engaged in the process, he said. Other members of the public who testified in the hearings, some of whom identified themselves as Peter Martin's employees, echoed these concerns.

CPAC members Jeri Dean and Dylan Payne, both of whom have ties to Martin's companies—Payne worked as a real estate agent for West Maui Land Company, while Dean's brother was the president of Martin's West Maui Construction company—urged the Council to make amendments to the plan so that it would better align with the Maui Island Plan. Jeri Dean, like Kyle Ginoza who testified before her, criticized the process.

I found it very interesting that there was often a disparity of time given to presenters on several occasions. There was a time when different developers were given just three minutes each to share what they probably spent a lot of time and money on with expert data and information, while other testifiers who were anti-development were given a minimum of 30 minutes each with encouragement of the chair and [Planning] Department. I had a sense there was an agenda throughout the process, and those who supported the plan had the unyielding floor, where[as] those members, both on the CPAC or community, who had questions or disagreements to the plan received verbal lashing, criticism, intimidation, and were even blatantly told that their input goes against the chair or the current plan.

Dean's brother, Joshua, also testified before the Council Committee.

A plan takes time because you are trying to do something and you have to find out: can it be done? Does it pencil out? Does the math work? You know, it doesn't take no time to scrap a plan. Because what does that involve? It involves doing nothing, and that's what this felt like. I was part of this community plan. I went to several meetings, and it was all about: "How can we erase things from the plan?"

Payne focused his criticism on aspects of the CPAC plan not in "alignment" with the Maui Island Plan.

We went through this at CPAC about why it doesn't have to agree completely, but there are certainly areas in the West Maui Community Plan areas, urban growth boundaries and rural growth boundaries, where there's absolutely zero designations that would allow for any urban or rural growth. So, I'm not saying those areas need to be totally painted in, but it does seem a bit, you know, contradictory. And if we set this precedent with the first community plan after the Island Plan update, it kind of begs the question, well, what's the Island Plan for?

Nishiki, who was one of the last people to testify before the County Council, rebuked the sentiments of those who called the process unfair, intimidating and hostile.

To hear developers and their employees complain that there wasn't ample community engagement and that developers weren't given a voice is ludicrous. In fact, developers and landowners had an entire meeting set aside for them to provide information on their projects and answer questions. [...] It seems to me, and most of our community, that we did indeed hear the developers' voices. And the problem isn't that they weren't heard; the problem for them is that we didn't do what they wanted. There is a huge difference. To me, they are acting like spoiled toddlers throwing a tantrum over not getting their candy.

Earlier in the meeting, following developers' claims of intimidation and bullying, Laʻakea Low pushed back against what he viewed as an attack on the process.

A lot of the opposition is from developers or people who work for developers. I think in terms of bullying, if you want to talk about bullying, we can talk about quiet title that the developers engage in on the island. We can talk about developers calling cops on wahine koa protecting kuleana lands, getting kidnapped by the police, illegally arrested by the police for protecting kuleana lands. If you want to talk about intimidation and bullying, I would say that a lot of the developers engage in that behavior more than anyone else on the island.

Another testifier, Jordan Hocker, echoed Nishiki's sentiments:

I would beg you to recognize the difference between people who have everything to lose versus people who have everything to gain. The West Maui Community Plan was drafted by people who had the most to lose, and I resent the implication that somehow a majority of the CPAC members now feel like they disagree with their own decisions.

* * *

In Low's testimony, he cautioned the County Council Committee about "removing the teeth from the community plan" by changing the language. The Council would need to resolve the high-stakes war over words. Some wanted the Community Plan to remain "visionary" with softer language. Others advocated for the opposite, reflecting back on the ineffectiveness of the 1996 West Maui Community Plan. Albert Perez of Maui Tomorrow commented,

We need to use strong language such as "shall" and "must" and "require" instead of saying things like "encourage" or "it would be nice." We can maximize the enforceability of the Community Plan if we word it properly. We also should not use words that claim limits to the plan's regulatory nature. If the Community Plan says that it is not regulatory in any way, then that will be construed as the intent, and it will become true. Let's not make that mistake. Please support the efforts of all the people who contributed to the West Maui Community Plan by making sure the language is clear and enforceable, and that it does not limit its own power.

Conversely, Joe Kent of the Grassroot Institute of Hawaii advocated to soften the language.

Our research shows the original West Maui Plan was 59 pages long, and the current draft is 170 pages long—that's about three times bigger. Also, the current draft is long and has many legalistic words that seem to guarantee it would create regulatory barriers to more housing. So, for example, "shall" appeared four times in the original plan, but now the word "shall" appears 64 times; same thing with "required"—that increased from six times to 19 times. We're just concerned that these words, like "shall" and "require" moved the document from a visionary document into more of a legal document and create conflicts. We suggest using words like "encourage," "promote," "foster" and "prioritize."

\* \* \*

Several first-time testifiers, some of whom identified themselves as Peter Martin's employees, advocated for affordable housing. Among them were Sham Vierra, a relative of Paltin, and Kalani Opunui, who tearfully shared his experience with homelessness and addiction. In a process that often drew participation from the same people representing the same interests, testimony from individuals like Opunui were uncommon.

Right now, I fight with two demons. One is addiction, which I'm currently okay right now; I'm still in recovery. The second thing is my past. What I'm asking is that you guys try to make housing a little bit easier to keep people off the streets, because right now the beaches is loaded. It's a lot of kids out there that are on the beach. It's sad for me to see that because I was there, and I no like go back there.

Many testifiers spoke in general terms about removing barriers for developers. Doing so, they reasoned, would make more homes available to the houseless and low- and middle-income residents. A smaller number of people, including farmer Kaipo Kekona, called for a pause in development. Kekona served as an agricultural resource person for the West Maui CPAC.

> If we're going to talk about any further growth from what's already projected, permitted, and approved, we don't have the water capacity here in Lahaina. The county doesn't have the water; these private entities with PUCs are complaining about not having the water. They're requesting for rate increases. The county is trying to drill out more wells out in the Mahinahina area to try and find more water sources. Nothing is a promise, especially drilling a well. There's all kinds of gambles involved in that too, to acquire more water, and nothing is a guarantee. Until we can even resolve those issues, I support plans that will hold this back.

## "On Many Issues, There's Division and People are Passionate"
### *February 9, 2021*

Committee Chairperson Tamara Paltin invited councilmembers to ask the Planning Department questions at the start of the meeting. Councilwoman Alice Lee asked Planning Director Michele McLean whether requiring developers to pay development and traffic impact fees made more sense than requiring them to pay for infrastructure, which would be contingent on progress made on the project.

> Do you think it's more efficient to have a development fee and a traffic fee? I can see the downside being waiting until enough development occurs to be able to pay for something. But then on the other hand, if one developer doesn't go forward with his project, then you get absolutely nothing. So which way is better? And you know, I don't think this council will ever file a development fee or a traffic fee study.

McLean agreed requiring impact fees is a better approach overall because the developers will know what the fees will be.

\* \* \*

During their proceedings, the Maui Planning Commission recommended a Rural Residential designation for the controversial Plantation Estates subdivision, paving the way for lot owners to seek a zoning change that would no longer require them to do agriculture. The decision went against the CPAC's and Planning Department's recommendation to keep the area in Agricultural designation. Nevertheless, the Planning Department changed its maps to reflect the commission's decision. However, at the February 4, 2021 meeting of the Maui County Council Committee, John Kindred, President of Plantation Estates Lot Owners Association, accused county planners of not assigning the Rural Residential designation for the entire Plantation Estates "neighborhood." According to Kindred, this neighborhood included Honolua Ridge.

> The Commission voted six to two to designate Plantation Estates as Rural Residential. They did not vote on only a portion of our neighborhood. We cannot understand why the Planning Department has produced an inaccurate map, which splits the designation of our neighborhood in a manner which is not only inconsistent with community harmony, but also appears arbitrary and unfair.

In the February 9, 2021 meeting, Councilmember Sinenci, referencing Kindred's testimony days prior, asked County Planner Jennifer Maydan to clarify why both subdivisions had not been granted the Rural Residential land designation. Maydan responded,

> Through the process with the Maui Planning Commission, it was always Plantation Estates that was referenced, so that's why the change is made in the draft plan as you have it before you having that part, the Plantation Estates, Rural Residential, and the Honolua Ridge as Ag.

\*   \*   \*

To encourage participation in the West Maui Community Planning process, county planners relied on community leaders, referred to as the Alaka'i group, to build trust and sustain engagement. Councilmember Sugimura questioned the makeup of the group, how they were selected and what their role was in shaping the plan. County Planner Jennifer Maydan responded,

> Their role is much more helping us connect with their community than dictating the content of the plan. Their role is to make sure that whoever they represent in their community, maybe there's somebody from the environmental program, maybe there's somebody from, you know, Homeless

Resource Center, maybe they're kanaka. But they're helping us reach the various facets in the community.

Paltin, who was an Alaka'i member, spoke to the group's involvement.

I would just share my recollection of that group. It wasn't really hand-selected; it was just the people that kept showing up. It was prior to the CPAC getting sat, so it was a way to get the word out about it. I know some of the testifiers or some even people were making the comment that the CPAC didn't know who those people were, or maybe they weren't community. But if you recall, it was real slim pickings of who to choose for the CPAC. And it wasn't because people didn't know what was going on; it was because of the distrust that Ms. Maydan was talking about. I think also the fear at previous plans being picked apart or not listened to by CPAC being the lowest level and then getting revised by the Planning Commission, then getting maybe rewritten by the council.

Later, Paltin asked the Planning Department to comment on the accusations of bullying and intimidation raised at a previous meeting. While Maydan acknowledged the division in the community on certain topics, she believed the CPAC process was "fair and orderly."

Of course the topics in the community plan are personal. It touches people deeply, and there's division within communities. I mean, you all know that. On many issues, there's division and people are passionate. [...] I believe our CPAC Chair, Kai Nishiki, did a great job of keeping order in the meetings and encouraging participation of all of the members. Attendance varied at meetings. You had some members that attended most, if not all, meetings; you had some members that did not have as shining attendance. But order in the meetings, I believe, was kept quite well. And as far as public involvement in the meetings, we had a lot of testimony at the CPAC meetings.

*   *   *

The Maui County Council committee, which was made up of some Hawaiian-language speakers, brought an additional layer of cultural sensitivity to the deliberations that came before them. Some of the earliest amendments included inserting Hawaiian place names into the description of West Maui.

Changes such as replacing "West Maui Mountains" with "Mauna Kahālāwai" resulted from amendments proposed by Rawlins-Fernandez and Paltin.

Hawaiian place names featured prominently in the plan following their revisions. "Hawaiian names describe the area and have information, which is why it's important to use the traditional names of places—because they contain additional information for people to understand the place without being there," commented Rawlins-Fernandez. "So Lahaina, as we know, is really hot, and that's why it was codified within the name of Lahaina." She explained "Lahaina" means cruel or merciless sun.

She later worked with county planning staff to revise historical sections of the plan. Previous versions of the plan presented Hawaiian history through a "colonized" lens, referencing the culture in relation to Western or European influence. Commented Rawlins-Fernandez,

> It is important how it's written because this is an official government document, and we would be approving some of the language that would be revising our history. And I am in strong opposition of revisionist history in a community plan.

\* \* \*

Earlier versions of the plan included what was at the time the projected sea level rise of 3.2 feet. However, Paltin pointed out that updated projections could render that height obsolete. She recommended replacing specific figures with the "sea-level rise exposure area (SLR-XA)." Councilmembers adopted this amendment by consensus.

## Enforceable Wording
### *February 18, 2021*

Adapting to sea-level rise would cost millions of dollars, and community plan leaders moved to protect the county from bearing the burden of these costs. Councilmembers Keani Rawlins-Fernandez and Tamara Paltin both introduced amendments to free Maui County and the State of Hawai'i from liability. Originally, they proposed to require waivers from property owners seeking to protect or maintain their properties in exposure areas, but decided to withdraw the waiver requirement pending a review by Corporation Counsel Michael Hopper. They also wanted to block shoreline hardening requests. Hopper commented,

It's just an odd situation, because the community plan does have the force and effect of law in the SMA. But under the Charter, the Planning Commission [is] the authority in the Coastal Zone Management Area. There [are] certainly things you can do through the community plan that will have an effect, but it's just a little bit different of a situation, because it's not like zoning ordinances where you can just implement the plan by adopting the zoning ordinance. It's a little bit different because you don't have as much control over the specific implementation in the rules.

Councilmembers settled for a compromise on the issue. They voted to incorporate some of the wording within existing policy. But references to waivers were withdrawn until Hopper could complete his review.

*   *   *

One of the biggest differences in the approach of the Planning Commission versus the Maui County Council and the voting majority of the West Maui CPAC was in the use of enforceable language. When the CPAC's draft version of the plan came before the commission for its review, some of the stronger word choices such as "require" were replaced by words such as "encourage."

At the start of deliberations, members of the Maui County Council committee indicated their intention to re-insert stronger language throughout the plan. One example of this was the amendment of Policy 2.1.10. The CPAC passed a version that read: "Require public and private water purveyors to coordinate water development in order to optimize pumpage, mitigate saltwater intrusion, prevent impacts to streams, and preserve regional resources." The Planning Commission changed the word "require" to "encourage," while the Council Committee changed the word back to "require." The Council Committee, at the request of Rawlins-Fernandez, went further in adding a sentence to protect Native Hawaiian access rights: "preserve traditional and customary rights protected under Hawai'i Constitution Article XII, Section 7." Councilmembers unanimously voted to approve these changes.

*   *   *

In a move to create additional protections for culturally sensitive areas, Paltin added specific areas in a policy meant to "preserve and protect the region's cultural resources and traditional lifestyles." Paltin's suggested additions included subsistence agriculture on DHHL lands, Honokowai, Kauaula Valley, Olowalu and Ukumehame—areas that stirred intense debate between community members. Fellow council members unanimously supported the amendment.

\* \* \*

Members of the Council Committee and CPAC placed protections on areas popular among residents but overrun with tourists. One such area was Hana-kaʻōʻō Beach Park, also known as Canoe Beach and often referred to as "the last locals' beach." Paltin proposed language to incorporate these protections into future master planning processes for the area.

\* \* \*

In a bid to bring more balance to the number of housing units available for residents and visitors, the West Maui CPAC's majority passed a policy to halt permitting for new visitor units unless an equal number of workforce units were created. Construction and real estate industry groups strongly criticized the proposed policy, and came out en masse to testify against it before the Planning Commission. Between the testimony and the commissioners' own reservations about the policy, the Commission voted by majority to change the policy completely, removing any reference to workforce housing. However, Chairperson Paltin, citing the shortage of workforce housing in West Maui, proposed to change it back.

> I would like to revert to the CPAC original language, which says, "No additional visitor units except bed and breakfast homes shall be permitted in West Maui unless an equal number of workforce housing units are concurrently developed in the same subarea." When they talk about amending 2.96 to provide more workforce housing and how that could prevent the creation of more housing, period, this takes it in a different direction if we don't really need more visitor units until we have more workforce housing.

Deputy Corporation Counsel Michael Hopper voiced his concern over whether the policy would require an amendment to the County Code to be implemented.

> I just wanted to try to clarify the intent. It reads, "No additional visitor units except bed and breakfast homes shall be permitted in West Maui unless an equal number of workforce housing units are concurrently developed in

the same subarea." Does that mean that if someone applies or has applied for an STRH [Short-Term Rental Home] permit, that permit would have to be denied unless they concurrently built a number of affordable housing units equal to the STRH unit? And that if a hotel, existing hotel, wanted to expand its units in the SMA [Special Management Area], that permit would have to be denied unless they concurrently built an equal number of affordable housing units?

"That's the intention, yes," Paltin replied. Hopper said he would need to review the policy because "that's certainly a significant change to the County Code." Councilmembers voted unanimously to adopt the change.

*    *    *

In a policy to support small-scale and subsistence farming, Paltin suggested adding in, "Agriculture shall not be discouraged or limited through CC&Rs" as a way to protect agricultural activities in areas redesignated from Agricultural to Rural Residential, such as Plantation Estates. Councilmembers unanimously supported the amendment.

## To Eliminate or to Minimize
### *March 4, 2021*

In their attempts to respond to the felt impacts of climate change, some members of the West Maui CPAC introduced action items to start the process of planning for managed retreat: a term used to describe moving existing buildings away from the shoreline to avoid rising sea levels. The CPAC's version of the action item read:

> Conduct a feasibility study on managed retreat of at-risk development in West Maui, to include an analysis of alternatives and interim steps to achieve managed retreat, identify incentives for proactive retreat, and develop programmatic environmental documents to assist in implementing managed retreat.

However, the Planning Commission changed the language at the request of county planners, who were concerned about their ability to implement the action. They added "consider" before "develop." During the County Council committee's proceedings, Rawlins-Fernandez proposed to revert back to the original CPAC wording. Planning Director Michele McLean offered her department's perspective:

> The reason we requested the softer language is because we've been striving for these plans to be realistic, and we take the implementing actions that are directed to the Planning Department as ones we intend to do. It's not necessarily the Planning Department's responsibility to do the environmental studies needed for managed retreat; it will depend on where that might occur.

Rawlins-Fernandez acknowledged McLean's point and offered a compromise to address the Planning Department's concerns while also giving the action item the right language. Ultimately, councilmembers and Planning staff agreed to use "support" instead of "consider."

Other climate-change-related actions recommended by subject areas and adopted by the CPAC were later removed by the Planning Commission. One of those actions stated, "Obtain funding for additional sea level rise exposure modeling, incorporating local data, for six feet or more of sea level rise to use in vulnerability assessments of critical infrastructure and facilities." Paltin and Rawlins-Fernandez re-introduced this action during their amendments.

\* \* \*

County staff and committee members sparred over whether to include an action to eliminate injection wells—devices the county used to place untreated wastewater underground. Division of Environmental Management staff argued eliminating the wells was unrealistic. After lengthy and heated discussion, the CPAC reached a compromise in the phrasing of the action:

> Study and implement other disposal means to strive to eliminate the use of underground injection control wells and transition from the use of wastewater injection control wells to appropriate, environmentally sound methods of wastewater disposal and promote beneficial use of wastewater effluent.

The Planning Commission revised the action to replace "to eliminate" with "to minimize." Their recommended action stated,

> Study and implement other disposal means to minimize the use of underground injection control wells and promote beneficial use of wastewater effluent.

Rawlins-Fernandez proposed to restore the CPAC language, and the County Council committee, with little discussion, voted unanimously to support the change.

\*   \*   \*

Councilmembers were notified of a tsunami watch after New Zealand experienced an 8.0 magnitude earthquake. They hurried to finish their business.

\*   \*   \*

Councilmember Shane W. Sinenci introduced two new action items related to cultural preservation. His fellow councilmembers vote unanimously to adopt them.

> Action 3.07: Expand the boundaries of the Historic Districts, and propose companion amendments to the National Historic Landmark District, should new cultural assets be identified.
>
> Action 3.08: Develop a cultural overlay map identifying the location of important historical events, known burial sites and archaeological resources, and known above-ground resources. Create a cultural overlay district to protect cultural assets and establish an efficient review process for property owners.

## "An Atrocious List of Noncompliance"

### *March 18, 2021*

The Maui County Council Committee overwhelmingly supported resurrecting key policies and actions passed by the CPAC's majority. They rejected several changes made by the Planning Commission in favor of stronger language meant to make more affordable housing available for full-time residents.

Perhaps the most contested of these action items was 5.08, which originally stated, "Propose legislation to amortize the short-term occupancy list and phase out short-term rental use to make more housing units available for long-term occupancy." Property owners and real estate agents strongly opposed this language, calling it misguided and unlawful. The Planning Commission ultimately sided with them and stripped the action of any reference to short-term rentals. The Commission's version stated, "Propose legislation to make more housing units available for long-term occupancy."

Councilmember Keani Rawlins-Fernandez proposed to restore the CPAC's version of the action, which councilmembers unanimously supported.

In the Planning Commission's review of the West Maui Community Plan, Commissioner Christian Tackett strongly opposed an action item that gave "special consideration" to modular housing as a solution for temporary farm-worker housing. He expressed concern about the units being improperly discarded or misused. Maui County Council Chairperson Tamara Paltin, however, brought this language back in the Council's amendments to the West Maui Community Plan.

> And the proposal would read as follows, "Identify," and then I added, "and propose amendments to," and then, existing language is, "existing barriers in laws, rules, and processes that prohibit the construction of safe, sanitary, and affordable on-farm employee housing for farm workers, with special consideration given to non-permanent modular housing as a solution." And this brings back a little bit of the original CPAC vision. I believe it was a recommendation that came out of the previous TIG [Temporary Investigative Committee] that my predecessor had put together, specifically non-permanent modular housing for farm workers.

\* \* \*

Councilmembers introduced new action items with important implications for development in West Maui. One proposed addition from Paltin aimed at creating transparency around the terms of conditional permits. Her proposal generated discussion among councilmembers, who acknowledged a need for oversight should developers neglect their permit commitments.

Councilmembers took turns citing examples of developers who were allowed to complete their projects despite a disregard for permit violations or noncompliance. Paltin proposed a new action item to develop a system in which all the conditions placed on conditional permits would be visible to the public.

> There needs to be a way where someone just coming into the Planning Department, or Public Works, or wherever they are, can easily see [the] conditions on it, and that they need to be complied with. [ . . . ] Because as we make up those conditions for a change in zoning, we put a lot of effort into it; we consult with Corp. Counsel. And then to see that some of them don't get complied with, but the project is still moving forward, is kind of disheartening to our community, as well as to me as the Chair who facilitates these conditions in change of zoning.

Councilmember Sugimura asked Planning Department Deputy Director Jordan Hart to respond to Paltin's comments. Hart said his department had been taking steps to better track the history of conditional permits. He voiced support for the proposal and emphasized the need for clarity in the conditions set by the county.

> We are already trying to figure out how to do this more comprehensively. It's kind of a long challenge just because of how many ordinances there have been over the life of the County. But it's also important to note most of those are construction-related, and only a specific few are long-lived or perpetual conditions that are more difficult to track. And then there's the odds and ends where projects don't kick off. We're open to it, and we are trying to figure out how to make this user-friendly.

Councilmember Lee raised the issue of other county departments imposing their own conditions on developers and how, in some cases, these added requirements caused projects to become financially unfeasible.

> It's incumbent upon the council as well to make it very clear on what every condition is. It's hard to require a developer to build in a timely manner when he has no control over what Public Works wants, over what the Water Department wants—maybe a reservoir, drill a new well, or whatever. There are many, many requirements put on a project: not only housing, tons of other requirements. For instance, Hale Mua in Waiehu—I'm sure you're familiar with that project, Jordan—where they were required to build a bridge, and a brand-new road, and a traffic signal, and the council put on it, and it never got off the ground. These are the kinds of things I worry about when the council puts conditions on a project and then ten years later, looks at the projects and—what happened? You guys owe us 500 units. Well, maybe some of the conditions were overly restrictive that made it difficult, if not impossible, for a project to move forward.

Councilmember Kelly King echoed Paltin's concerns, saying the oversight of conditional permits was an island-wide issue needing attention. She cited some specific examples of projects allowed to proceed despite violating conditional permits.

> We have to make sure we set clear conditions that are understandable. Sometimes the conditions should have timelines on them, because when

I look at what happened with Wailea 670, there's an atrocious list of non-compliance on those conditions, and yet they were marching forward. At some point, it should've just been stopped and the zoning reversed because it was so far out of compliance. [...] To me, this is a countywide issue, not just a West Maui issue.

In the end, the proposed action item was amended to remove "in a timely manner," and adopted unanimously. The final language stated, "Develop a monitoring, enforcement, and public reporting system that ensures more transparency and compliance with conditional zoning."

\* \* \*

Concerns over the loss of public access to West Maui's shoreline prompted Rawlins-Fernandez to propose a new action item to require public access as a permit condition for certain projects. Paltin cited a recent example of the problem of losing shoreline access when the west side of Puamana Beach Park was closed due to shoreline erosion and the discovery of iwi kūpuna. While the Puamana gated subdivision is next to the park, residents could not access the subdivision as a means to getting to the park. Paltin commented,

> This action item would trigger any shoreline property which currently does not provide public access to develop it whenever they come in for any permit. Currently, it is a discretionary decision by a Coastal Zone Management Planner. This is very relevant to the west side with Puamana Beach Park being shut down due to shoreline erosion and the discovery of iwi kūpuna. A lot of folks are unable to access the shoreline over there. Puamana gated subdivision is right next door, but there is some issue with accessing shoreline.

Deputy Corporation Counsel Michael Hopper cautioned against having a blanketed requirement to establish shoreline access, saying there may be cases where such a requirement would be unconstitutional.

> You can require as a condition of development permits to provide public beach or public shoreline access. That has been done from time to time. However, it may not be permissible in all cases. There are U.S. Supreme Court decisions on this that talk about if you are exacting from a landowner a public access right, that has to be proportional to the development that

they're doing, and have a nexus toward the permit that's being granted. So there may be, certainly, cases where as a condition of an SMA permit, public shoreline access is required. However, there may be cases where that would be problematic and potentially unconstitutional. If there's cases like Member Rawlins-Fernandez had talked about where there are public trust issues or there are gathering issues involved in a particular case, that can certainly be an item that's allowed. This would appear to just say blanketly, no matter what the facts are of a particular case, that you can't have an SMA permit granted unless there's some type of public access on every single parcel involving that. I don't know if there is a way to maybe more closely tie this to the Hawai'i State Constitution dealing with public trust or gathering right issues in particular cases, and have language that states, maybe, "to the extent permitted by law."

The committee debated what conditions should trigger a shoreline access requirement and sought clarity in the language. "Unfortunately, I would interpret that to mean anytime somebody applies for a permit, we take shoreline access from them," said Planning Deputy Director Jordan Hart. In response, Hopper suggested adding a clause to the requirement that would only require shoreline access if the potential for impacting shoreline access were present.

In the midst of discussion, Councilmember Rawlins-Fernandez questioned Hart's potential conflict of interest given his past ties with clients who sought SMA permits. Hart replied,

> I did have to divest all my ownership of Chris Hart and Partners, and did go to the Board of Ethics for direction on how to perform my duties as Deputy. I basically recuse myself from all projects that are associated with Chris Hart and Partners, or previously worked on. But there were definitely clients. I do have a good amount of experience on this subject.

Rawlins-Fernandez pressed further: "So you have to recuse yourself when discussing former clients? And so would this discussion involve former clients?" Hart remarked,

> Actually, I did ask the Board of Ethics for direction on how to handle government plans that I might have participated [in] before entering the county, for instance the SMA and Shoreline Rules for the Maui Planning Commission, and I was instructed that because I was monitoring that on

behalf of clients, I had to recuse myself. This was not something that I had been working on or monitoring prior. So as far as my past direction from the Board of Ethics, this wouldn't pertain [to] that.

Given the number of questions raised about the conditions triggering shoreline access, Committee Chairperson Paltin suggested councilmembers revisit the proposal at a later time.

## Discouraging "Gentleman's Estates"
### *May 20, 2021*

In this most recent iteration of the West Maui Community Plan, the county's Planning Department unveiled new community plan designations that aimed to encourage mixed uses, incorporating the latest in "Smart Growth" principles. These designations would have the greatest impact on growth in West Maui because they would ultimately determine what zoning and growth would be allowed. But not everyone supported the new designations.

Councilmember Kelly Takaya King, Albert Perez of Maui Tomorrow, and others worried that the community did not have adequate time to understand and provide feedback on them. He said the designations were a kind of Form-Based Codes or Form-Based Land Use Planning, which focuses on the form of buildings and their relationship to each other. Commented Perez,

> I think this needs to be much more widely discussed, because it's a major change. I did some research on Form-Based Codes, and I found a couple things. One is, in actual application, they depend on the subjective application by the planner, especially when you're talking about mixed uses. They tend to hinder planning participation by the public, and they're much more difficult to enforce than traditional zoning. For this reason, it's also more prone to litigation than traditional zoning.

One of the new plan designations combined "single-family" and "multi-family" into one "residential" category. "This designation encourages a range of housing types to provide mixed neighborhoods and affordability," explained Maydan. Councilmember Rawlins-Fernandez said she liked the new designations and the intention behind them. Councilmember Gabe Johnson asked the Planning Department to expand on its reasoning for creating a "residential" designation:

I've been reading this wonderful book, *The Death and Life of Great American Cities* by Jane Jacobs, and one thing she mentions about the dense, mixed use of residential areas that have that "eyes on the street," right. Does the Department recognize that single-family home zoning creates problems to low-income, working-class and minorities by redlining, keeping mortgages out of reach, and creating oversized lots and gated communities that non-resident investors will snatch up? Is that a factor that you considered? [Is that] why you guys lumped them all together? Can you expand on that, Department?

Maydan said the points Johnson raised were part of the department's discussion.

This has been part of our conversation in realizing that we really need to change our community plan designations, and almost even more importantly, changing our zoning code. It is so exciting that this is happening in our county right now. We fully acknowledge that this is a big shift. Change is hard. We are used to the Community Plan Designations we have, and we're used to the zoning we have. But we need to also recognize that it's time to evolve—that there are many benefits to evolving to designations and zoning districts that promote more complete communities, that promote [a] mix of uses, and try to right some of the wrongs of the past as far as segregating neighborhoods, redlining, having a really negative impact on those in our community that really are underserved—that get pushed out of housing options. So that absolutely was a part of our conversation. Affordable housing is such an incredible challenge that I don't need to say that to you all. I know you deal with that all the time. This shift in the community plan is one step in the right direction in addressing our affordable housing problems in our county.

\*   \*   \*

The Council Committee revisited the contentious subject of maintaining agricultural land use designations as a way to discourage "gentleman's estates," those on which farming or ranching is done for pleasure or to meet minimum zoning requirements rather than profit or sustenance. This subject generated public testimony both for and against keeping agricultural designations, as well as conversation between members of the CPAC and the Planning Commission.

When Councilmember Mike Molina asked Planning Director Michele

McLean whether the draft plan increased ag designations and what her thoughts were on discouraging gentleman's estates, she said she believed the community plan was "pretty strong in supporting agriculture and restricting any further gentleman's estates." Maydan added that, compared to the 1996 Plan, the current West Maui Community Plan decreased agricultural lands to accommodate projected growth. Paltin chimed in on the conversation, clarifying the thought process behind actions to support agriculture and the challenges that councilmembers would face in their decision making on the subject.

> The way that I see it, you know, the Ag designation is what protects ag. In Rural, there isn't the same requirement to farm that Ag has. Ag has the requirement to farm; Rural, you can farm. In Rural, you can make HOA designations that limit farming; in Ag, you cannot do that. If it looks like rural, but you want to protect ag, Ag would be the designation. If you change Ag to Rural, there's no protection against a homeowner association passing rules that would limit farming in some way. There's no requirement to farm, thus making it be open to gentleman's estates. So that's kind of my interpretation. You know, I think throughout the entire county, as a policy, this is a decision that we will be faced with because of all the ag subdivisions that never underwent a public hearing.
>
> There was that sliding scale requirement, and then now we have landowners [who] want to further subdivide. But because of the sliding scale requirements, now they have to go through an open and public process, whereas initially, with the large tracts of ag land that they own, there was no public process. I'm sure we'll have plenty of folks saying that I can't farm because there's no water; I can't farm because there's black plastic. That's an island-wide kind of concern. It would be a decision we're making for the West Maui Community Plan. But ultimately, it's an island-wide policy we'll be making as well. You know, if people in one area can't farm for whatever reason, and we say you have to farm, whereas other people don't have to anymore, it doesn't seem fair, you know? I think we're making decisions within the West Maui Community Plan area, but we need to look ahead and be consistent, you know, in the decisions that we do make.

*       *       *

A move to strengthen the authority of community plans by amending the County Code began to gain steam. The effort was spearheaded by Perez and others. Citing Perez's written testimony on the topic, Councilmember

Rawlins-Fernandez and councilmember Shane Sinenci voiced their early
support for the concept.

## "We Always Presented our Neighborhood as One Neighborhood"

### *June 3, 2021*

The Council Committee opened a brief period for oral testimony in an attempt
to gain back time for review and changes to the designations and maps. They
received testimonies from John Kindred, president of the Plantation Estates Lot
Owners Association, former Planning Director Will Spence, and Dick Mayer.
Spence and Kindred repeated their case for a Rural Residential designation for
Plantation Estates. Further, Kindred asked the Council Committee to address
what he viewed as an error of the Planning Department.

> The Rural Residential designation, as I mentioned a moment ago, was
> adopted by the Maui Planning Commission. However, the map was not
> drawn in such a way that reflects the entirety of our neighborhood in Rural
> Residential, which was very surprising. We've laid out a number of reasons
> to the Planning Commission as to why it made sense to be Rural Residen-
> tial, and they adopted that by a majority. The map being drawn in error, I
> think, is a big problem. It splits our neighborhood in half. We always pre-
> sented our neighborhood as one neighborhood. We have one CC&Rs; we
> have one Homeowner Association.

## "Million-dollar Homes Would be Built"

### *June 14, 2021*

Among the new land use designations proposed by the Planning Department was
a combined category for Parks and Open Space. The CPAC used this combined
designation throughout the growth map exercise. However, the Maui County
Council Committee wanted to separate this designation into two: one for Parks
and one for Open Space. Committee Chairperson Tamara Paltin argued that sep-
arating the two and applying them to the maps would better enable the county
to represent residents' desires for these areas. Paltin commented,

> Some of the areas, Olowalu to Launiupoko and Olowalu to Ukumehame, the
> CPAC designated as Park/Open Space. And as I look at the existing county

zoning for those areas, it appears to me to be Agriculture currently. To me, it would be good to clarify if the intent is for this Community Plan Designation to be Park, or is it for it to be Open Space, because the current zoning is Ag.

Planner Jennifer Maydan explained her department opted to combine the two designations because they shared more similarities than differences. She said the task of choosing a designation, especially for those newly designated areas, would be difficult because some of them did not have developed plans. One example of this was the more than 300 acres of Park/Open Space-designated land between the Pali and Puamana.

That's an example of where I'm saying this is quite a task at this point in time to split Park and Open Space into two designations, specifically for new areas that are not existing zoned Park or Open Space, but areas that are existing mostly zoned Agriculture. So that's an area where I would guess that the Parks Department is not at the level of identifying the particular uses on the land.

Later in the discussion, after Vice Chairperson King made a motion to separate Park/Open Space into two separate community plan designations, Deputy Planning Director Jordan Hart pushed back against adding too much detail.

If you pursue an approach of making the community plans almost as detailed as the zoning, you may unintentionally create a lot of conflicts, especially when you get into subdivision and special management areas where you thought you were doing something that was going to be clear, but it creates another layer of constraint. And so let's say that the council decided, "We need to fine tune something; this zone is not working." You may find that you're going to have to tweak the community plan and the zone if you put too much detail in the community plan. [...] But while you're in the community plan process, what you could do is you could add language to associate with a specific location on a map. Let's say that you wanted to designate a certain area Open Space, but you wanted no permanent structures. You could add a section that describes the designation of that area, that puts further limitations on it. [...]

In her second and final testimony prior to the County Committee taking a vote on whether to separate Park and Open Space into two designations, Vice

Chairperson King called Hart's argument to keep the designation combined "incongruous."

> It was kind of interesting because the advocating for not getting too deep, and then suggesting that we put in the specific areas that have specific details on them, seems to be a little incongruous. But one of the things that's really important about making these Community Plan Designations as clear as possible right now is we just went through this thing in South Maui with the Planning Commission and their approval of the Maui Coast Hotel; 95 percent of the community came out and said don't do it, and they passed it anyway. Two of the things that were said was one, the community plan is not clear enough so we don't think we're violating it by going up six stories because there was a section in the Community Plan that talked about view planes, and they didn't see that as clear enough to prevent blocking that view plane. And the other thing was one of the Planning Commission members said that the council needs to give us more direction—you know, complaining that we're putting this decision on them about the SMA permit, and that we hadn't given them enough direction.

The motion to separate Parks and Open Space into two community plan designations passed with six votes, with councilmembers Sugimura and Kama opposed.

Immediately after voting on this decision, councilmembers voted unanimously to designate the areas between Launiupoko to Olowalu and Olowalu to Ukumehame—an area within the 3.2-foot sea-level rise exposure area—as Open Space. Prior to the decision, the area was assigned a combined Park/Open Space designation.

*       *       *

The future growth and character of Lahaina Town was extensively discussed among members of the CPAC, Planning Commission and Council Committee. Through at least two amendments to the community plan maps, the Council Committee sided with the majority CPAC view and pushed for managed growth in Lahaina. Both amendments passed unanimously. One change removed "Industrial" designation from a parcel in town after councilmembers voiced their concern about allowing heavy industrial use among homes, churches and businesses. The other amendment, proposed by Paltin, was to change the name of "Urban Center Corridor" to "Transit-Oriented Corridor."

My reasoning behind that is people come to Maui County from all over the world, and the image that they have in their mind when they picture "urban" may be largely different than what we picture when we say "urban." The images of, like, New York City or downtown Waikiki come to mind sometimes when you talk about "urban." And that's definitely, I don't think, what anyone [wants] for Lahaina.

\* \* \*

As a matter of policy, gulches and streams were designated as Open Space to keep them clear and protected from future development. The CPAC, Planning Commission and County Planners all supported this policy and applied the designation across West Maui.

Two of the parcels designated as Open Space for its gulches and to set aside land for a park near Lahaina Town were owned by Kamehameha Schools (KS). Dana Sato, KS director of leasing and transactions, opposed this new designation and asked councilmembers to restore the Agricultural designation. Sato said the organization was concerned the new designation would limit their ability to farm lo'i kalo. She maintained these concerns even after Corporation Counsel Mike Hopper clarified that Open Space zoning allows Native Hawaiian customary and traditional uses.

Councilmember Yuki Sugimura introduced a motion to change the designation back to Agricultural, and Councilmember Rawlins-Fernandez amended the motion to keep the gulches as Open Space and allow the remaining land to stay as Agricultural.

> We already came to consensus on that policy of what we would like to see and not see in gulches, and that would be consistent throughout the entirety of West Maui and not just on this one particular parcel. What we're looking at is consistency throughout the district so that all the gulches throughout the district would be Open Space gulches and streams. And I'm not opposed to farming kalo, so having lo'i kalo in or around the area. But I would be opposed to other permissible activities allowed on Ag-zoned land, which is the building of structures and other things that is permissible.

A motion to designate the gulches and streams within the Kamehameha Schools' parcels as Open Space passed with six votes in favor and councilmembers Kama, Lee and Sugimura opposed. A subsequent motion to designate the remaining areas of the same parcels as Agricultural passed in a 5–4 vote with Paltin, King, Sineci and Johnson opposed.

*   *   *

One of the largest developments referenced in the West Maui Community Plan was Ka'anapali 2020. The decades-old proposed development project located on the mauka side of Hanaka'ō'ō Beach Park and the Kā'anapali resort area had a controversial history. After failed attempts to gain approval for the project in the '90s, the developer convened a community advisory group in 1999 to put together a master plan they hoped would be more palpable to the larger community. Two West Maui CPAC members, Hans Michel and Joe Pluta, as well as some community leaders like Ed Lindsay, served in the group. The original plan presented to the CPAC sought to build a "limited-resort-type" hotel mauka of Hanaka'ō'ō Beach Park. After facing pushback on this idea, Chad Fukunaga from the Kaanapali Land Management Corporation said the developers revised their plans before bringing them to the Maui County Council Committee.

County planners presented five different scenarios for Ka'anapali 2020 to the CPAC. Despite the endorsement of some prominent community members, the CPAC majority (by a 6–1 vote) approved a version designating a large swath of land as Park, Open Space and Agriculture above Hanaka'ō'ō Beach Park. CPAC Chairperson Kai Nishiki elaborated on the decision:

> Amongst other considerations, the CPAC was asked to plan for 3.2 foot of sea-level rise in our deliberations, and we were asked to imagine a time when the entire park and cemetery is underwater, and the new shoreline is mauka of the highway. We are tasked with putting into place plans for our grandchildren, the future generations, to continue to have access to the shoreline and celebrate and honor their culture. We also received a presentation by the Parks Department, and I ask you to reference the technical resource paper provided by them, which highlights that West Maui has the highest number of average daily visitor population in our county, and that beach parks are highly used by both visitors and residents alike. The most popular recreation in West Maui, according to a survey conducted by the Parks Department, is utilizing the ocean and beach parks. A shortage of beach parks and parks in general in West Maui was identified, in addition to the projected loss of up to 40 percent of our beach parks in the future.

The expansion of park space was the biggest difference between what Fukunaga was proposing and what the CPAC and the Planning Commission adopted. By contrast, the developers' plans called for a 10-acre park above Hanaka'ō'ō Beach Park—enough space to protect the view plane, Fukunaga said. Speaking in support of a motion to adopt the designations passed by the CPAC and the Planning Commission, Paltin said,

> This project has been in the works for at least 30 years. You know, there are living Ka'anapali 2020 members on both sides of the issue. Spoke to Uncle Walter Delos Reyes, Uncle John Kuia, who were original members, and they love the idea of Hanaka'ō'ō Mauka. They shared with me [that] Charlie Fox, who was one of the original proponents of a master plan, was really about the community having a voice. And while I respect those that put in so much time and effort and passed away, it's my understanding that we're planning for those that are living, and in the context of what is going on right now with sea-level rise and whatnot.

Councilmember Lee spoke out against the motion:

> I'll be voting no, because I don't believe that Ka'anapali 2020 sees this as a win-win. It's more like a lose-lose for them, because this is not what they wanted. And I'm always cautious about lopping off large portions of people's lands and downgrading them.

Councilmembers voted 5–4 to pass the motion for the CPAC and Planning Commission's version of the Ka'anapali 2020 designations. Members Kama, Lee, Molina and Sugimura opposed.

\* \* \*

The contentious issue of what designation to give to Plantation Estates was now before councilmembers. Those who opposed the change viewed the decision as a symbolic one, with larger implications for all of Maui. Paltin described the context of the decision and voiced her opinion on the matter prior to entertaining a motion.

> So to me, it's really a policy decision that's going to affect the county. If those are criteria by which we allow Agricultural subdivisions to be taken out of Ag

subdivision status, then we'll be populated wildly with gentleman's estates. There were comments made when we watched the Maui Planning Commission—statements made by Commissioner Hipolito really kind of were a turning point in my making of a decision. When he spoke as a former Maui Land & Pine employee of farming that area up there, and when he spoke of the winds converging from mauka and makai, and the mist that it created, and you hear the nostalgia of how he talked about farming those lands, that was a turning point for me in not being able to make a decision to being able to make a decision. And so my recommendation would be to remain in Ag.

Some of the testifying landowners argued the land was not suitable for farming, despite the fact that it had been cultivated for commercial farming for decades. Others sought the change to fully enforce their homeowners' association rules and thus increase their property values. The Planning Department, in making its recommendation that Plantation Estates remain under agriculture community plan designation, cited the strong opposition to the change by the greater West Maui community. Planner Jennifer Maydan explained,

> I think this has been the most discussed item in the Community Plan, whether this area should be Rural Residential or remain as Ag. The department took this very seriously in weighing this, because of course, there are areas outside of this Community Plan area, as we move forward with updates, where we are going to continue, and the council is going to continue to grapple with this issue. We ultimately came forth with the department's recommendation to leave it as Ag because we did hear very loud and clear from a lot of folks in the West Maui community that it was important for them to retain this area in agriculture.

The Maui County Council Planning and Sustainable Land Use Committee debated at length about the request for a change, as the CPAC and Planning Commission had done before them. Councilmember Sugimura introduced a motion to change Plantation Estates, including Honolua Ridge, to Rural Residential. She said doing so would generate more property taxes and better align with the character of the neighborhood.

> I see this upcountry, where you have people who are designated Ag and have to figure out how to do Ag because that's what they have to fit into, but they're not necessarily Ag. And I see this Plantation Estates community

the same way, where they're really a residential community. And yep, if we change it, then their highest and best use would then go to higher taxes.

Councilmember Rawlins-Fernandez, who spoke against Sugimura's motion, remarked on the implications of their decision. She moved to amend the motion to designate the area as Agricultural.

I'm sure there were community members who opposed this development, knowing that in the future this is exactly what would've happened. Million-dollar homes would be built, and then those million-dollar homes can afford million-dollar attorneys, and million-dollar CPAs that can give them million-dollar advice on how to go about getting their way, which was in opposition to the community that opposed it back then. [They] wanted to protect what they had in their town, wanted to protect the character of their town, and slowly by slowly lost so much. And it's heartbreaking. So I speak against the motion.

After deliberation, the councilmembers voted by majority to keep the area's Agricultural designation. Councilmembers Kama, Lee and Sugimura opposed.

## "PUBLIC BEACH ACCESS SHALL BE PROVIDED"

### *June 15, 2021*

After six hours of deliberation over its growth map designations, the Council Committee turned its attention toward the wording of the designations themselves and how the plan would be implemented.

Maui Tomorrow's Albert Perez submitted several proposed revisions to the language. One that generated discussion attempted to address the conflicts between the zoning ordinance and Community Plan: "In the event of a conflict between the Community Plan Designation and the zoning, the community plan shall rule." Deputy Corporation Counsel Michael Hopper commented,

I think some of the language, though—there's been this sort of longstanding discussion over which one rules over the other, or which one is supreme. And the actual answer is, both apply at the same time—it's just that the community plan is going to apply with the force and effect of law only in certain cases. So if you need an SMA permit, for example, you need to comply with both. You need to comply with the community plan, and you

need to comply with your zoning. And so one really never supersedes the
other in that case.

Siding with Hopper's argument, then-Planning Director Michele McLean
discouraged the Council Committee from adding language of that nature to
the plan.

> Certainly, there are ways for community plans to have more teeth. I don't
> think putting it in the text of one particular community plan is the right way
> to do that, because that language would then conflict with current language
> of the County Code 2.80B. The way the system works now—and I'm not
> defending this system by any means—is that if you change your zoning,
> it has to match the community plan. When a community plan update is
> done, it can create mismatches. It doesn't have to match the zoning. That's
> why community plans are this overarching guide.

Later, in responding to Hopper's concerns about adding language to give
more authority to the community plan, Vice Chair Kelly Takaya King suggests
adding a sentence that reads: "In the event of a conflict between the Community Plan Designation and zoning, where the law does not specify the authority
of zoning, the community plan shall rule." In response, Hopper said, "any language that talks about one sort of superseding the other, I'd have an issue with."

Paltin suggested a compromise: "So maybe something like in the event of
a conflict between the Community Plan Designation and the zoning, efforts
should be made to bring community plan and zoning into alignment." The
discussion that followed hinted at the need for comprehensive zoning. Councilmember Molina:

> I kind of looked at Appendix C on page 142, and it notes that the zoning
> code is not providing decision makers with the tools necessary to create the
> safe, healthy, affordable, and vibrant communities that Maui wants. And
> I find it troubling because as we are developing a revised community plan
> with new designations, the question for me is, how do we make an updated
> community plan work with a broken zoning ordinance? And this whole
> process is frustrating, and I know there's no real easy answer to it.

Hopper said the Maui County Council avoided comprehensive zoning in
the past because of its complex and controversial nature.

That's historically why that has not always happened, meaning that once the community plan is adopted, you do not often—or at least I don't know of any time in Maui County where there's been a comprehensive zoning ordinance adopted that would bring all of the misaligned zonings and community plans into matching with each other. But that is something that if you adopt the community plan, and you've got a bunch of community plan designations that are new, and the zoning doesn't track them, to then follow up with the zoning ordinance to make the zonings all change to be consistent with the community plan. But like I said, I don't think that often happens because you can't really condition those, so I think that's something the council has historically not wanted to do. Also, with comprehensive zoning, you don't necessarily notify property owners. You know, I think you can do it, but I don't think it's legally required. So comprehensive zoning—I think back to the Rural Bill and the Ag Bill—can be controversial because you're rezoning properties without notice, necessarily, to all the owners that are affected. I think historically that's a reason that comprehensive zoning hasn't happened.

This Council Committee, however, appeared supportive of the move and voiced their intentions to introduce comprehensive zoning efforts alongside its review and approval of community plans for the rest of Maui County. Lee warned such efforts would encounter resistance. "I am a believer in comprehensive zoning, but mark my words, you're going to run into a lot of resistance from other people who prefer to have multiple bites at the apple." Paltin suggested the committee defer action on changing the language related to zoning and community plans.

\* \* \*

Concerns often were raised over the loss of public beach access for residents. Councilmembers spoke of the need to add language, where they could, to protect this access. For the Resort Hotel Community Plan designation, councilmembers adopted by consensus a statement that read, "Public beach access shall be provided as required by law, and will not be discouraged." Councilmember Sinenci remarked,

Because in Lahaina, they have all the walkways that go in front of the hotels; however, they might be state properties or public access that has not been dedicated. [ . . . ] The question is [how to] keep these access areas open—not just for visitors, but also for the general public.

Paltin noted that while public access may have been provided in some cases, the use of them was discouraged. "Because one of the ugly parts about living in West Maui and having a bunch of kids, you see certain kids with a certain skin color having free access everywhere, and other kids being discouraged or kind of kept out where other local kids blend in freely. I think we do need to have a statement that [public access] shouldn't be discouraged."

\* \* \*

Plantation Estates lot owners relied heavily on the newly updated land use designation "Rural Residential" in their bid to seek a designation change. They cited the Planning Department's definition as the most accurate representation of their subdivision. However, some councilmembers and community members were concerned the definition created a loophole that encouraged the development of more gentleman's estates on agricultural land. The original language stated, "Rural Residential areas are generally developed with large lot subdivisions, family farms and estates." Councilmember Sinenci supported Perez's suggestion to take out the sentence.

With broad support for these changes, the County Committee adopted the changes to the language that included the deletion of "estates" from the definition of "Rural Residential" and a clarification that such a designation would serve as a buffer area between agricultural and more urban development.

Councilmembers also agreed by consensus to add a new clause in the Agricultural Land Use Designation, stating, "Gentleman estate-type subdivisions with lots that are not used for active agricultural production are prohibited, and long-term leaseholds are encouraged for farming." Hopper encouraged councilmembers to consider revising Maui County's agricultural zoning ordinance 19.30a to prohibit undesirable activities.

\* \* \*

A point of growing frustration among community members was the number of uncompleted yet entitled development projects, which were often approved with affordable housing requirements. This lack of progress both complicated Maui County's planning efforts and angered West Maui residents who wanted to see more affordable homes constructed. This issue surfaced throughout the process of developing the West Maui Community Plan. Paltin requested the assistance of the County Council's legislative attorneys in drafting additional language specifically for the Kapalua section that would allow the county to revert a conditional zoning designation for projects that did not commence within five years.

The landowner, Maui Land & Pine, received conditional zoning for the Kapalua Mauka Project in 2006, and sold a portion of the project, Mahana Estates, to Nan Inc. Nan Inc. completed the Mahana Estates Project about five years ago. To this date however, Maui Land & Pine has not started development of the Kapalua Mauka Project, which excludes the Mahana Estates. When the county grants conditional zoning, it does so subject to projects proceeding within five years. Under the County Code, the Council retains the right to revert a conditional zoning designation to the prior zoning designation if a project does not commence construction within five years.

Hopper cautioned that such a blanket time period may not apply to all projects.

The conditions without a time frame are supposed to be fulfilled in five years. But the general statement that all projects with conditional zoning have to proceed within five years isn't necessarily correct. There could be conditions saying prior to subdivision, something has to be done. I think that's a little bit of a general statement with the five-year time frame. I mean, the general idea of not wanting projects to linger for a substantial amount of time, I think you could say.

Given his concerns, Paltin called upon David Raatz, supervising legislative attorney, to work with Hopper to revisit and rework the language. Councilmembers supported this step.

\* \* \*

In amending the definition of the Residential designation, councilmembers spoke about their desire to encourage locally owned businesses versus franchises or big-box stores in areas designated Residential. Paltin proposed to incorporate this wording into the designation, with support from her fellow councilmembers. Commented Kama,

I like having mom-and-pop stores. We don't have them anymore, and that's the problem that we have today with the big-box stores. So whatever we can do through economic development in supporting our local communities and our members, and our constituents to be able to get out there and create something with their blessed gifts that they've been given and their talents, we should help them make that happen.

Councilmember Lee spoke on the side of big businesses. She pointed out that many of them hire local people. "Please don't excuse them simply because they're not mom-and-pop, because they certainly provide a tremendous service to the community by hiring our local folks." Others chimed in to say they were not discouraging big businesses but had a preference for small business in Residential-designated areas. The Council Committee adopted new language to encourage walkability and to support small, local businesses.

## "START COLLECTING THE MONEY FOR MANAGED RETREAT"
### *June 16, 2021*

Citing a recently approved plan to build a six-story hotel in Central Maui, councilmember Kelly King sought to include height limits for buildings in the West Maui Community Plan. King said the Planning Commission approved the plan despite opposition from area residents. In its decision, the commission cited a lack of guidance, specifically height restrictions, that would prohibit the hotel's construction. "There's really no clear directive of what does meet that scale and character," she said.

Ultimately, while this topic generated discussion among councilmembers, the Planning Department staff successfully argued such specific language belonged in the zoning code, and amending the zoning code was the best way to address King's concerns.

Nonetheless, the discussion led councilmembers to unanimously approve the addition: "Development in [community plan designation] must follow the scale and character of the surrounding area until design standards are created." They approved this for four community plan designations: Neighborhood Center, Small Town Center, Employment Center, and Transit-Oriented Corridor.

\*   \*   \*

To close out their revisions to Section 3 of the West Maui Community Plan, councilmembers unanimously approved a motion by chairperson Paltin to change "should" to "must" in a sentence on page 64 that would direct developers and landowners to use the community plan map.

\*   \*   \*

Councilmember Rawlins-Fernandez inquired about including a list of topics and participants from the CPAC and Planning Commission meetings.

In looking back at, you know, like the plans in the '90s, in doing research, it was something that would have been really helpful to know who in the community participated in the drafting of the plan, and it's part of history. You know, like if my grandparents participated, It would have been good information to have, and then I would have been able to ask them, "Did you attend this meeting during this process? And "What were the feelings and the comments that were shared?"

Senior Planner Jennifer Maydan explained the difficulty in doing so, because not every participant signed into the meeting, or those who did, did not necessarily testify at them. She said all of the meetings, agendas and minutes were posted online at the wearewestmaui.org website.

Member Kama supported Rawlins-Fernandez's request to at least include a participant list as a historical record.

But over time, I've worked on different projects, and one of the things we always like to have is a participant list. Because now, when I go back and look at the Native Hawaiian Study Commission that happened in 1983— and I look at all my friends, and I look at all the kūpuna that was alive at that time, and they participated and it quotes what they said in the book—when I read it today, I know now why I am where I am. I anticipate that people in the West Maui community…this should be part of their education in that community.

\* \* \*

The Council Committee was divided on the subject of whether to allow an exemption related to a policy[1] aimed at promoting shoreline retreat. Councilmembers already unanimously approved deleting the words "for reasonable development" at the end of the first sentence in the policy. They now needed to decide whether to include an exemption for beach restoration projects, such as the installation of t-groins at Kahana Bay. T-groins are structures built to trap sánd along the shoreline to prevent erosion. Councilmember

---

1. "To minimize impacts from future coastal erosion, new permanent structures must be located landward of the State-recognized SLR-XA for coastal erosion, except a minimum buildable area must be provided. This restriction does not apply to structures needed as part of an approved beach restoration project or cultural project, such as loko i'a [Hawaiian fishponds], and which must be evaluated on a case-by-case basis."

Rawlins-Fernandez made a motion to approve the policy without the exemption. She feared such an exemption would allow property owners to propose restoration projects. Councilmember Sugimura disagreed:

> I just wanted to bring up that it's not only Kahana Bay. We did hear Nāpili Bay also coming forward, saying that they needed assistance. And islandwide there's other communities that are being affected by it, including Māʻalaea, who have asked for and they're trying to find their own solutions. But this is a situation…or that our residents are being affected by it. So I stand against the motion, because I think it's something that we need to address.

Councilmember Lee also opposed excluding the exemption, because she said the County Council had been informally and formally discussing the project for Kahana Bay. "I think it would have been fair to them if we told them that we were thinking of not allowing what they're trying to do, and not wait until now to come up with this kind of a policy."

Paltin, who said the County Council could no longer bury its head on the issue, signaled she would be open to supporting t-groins on the condition that property owners committed to planning for managed retreat.

> I like to have that type of leverage to say, "Okay, I could possibly go along with this t-groin idea if there's a firm commitment to retreat." It'll take how many years to build the t-groin and do all that; in the meantime, also start collecting the money for managed retreat.

Rawlins-Fernandez's motion to exclude an exemption from the policy failed in a 4–5 vote. Councilmembers Paltin, Lee, Sugimura, Molina and Kama opposed. A subsequent motion, also introduced by Rawlins-Fernandez, to include cultural projects such as loko iʻa in the exemption passed unanimously.

* * *

With West Maui dealing with worsening drought conditions, Councilmember Sinenci proposed a new policy to "restrict the use of water developed within or imported into the West Maui Community Plan area to use within the West Maui Community Plan area." While his proposal renewed discussions about water management countywide, fellow councilmembers and county planners pushed back against the idea of a blanket prohibition that would restrict water across district lines. They expressed concern that it could set an unjust precedence over water use on Maui. Vice Chair King and Councilmember Sugimura spoke on the proposal. King commented,

> I have reservations about this, especially since it allows importing but it doesn't allow exporting. It sounds like the community wants to take water from other areas, but doesn't want to give any of its water to any other areas in return. We always looked at ourselves as an entire community, and, you know, one of the things that has always been pointed out in budget sessions previously is how much of the tax revenue comes from West Maui and South Maui. And I would hate to see the communities say that the tax revenue has to stay within South Maui that's gathered in South Maui, or stay in West Maui that's gathered in West Maui.

Councilmember Sugimura added, "I'm going to be voting against this although I understand the intention. But I believe that we're an island and that unfortunately, we got to share. By us excluding doing that and only taking, then, you know, it creates the imbalance or problems that we could have in the future."

The discussion surfaced concerns over private companies bottling water in various areas of Maui, which prompted Sinenci to amend his original motion to state, "Prohibit the water bottling of one liter or less from the West Maui Community Plan area for export, and restrict five-gallon bottling of water resources from the West Maui Community Plan out of the County." The Council Committee voted unanimously to adopt the policy as amended.

## Known Sensitive Archaeological Areas

### June 17, 2021

Archaeologist Janet Six appeared before the Council Committee to share information previously unknown to councilmembers about the area known as Lahaina Town South—an area that had been designated for residential and commercial development. She disclosed a number of known post-contact and pre-contact burial sites, and shared the largely unknown results of a survey commissioned by Alexander & Baldwin. Six's overview sparked a conversation about how the community plan could include a layer of protection for significant archaeological or historical sites. Six remarked,

> Working with the county, we have lots of issues with Puamana right now and iwi coming out. [...] We have burials in the area very close. This seems

to be kind of an area that people wanted to be interred in. That doesn't mean you can't develop it. But what it does mean is that this area would likely go under a 6E Review for whatever development would go in. And I would imagine that the SHPD [State Historic Preservation Division]—I can't speak for them—they are the authority; they also license and permit me—would want a very rigorous archaeological inventory survey for the proposed project area. Alexander & Baldwin did a survey in this area over here roughly, and they never submitted it to the State because they decided to abandon the development project. But they did find three inadvertent finds. I've seen that report even though it was never submitted. So they don't show up on this map, but there was a post-contact burial. We know that because it had a coffin, and there were two they thought were pre-contact. And then if you were following the pipeline, they also hit disturbed human remains. So what I can tell you about this area is while there's no immediate burials in this area that we can see, other than the known cemeteries, had that report been turned in, they would show three inadvertents in this area.

Six later commented that the "inadvertent finds" were not surprising given their proximity to Moku'ula[2]—"an important power center and a piko [summit]" for pre-contact Native Hawaiian communities. Councilmembers peppered Six with questions, including why the Alexander & Baldwin-commissioned survey was never submitted and how burials could go undetected in areas heavily farmed at one time.

She explained that because Alexander & Baldwin never moved forward with their project, they did not submit the findings from the 2009 survey. Those who farmed pineapple and sugar did not have to dig more than a few inches below the surface, which was not far enough to disturb interred remains buried 10 inches or deeper. By contrast, the development of buildings, which required a deeper level of digging, was more likely to come into contact with and disturb bones or iwi kūpuna.

Committee Chairperson Tamara Paltin, who represented West Maui, was concerned about the conflict over the disturbance of burial sites. She cited an incident in late 2020 when Native Hawaiian elders threw themselves between the ground and heavy machinery after bones surfaced at one of Peter Martin's development project sites. Paltin introduced the idea of creating a new commu-

2. Moku'ula was the private residence of King Kamehameha III from 1837 to 1845 and the burial site of several Hawaiian royals.

nity plan designation to offer an additional level of protection for historically significant sites throughout West Maui.

> What I just drafted was a Cultural Reserve Community Plan designation intended to preserve and manage lands for native Hawaiian traditional and customary uses while protecting sensitive and significant cultural areas such as heiau, iwi kūpuna, et cetera. Areas in West Maui that would fit within this designation include, but are not limited to, Moku'ula, Mokuhinia, Lahaina Town South known cemeteries and inadvertent burial finds, Honokahua Burial Preserve, I know of some family burials in Kahana makai of Highway 30, mauka of Lower Honoapi'ilani Road, and north of Hui D Road. There's a heiau in Honolua that's called Honua'ula. Dr. Six mentioned Pu'upiha Cemetery and Puehuehueiki Cemetery. I know that Nāpili Kai also has some burials. I think it's by Puna Point over there. So there's a lot of areas that could fit inside of this new type of designation. Olowalu has many significant sites, and I believe a heiau over there. And, you know, this could also translate to countywide. I'm not sure if it's too late at this stage for West Maui Community Plan to get a Cultural Reserve designation for the Community Plan. And my start on the idea was, you know, any type of actions taken in this designation area would require, at a minimum, licensed archaeological monitoring.

Her idea did not gain enough support to move forward. Instead, as a compromise, Paltin sought to reduce the amount of land designated as Residential in the Waine'e area from 64 acres to 20 acres. Paltin said she would accept an Open Space designation for the rest of the land, because it was the most restrictive option available.

> I know we need affordable housing. I have concerns how affordable it can be with the archaeological monitoring and inventory survey plan needed. For me, I'm kind of leaning towards leaving it as is and not expanding it. I guess, you know, the experience that we had with this developer, we've already seen it this past December. That information was known to them, the three cemeteries, the inadvertent finds. And then there was another inadvertent find with grandmothers being arrested for trying to step into the way of desecrating the bones. And they're still going to court over that one incident right now. And it really is tearing up the community with folks taking sides and whatnot. So I'm just asking us as leaders to take steps to not

enable that kind of division within our community. And I'm not sure of the best way to do it. I mean, if it were easy, everybody would be up in this seat, right? But that's my main concern. You know, I would love for my community to get along, to work together towards a shared goal. And I don't see that being able to happen when certain folks' bones are protected by virtue of them being in a marked cemetery, and other folks' bones are not afforded that same level of protection, where this company in particular, the lineal descendants have been in kind of an antagonistic relationship within the community. [ . . . ] It's hard. The compromise for me would be to leave it as it is, and then have additional protections, not expand it. That would be the compromise. My ideal would be, you know, Open Space—most restrictive.

The Council Committee voted unanimously to adopt two separate motions. The first amended the Residential designation from the Maui Planning Commission version to the existing Residential designation for 20 acres as opposed to 64 acres, and the second amended the other 44 acres as Open Space designation.

A pair of related action items[3], which the Council Committee unanimously supported, accompanied these motions. One would prioritize the development of a cultural overlay map, and the other would reference sites to be included in this overlay. Both actions were created to put in place timely protections for known sensitive archaeological areas. Areas identified by the map and in the list would be subject to survey requirements.

## "If Something is Not Required, it Can be Avoided"
### *November 18, 2021*

Nearly everyone who testified at the first public hearing of the West Maui Community Plan had been involved in the process for years, represented special interest groups and testified in prior public hearings. They fell into one of four camps: employees, contractors or supporters of large land developers; property owners seeking redesignation for their lands; representatives of non-

---

3. "[D]evelop a cultural overlay map, identifying known above-ground resources, the location of important historic events, known burials, and known archaeological resources, and create a cultural overlay district to protect cultural assets and establish an efficient review process for property owners." "Incorporate appropriate sites on the ascription list in appendix f into a council-established cultural overlay through a public process."

profit groups; and hotel/hospitality industry companies. Several individuals represented themselves as interested citizens. CPAC Chairperson Kai Nishiki remarked on the people in attendance.

> It seems like there are a lot of paid consultants, developers, realtors, land speculators and lawyers here tonight opposing the plan during this public meeting. I always find it interesting when you see a bunch of paid guys opposing the community plan, our West Maui Community Plan, which really took a monumental effort on behalf of the Long-Range Division within the Planning Department doing extensive outreach with many stakeholders in West Maui for years, two or three years.

A petition circulated by consultants to adopt the Kaʻanapali 2020 project in its entirety garnered more than 300 signatures. While the Council Committee kept the entitled portion of the project intact, they supported Open Space and Park designations for the southern—a move opposed by those involved in the project. Members of the project's community advisory group, including CPAC members Joe Pluta and Hans Michel, testified in support of the company's vision for the project. Employees and consultants of Kaanapali Land Management Company, including Chad Fukunaga and Mandy Saito, also showed up to advocate for the project. Former councilmember Elle Cochran, who organized the petition in support of the project, commented:

> I want to hone in on Kāʻanapali 2020 plan, which I wholeheartedly support—and please keep it in its entirety. I got real-time feedback today, in particular our millennials—our young future generation [...] people who never heard of this plan. I showed it to them; I gave them details about it [...] they loved it. They thought, "Oh my god, I have hope—there's opportunity for us to finally, to possibly have a home." They love to have the connectivity there, how it created, really, family atmosphere: the integrated parks, right, the connectivity where you can walk, and play, and go to your mixed-use. There's a bus transit; there's a church; there's a school—there's so many things. [...] I feel like this needs to be in place. A millennial said, "If you cut out this Kāʻanapali South portion, isn't it really going to kill the whole plan? Doesn't the infrastructure need to connect?" I'm like, "You got it." [...] Our up-and-coming future generations see it. And this plan does address SLR—this plan addresses sea-level rise and managed retreat issues. [...] This entire project is mauka of the highway.

One person, Junya Nakoa, criticized the project for its lack of progress and unfulfilled promises to build affordable housing.

> The Ka'anapali 2020 was supposed to have choke affordable homes, work- force housing homes built, but zero was built. Not one single home was built. Okay, and then now they going try push the Pu'ukoli'i Mauka, and then now you get 51 percent of that, and you know what, they not building nothing. They not taking care of the local people.

*   *   *

A handful of Martin's associates criticized a policy that prohibited the development of gentleman's estates and the use of the State 201H or County 2.97 in the Areas of Stability. Two days before the first public hearing for the West Maui Community Plan, Martin sent an email urging his supporters to submit testimony in favor of his projects. "It has been my goal for the last 25 years to try to get single-family homes on these lands for our residents. I need your help," he wrote. "Our citizens and our children should be able to have homes with a yard for their families on this beautiful land. If the WMCP is adopted in the current form, there will be no housing for our families in the next 20 years on the lands of Olowalu and Launiupoko."

About 23 written testimonies were submitted in support of residential development in Olowalu and Launiupoko. Councilmembers voted unanimously to include all written testimony in the meeting record. Nearly all of the submissions were brief, one to three paragraphs long, and all cited a shortage of homes. Those who wrote in support of Martin's vision included a pastor, a local fireman, high school and college students, real estate agents and his employees. Dylan Payne, a CPAC member and real estate salesperson for West Maui Land Company, stated,

> I would really plead with you to remove Policy 3.4.2 that prohibits and just really discourages workforce housing south of Puamana. I would say get rid of that. If you do that, that doesn't mean that there's going to be a bunch of housing built in those areas. But it means that you're going to give it a chance.—that you're going to listen to it in the future. You can still say no, 'cause quite frankly, all of those proposals will come right back to you and this body for approval at that given time.

Another testifier, Lori Gomez-Karinen, who identified herself as a retired educator who grew up in Lahaina, wrote:

I have seen my homeland evolve from a plantation community to a tourist destination community. Also flourishing are local businesses and service-minded establishments. It goes without saying that affordable housing for West Maui has always been an issue. Workers need housing to remain in West Maui—affordable housing. COVID-19 has only exacerbated our housing problems. I implore you to designate the areas of Olowalu and Launiupoko as "affordable/workforce housing." To do otherwise would be to see an influx of locals and workforce employees leave Maui.

In his outreach to supporters, Martin did not mention why his projects in those areas encountered years of opposition from a wide range of people, among them coral reef scientists, area descendants and county planners. They cited the lack of infrastructure, the threat to Maui's most pristine coral reef ecosystem, and the threat of desecration to burial and historical sites. A handful of testifiers, such as Victoria Kaluna Palafox, spoke on these issues and opposed development in Olowalu.

I am against Mr. Peter Martin and his development in Olowalu for such disrespect. For many, many years, I worked over there in Olowalu, way before his development came in. And there were DLNR sites, boulders that labeled the areas where Camp PECUSA is to not to touch. There were three big stones. And I talked before with DLNR and I reported this so much. Nobody cared about it. The development went in and took all those site numbers away. Those site numbers also said "do not remove." Today you cannot find that. My grandfather's place, where he was buried, is not there anymore. He plowed over. So how come?

Olowalu is a very sensitive area, especially by our ocean. When we were younger, we used to dive there—so much baby fishes used to come from there. I remember. Today when we go and dive, our children, 'cause I cannot go in the water, there are still none, and they are trying to thrive; they are trying to replenish—especially the uhu [parrotfish], the one who creates the sand for us. That is important. Olowalu was ace for the uhu before.

But anyway, e kala mai [sorry], I am against any projects going on in Olowalu because of the sensitivity of that area. I agree that he wants to make it only for the rich. And I've never seen him ever build affordable houses in Lahaina. What I saw him do, though, is offer land to his employees or people of his choice to purchase lands for him in private areas. And we find these private areas are kuleana owned by families that are still living in Lahaina. If that's the kind of development Mr. Peter Martin brings to Lahaina, no thank you.

Some criticized Martin's tactics as deceptive and predatory. Among those voices was Kahala Johnson, who claimed lineage to Olowalu through his father Kekahuna.

The proposed development in Olowalu is against the consent of the community. A small vocal minority of rich, entitled developers, together with their paid lawyers, consultants and collaborators, continue to repeat and disseminate a savage conspiracy maintaining otherwise. While a few of these loud, vocal minorities have expressed emotionally overwhelmed opinions in the past, we cannot let tear-streaked tantrums and colonial visions overrule the voices of the community who have already spoken on this issue.

Lahaina resident Jade Chihara spoke in support of responsible development and prioritizing the health of the environment and protection of cultural sites.

As a member of my age bracket and this generation, I'd like to speak on behalf of what matters to me, and that's to ensure sustainability and just management of our natural resources while these plans are on the table. If living with my family for a little bit longer, and that means that the island remains in its beauty and its stability, I'm okay with that, while we figure it out in a just way. I do want affordable housing; I love our local people too, but not in a manner that is detrimental to burial sites, to our natural resources and our streams and our oceans—historically important areas to the entire community consent and important areas and open spaces.

\* \* \*

Property owners and associates of the Plantation Estates Lot Owners Association made their final pleas to the Maui County Council Committee to change the subdivision's community plan designation from Agricultural to Rural Residential.

West Maui CPAC members Karen Comcowich and Dawn Hegger-Nordblom both mentioned Plantation Estates in their remarks to the Maui County Council. Both supported retaining the Agricultural designation for the area. Hegger-Nordblom commented,

I did get a chance to talk to Plantation Estates regarding the ag versus rural designation. And because I worked for DLNR in the past, in the conservation district as a regulatory planner, I do feel that ag should remain in ag. And the reason why I say that is because from a state level, you don't want to keep perpetuating gentleman lots or gentleman farms.

\* \* \*

Representatives from West Maui's hotel companies criticized the council's inclusion of policies aimed at addressing projected sea-level rise. Coastal management, they argued, fell under the purview of the Maui Planning Commission. In their testimonies they stated that the concept of managed retreat was one that needed more detail and community input. Despite pressure from the hotel industry to walk back their policies to address sea-level rise, the council stood firm in their policy to require new development to be landward of the Sea Level Rise Exposure Area ("SLR-XA").

\* \* \*

Advocates and representatives for other community projects, such as the West Maui Greenway and Honokowai Homestead project, appealed to councilmembers to revise plan language to support their efforts. DHHL planner Julie-Ann Cochola requested revisions to match the master plan to its project's master plan.

Greenway advocates asked councilmembers to include language in the plan to require all new development projects to incorporate the Greenway into its plans. Donna Clayton remarked,

> If something is not required, it can be avoided. The West Maui Greenway is a high priority in West Maui and part of the West Maui transit corridor design that is in progress at this time. Once the route is determined, this additional wording will help ensure that working together, the county, state and community—we can make the West Maui Greenway a reality.

In the final readings for the plan, councilmembers unanimously voted to incorporate both the West Maui Greenway requirement and the language from DHHL's project.

## "Much-needed Housing Never Transpired"
### *December 3, 2021*

The community had been living with the COVID-19 pandemic for more than a year. Hawai'i had put in place costly and strict barriers to traveling safely to the islands, which dramatically reduced visitation and eased the pressure placed on the state's natural resources and infrastructure. Residents and local government had the space to conceive of a different approach to tourism.

In the context of this period, at the same time as the first reading to adopt the West Maui Community Plan, the Maui County Council also introduced Bill 148 to place a moratorium on the construction of new transient accommodation. Many of the same people who testified against restrictive aspects of the community plan also came out against the moratorium. For the most part, councilmembers heard from the same individuals and interests as they had when they started the process. As had happened with the final vote on the plan for the CPAC and the Planning Commission, last-minute efforts were made to change the content of the plan.

Councilmember Yuki Lei Sugimura introduced amendments on two contested issues. One amendment sought to change the designation of Plantation Estates lots to Rural Residential, and the other amendment sought to align the plan designations with the wishes of the Ka'anapali 2020 group.

"I think there was one parcel that was actually doing agriculture. But the terrain and the use is really, really Rural Residential. So, I want to make that motion," Sugimura said. Councilmember Tamara Paltin argued against the motion, saying the push to change the designation was a way to avoid public hearings on the matter. She said the community had long opposed development above Honolua Bay but were robbed of the opportunity to speak on the matter.

> This area is Honolua Ridge, Plantation Estates, above Honolua Bay. This is the whole reason the community galvanized back in 2007, 2014, and it looks like they may need to galvanize in 2021. It's like a seven-year cycle. The community never wanted houses there, never got the opportunity to weigh in on this ag subdivision bait-and-switch by Maui Land & Pine. People that don't want to live in the ag subdivision, there's Mahana Estates right down the way that is all rural.

The final attempt to change the Plantation Estates lot designation from Agricultural to Rural Residential failed by a vote of 5–4, with councilmembers Paltin, Johnson, Rawlins-Fernandez, Sinenci and Molina opposed.

Immediately following the vote on Plantation Estates, Sugimura introduced a motion to adopt designation changes for Ka'anapali 2020. The first amendment sought to redesignate 100 acres from Agricultural to Small Town Center. The second amendment would reduce the amount of land designated as Park/Open Space above Honoapi'ilani Highway from 97 acres to 10 acres.

During oral testimony, supporters, employees and paid consultants for the development project pleaded with the council to make these changes. Kimo Falconer and others argued the county did not have the resources to manage a large park. Chad Fukunaga, the project representative, said the designations would jeopardize the rest of the project. Commented Sugimura,

> The community plan, the Ka'anapali 2020 Community Planning Group-approved map, is consistent with the Maui Island Plan and includes a 10-acre park immediately mauka of Hanaka'ō'ō Beach Park, Canoe Beach, while also providing much-needed housing in a well planned, complete community. So this is the amendment, and it supports the vision and direction that the Kā'anapali 2020 Master Plan had.

Once again, Paltin voiced her opposition, remarking,

> This land was designated Park/Open Space through the Community Plan process. It was retained through the Maui Planning Commission process, and I'm not about to overturn the community's decision, or overturn the Maui Planning Commission's decision, for a bunch of folks that have financial interest in having it be different.
>
> Like Lanny Tihada [testifier] said, I also support Kā'anapali 2020's full plan. The most important part of that plan had people living in houses in 2020. Everything else doesn't matter, because nobody's living in houses in 2020. I don't even know if they'll be living in houses in 2030 or 2040. They have entitled land. Pu'ukoli'i Village Mauka was entitled since 2005. The state's priority is not the bypass right now. They got 22 million for realigning the highway, because if you can't get to the southern terminus of the bypass, it doesn't matter where the northern terminus is.

Councilmembers expressed heartache over the matter. They were torn over whether to support a community-driven vision from decades past or to update it in light of sea-level rise and a changed West Maui landscape. Molina commented,

> I gotta say, this one kind of pulls at my heartstrings 'cause this was one real...I don't want to call it a tragedy. But it's just from years before, a lot of great intentions and a lot of hope, and a lot of good people, a lot of kūpuna who passed on that put their heart and soul into this. And for whatever reason, as time evolved, I guess the goals and objectives to getting the

much-needed housing never transpired. And of course, now, we're in a bit of a quagmire, especially for West Maui with the need for affordable housing.

Similarly, Councilmember King said she struggled with her feelings about the project.

What really bothers me the most about it is, we've been told that they'd like to do affordable housing. But we haven't been offered any assurances of what percentage will be affordable housing, where the affordability will be, what AMI [area median income] levels. I've seen these kinds of promises happen when they're given verbally, and not manifest themselves when the actual development is happening. So I'm having a really hard time supporting it without that caveat in there.

The motion to amend policies related to the Ka'anapali 2020 project failed by a 6–3 vote with councilmembers King, Johnson, Molina, Paltin, Sinenci, and Vice Chair RawlinsFernandez opposed. A subsequent motion to change the land designated as Park/Open Space to Agriculture also failed to garner enough votes to pass.

*       *       *

One new proposed amendment emerged in the final meetings of the council. The Kahoma Villages project was an approved 201H project designated in the 1996 Community Plan. The plan detailed the developer's obligations[4] to the

---

4.   The existing language about the Kahoma Villages Project from the 1996 West Maui Community Plan, and which was carried over into the 2022 plan, stated: "For the area between Front Street and Honoapi'ilani Highway from Kahoma Stream to Kenui Street, the following policies and objectives from the 1996 West Maui Community Plan continue to apply (with page references to the existing community plan in parentheses): (1) concentrate multifamily dwelling units around the central commercial district. (2) a new community-oriented park along the south bank of Kahoma Street and between Front Street and Honoapi'ilani Highway. (page 18.) (3) the new park along the south edge of Kahoma Stream should be recognized as major entry features to Lahaina Town with appropriate landscape planting treatment. (page 33.) (4) the south-side of the Kahoma Stream channel should incorporate a 20-foot-wide landscape linear park or greenway, including pedestrian and bike ways, to provide visual and open space continuity between Front Street and the Honoapi'ilani Highway. (page 33.) (5) establish major recreation ways for pedestrians and bicycles along the southern side of Kahoma Stream. (page 37.) (6) there shall also be 6 acres of park land within the project district, including a linear park or greenway adjacent to the south bank of Kahoma Stream,

community as part of its entitlements. But the developer failed to meet these obligations—namely, the construction of a six-acre park.

The Protect and Preserve Kahoma Ahupua'a Association sued the developer, Stanford Carr Development, and the Maui Planning Commission to hold them accountable to the commitments made in the 1996 plan. Both the Intermediate Court of Appeals and the Hawai'i Supreme Court sided with the Association, sending the developer back to the Maui Planning Commission to determine how to proceed on the already-completed project. But without the same language about the project in the new community plan, the community did not have a procedural path forward for addressing the issue. The Association was now appealing to the Maui County Council to include the same language about the project from the 1996 plan. Association President Michele Lincoln testified in support of the amendment:

> The ultimate goal is to hold the developer accountable for following proper protocols regarding community plan amendments. Not only will this ensure that justice is served, but it will help with the enforcement of new community plans in the future. Think about it: if developers can circumvent laws and disregard rulings of the highest court and avoid any consequences for violations, then it sets a dangerous precedent.

Attorney Lance Collins, who represented Lincoln and the Association in a *pro se* manner, elaborated on the issue.

> Obviously, it's not possible to have the six-acre park in that area anymore, but that's actually not the point. The point is that the developer needs to do a community plan amendment as is the consequence of the Supreme Court's decision. It needs to do a community plan amendment so that the community has a sufficient opportunity in a transparent and meaningful way to work with the developer to basically come to a resolution of this problem. The answer is not to simply erase all of this and allow the developer

---

from Honoapi'ilani Highway to Front Street, at least 60 feet wide and approximately 1.5 acres in size. The extension of Wainee Street from its present terminus at Kenui Street to Front Street, as well as the realignment of Kenui Street shall also be considered. Said roadway improvements should be developed and funded in conjunction with appropriate government agencies. The remaining acres in the project district shall be evenly divided between the commercial business uses, and multi-family and senior citizen residential uses, to the greatest extent practicable. (page 50.)"

to get a "get out of jail free" card because the Administration and Corporation Counsel gave wrong advice about the limits of the County Council's authority with respect to this issue.

Lucienne de Naie, a resident who regularly participated at council meetings, spoke in support of the amendment.

> I also want to speak to what Lance Collins spoke to the area around Mala Wharf, the 'Alamihi Fishpond. That area, you definitely should do exactly what he said and keep the old language in the plan. It is a travesty that people just forge ahead because they have the money to do so, run all over the public process. Our agencies feel their hands are tied and just rubber-stamp everything. And then the courts say no, you didn't do it right, and now it's built. The citizens should have some recourse to get that six-acre park someplace. And having language in the community plan that says that's a requirement means that they should get a community plan amendment that allows a process for justice to be served.

Paltin introduced a motion to carry over the language from the 1996 plan into the current plan. Her fellow councilmembers were divided on whether to approve the amendment. Those against the proposed amendment were resigned to the fact that the project had already been built. "I'll be voting no on this one because it doesn't make sense to have a requirement, well, park, where homes are currently existing," said Chair Alice Lee. "And I don't know why we're getting involved in a court case that is really between separate parties."

Corporate Counsel Michael Hopper said he would not sign the bill to adopt the West Maui Community Plan if the Maui County Council included Kahoma Villages.

> The main concern I think that we had was that this is requiring six acres of park in an area where there's existing homes right now. And I think if that was something proposed for any community plan area, we have concerns with it. We have additional concerns. We could go to executive session and discuss that, but for now, I would be unable to approve the plan as to form and legality because of this.

For those councilmembers who voted in support of the bill, they viewed their support as legitimizing community plans and a step toward holding developers accountable to the agreements they made. Councilmember Kelly King spoke in support of the amendment, citing the need to hold developers accountable to the community plan.

> We can't keep allowing developers to build in a way that's contrary to our community plans and then just sweeping it under the rug. That's been going on for too long, because we haven't really taken the community plan seriously. But we're voting this into ordinance, so this is basically law. So the intent of this is to have the developers mitigate the issue after the fact, because we can't do it before the fact. But I think this is the only way we're going to do that, so I'm going to support it.

The motion to adopt the addition of the language on the Kahoma Villages Project passed by a 5–4 vote, with councilmembers Mike Molina, Tasha Kama, Yuki Lei Sugimura and Lee opposing.

\* \* \*

Hotel industry representatives who testified also questioned the legality of Policy 2.4.2[5] to require one affordable housing unit to be built for each new transient accommodation unit—a policy developed originally by the CPAC in response to concerns over the disproportionate ratio of visitor to resident units and the lack of workforce housing. Councilmembers pulled back on this wording at the final hearing for the West Maui Community Plan. After hearing from Corporation Counsel, councilmember Tamara Paltin decided the issue would be best addressed by amending the County Code.

> In discussion with Corporation Counsel, we decided that the policy in the posted bill would be more effectively incorporated with amendments to the Residential Workforce Housing Plan, which I intend to propose. And this would be strictly limited to the transient accommodations. And so because we just passed the moratorium[6] and it's on for two years, I'm

---

5. The final version of policy 2.4.2 read: "Developers of transient accommodation units must comply with the County's affordable housing requirements and prioritize fulfillment of affordable housing obligations within the boundaries of the West Maui Community Plan area."
6. On January 22, 2022, Maui County Council voted 6–3 to override Mayor Michael Victorino's veto of Bill 148 to place a moratorium on new transient units until the council implements recommendations by a Tourism Management Temporary Investigative Group, or in two years, whichever is sooner.

thinking within the two years we can enact this into the code rather than just the community plan.

Councilmembers unanimously approved a motion by Paltin to revise the policy to reference the county's Affordable Housing Requirements.

*    *    *

In spite of the council's divergent views on many topics, they voted 7–2, with councilmembers Sugimura and Kama voting no, to pass the West Maui Community Plan on first reading.

## "The Paradigm has Certainly Shifted."
### *December 17, 2021*

At the second and final reading of the West Maui Community Plan, councilmember Sugimura introduced a motion to delete the reference to the Kahoma Villages Project. No one seconded the motion and it did not move forward.

*    *    *

"I think the overwhelming sentiment I heard was although the plan isn't perfect, it is a great start and a great success in conducting multiple community meetings and getting consensus on community plan," said Councilmember Shane Sinenci in his final remarks prior to taking the vote to adopt the West Maui Community Plan. He said he was proud of the way the plan expanded historical districts and perpetuated culture.

Paltin, who led the process as West Maui's representative, said the plan was, for her, the culmination of a 15-year commitment. By the end of the process, two CPAC members had resigned from their positions. She acknowledged all the people who contributed to the plan and said she hoped they would see that their efforts mattered: "We heard what they said, and we did our best to keep it in the plan."

Deputy Corporation Counsel Michael Hopper refused to approve the bill for an ordinance citing his concern over the Kahoma Villages Project amendment and its implications for already-developed areas. Chairperson Lee said she supported the bill with reservations. "I just want to let you know that I have serious reservations about certain aspects of this plan. I will vote in favor of it, 'cause generally, I support it. But the idea of designating a property that's already in existence as park is, to me, a taking," said Lee. Similarly, Sugimura expressed her reservations:

> I have grave reservations about that. And I also have reservations about not recognizing the Maui Island Plan and all the people who worked and put that together through testimony that we received from the community—that they're saying this is the plan, and not necessarily looking at what was said before. And I have a grave concern about Kā'anapali 2020 and what they were trying to do in terms of affordable housing and planning for the West Maui community.

Councilmember Mike Molina observed the shift in community sentiment reflected in the plan and the individuals who helped shape it:

> What I found very fascinating about this process was to see the amount of younger generations of folks wanting to participate, because that was so important. Because the whole landscape has changed from one time, as you had mentioned, Member Paltin, West Maui being viewed as a recreational area that promoted tourism. And the mindset has changed to more of let's look at the quality-of-life concerns—that's really reflected in this West Maui Community Plan, as well as cultural preservation for an area that was once the seat of the royal kingdom. So the paradigm has certainly shifted.

The Maui County Council voted 7 to 1 to pass the West Maui Community Plan at final reading. Sugimura was the sole dissenting vote. Kama was excused.

# Afterword
*Brian Richardson*

## 'O ia mau nō

For over a century, sugar companies have had plans for West Maui. In the 1950s, the planning became more state-sponsored and focused on framing the development of the Lahaina Historic District and massive hotels north of Lahaina, and organizing government-funded infrastructure to support those developments. By the 1970s, there was a sense that broader community involvement was important, even if the dominant voices remained the large landowners and corporations. The points of controversy by the 1980s centered on what could happen with the land and resources that had been tied solely to the production of sugarcane but that were now available for other uses. Massive profits were possible for some; however, for many others, the existing community was threatened.

In a sense, modern community plans are attempts to limit the impact of people with money to simply do whatever they want. Those limits often fail, largely because community plans can be ineffectual or can provide resources to help developers make money by funding infrastructure and keeping community challenges at bay. The planning process is a contest between many interests—some local, some distant, some well-funded, some impoverished, some welcomed to the process, others marginalized. Local planning is like a game based on flexible or inconsistent rules that some people can ignore. At times, different people are playing different games, even if they seem to be using the same board. The main reason the different games come together is that they are fighting over the plan, largely because the plan helps set up future contests, empowering some people in the process and providing material support for certain types of change.

A community plan is not simply a document with a rational origin and a straightforward impact. It is more contentious, ambiguous, and fluid than that. Not only is creating the plan a messy process, but the plan itself is often ambiguous, contentious, and applied selectively. Some people win, some people lose. The plan, and therefore the planning process, is part of the larger game of who gets to do what. Key to understanding a process as a game is determining what players and resources make up the game's dynamics.

For example, the game Monopoly has properties, cash, and the randomness of dice throws. Checkers has pieces, a board, and rules that govern how the pieces can move. In our context, the situation is more complicated in the sense that there is a game that creates the plan, and then the plan itself becomes part of a larger game about what happens in the community. The planning process must manage many conflicts, issues, and resources. The plan can be ignored, but it is easier, and cheaper, if the plan already supports what certain players want. To understand the game, players are required to pay attention to factors such as money, people, and values that matter in the debate and to also understand what the focus of the debate should be, such as housing, work, the environment, and well-being.

The process is additionally often complicated by the lack of public information about what is happening. There are many private conversations, hidden agendas, unspoken goals, and invisible players. Sometimes, hidden agendas become visible when committee members accuse each other of conflicts of interest. One example occurred at the November 21, 2019 CPAC meeting, when Kai Nishiki discouraged Dylan Payne from commenting on properties owned by his employer, West Maui Land Company. There are sometimes conflicts over who is able to participate in a meeting: meetings can be scheduled to make it difficult for working people to attend, speakers can present themselves as representing this group or that, and people can engage in theatrics of all sorts. And if someone thinks that the process is not going their way, they can complain that it is unfair, which sometimes it is, or attempt to weaken parts of the plan to make it less effective. The planning process has few and frequently adaptable rules, and the result can become less about a thoughtful plan and more about the political struggle over whose interests are favored—and, ultimately, who can participate in designing the land, and therefore the community.

\*   \*   \*

Let's go back a few decades and look at a project that illustrates how these dynamics and outcomes play out. In 1987, L. P. Liem purchased a 10-acre parcel of land on Hāwea Point between what is now the Kapalua Bay Hotel and the Bay Villas resort homes for $2.4 million. The land, which is the location of the Hāwea Point Lighthouse, was owned by the federal government and sold at auction, where it was purchased for well over the estimated sale price. After the auction, some local politicians proposed to condemn the land to create a park, in part to ensure beach access. At the time, the property was zoned as Conservation and was designated as open space in the Lahaina Community Business Plan (*Lahaina News,* August 12, 1987, page 1). Liem's local representative, Edward Frankel, indicated the land was going to be used to build a residence and that it would be "harmonious with its surroundings and we would take into consideration our neighbors." That was not a legally binding statement.

At the auction, State Senator Rick Reed opposed the purchase and afterwards warned that it would be difficult to gain approval for even a single-family house on the property given the need for an environmental impact assessment, approval from the State Land Use Commission, and approval from the Department of Land and Natural Resources. In addition, Reed noted the need for a public hearing and referenced "strong community opposition."

It turned out Reed's sense of the project's future was wrong. The house, at 9 Beach Drive, was completed in 1996 following a long conflict over permissions and permits. At over 6,600 square feet, the house has seven bedrooms, nine bathrooms, and three garage spaces. The buildings were not as large as initially proposed, and members of the public were still allowed to access the ocean at the edge of the property. In December 2020, the house sold for $24 million and was listed for significantly more in 2022. Liem clearly won. An investment of $2.4 million plus the cost of the building yielded close to $20 million in profits over 25 years. Beyond that, Liem was able to create a highly isolated property along the lines of what is now happening in places like Kaua'i and the Big Island, where the occupants are protected from incursions but can also access public services and people at will. In return, he had to do little more than pay his property taxes.

The impact of Liem's money meant that the property was organized to the detriment of the community, and the use of the land ended up being greatly different from what was in the community plan at that time. It is not simply that the parcel of land became private, but also that the regulations that connect a parcel of land to the community were largely ignored, waived, or weakened.

The development was created by the highest bidder.

A detailed account of what happened would shed light on how money, government, and the community interact to determine how land is used. Scraps of newspaper articles provide only hints. The process and conversations are largely lost. However, there are a few points worth noting here.

The process itself involved the interaction of not only the relevant laws, regulations, and procedures, but also players who are typically involved whenever a significant development is proposed: the owner and his lawyers and representatives; politicians, some making public statements, others possibly making private deals; people in government agencies who decide if a project can move forward; and members of the community, some of whom attended public hearings and some of whom joined the Friends of Hāwea Point, organized by Scott Northrop.

By February 1990, local politicians, including Maui Mayor Tavares and State Representative Rosalyn Baker, joined State Senator Reed in opposition. At the time, Tavares and members of the Maui Council floated the idea of condemning the land and then purchasing it from Liem. These efforts went nowhere.

By November 1990, the *Lahaina News* reported that the conflict between Liem and the Friends of Hāwea Point had been resolved. A Maui Open Space Trust was to be established to manage part of Hāwea Point, and Liem contributed $40,000 to the trust. In addition, the area along the coast was to be designated as "open space" but also closed to the public. There would be nothing constructed in areas where nothing was probably going to be constructed anyway. Open space here was more like open views from the house. Beach access, however, would be allowed in specific areas. Finally, the agreement was to last for 10 years, and at that point any changes to the property required the agreement of a certain percentage of owners at Kapalua Bay Villas (*Lahaina News*, November 11, 1990, pages 3, 4).

The owners at Kapalua Bay Villas figure highly in the resolution. When the land was first purchased, Liem's representative Frankel had noted that Liem would take into consideration the property's "neighbors," a statement that foreshadowed how the debates over the property would proceed. The neighbors in this case were primarily owners at Kapalua Bay Villas, who share a concern for limiting beach access to people who do not live in the immediate area. Outsiders, meaning those who lived in the larger community, were not welcome members of the conversation.

Disputes arose over access to the beach even before the house was completed. By 1994, The Friends of Hāwea Point no longer existed, but other groups challenged how the building had been designed to the detriment of the community (*Lahaina News*, September 9, 1994, pages 1, 3). Kapalua Bay Hotel and Kapalua Bay Villas were also criticized at the time for limiting public access to the beaches.

And the disputes continue. In early 2022, tech millionaire Jonathan Yantis, then the owner of 6 Beach Drive, called the police several times to complain about the noise and alcohol at the beach, and also stationed a guard at the beach access point. Tension is ongoing as the property owner pushes for privacy and the greater community pushes for access.

In the case of 6 Beach Drive, the conflict has become limited to specific beach access issues because the building and the general pattern of land use were established by the early 1990s and could not be changed without significant legal challenges and costs. In other places, conversations have long ended, and it is too late to fix past problems. With many, there was never a conversation in the first place. And in still others the conversations are only starting or are happening in terms of general planning documents that help create the conditions under which land could change in the future.

## What Matters?

If the property purchased by Liem is any indication, money is the fundamental factor in deciding what happens to the land. The community plan in this case was largely ignored, and the limits to Liem's initial plan arose in part from community outrage and threats of potential action from politicians. The market, or more broadly the economy, is key to the discussion. Rents are high. The cost of home ownership is high. Local people are priced out of their communities. While few would loudly argue that this is acceptable, many, especially those who are wealthy, likely approve because it increases their land values and allows money to filter out undesirable residents. A system based on money is simply a question of who is the highest bidder, and if you are either selling something or have the money to buy something, then an unregulated auction is a suitable process. It's a free market.

Of course, there are challenges to the idea that people with money should be able to do whatever they want. Why should access to money determine how land is developed? In fact, even wealthy people do not want other people with money to be free to do whatever they want. If someone has created a comfortable fake farm, growing a few mango trees and tending to their collection of sports cars, the last thing they want is for someone to come along and build a high-density tourist development next door—or even worse, to actually engage in farming, with piles of manure and loud machines. In the case of Plantation Estates Lot Owners, at the January 23, 2020 meeting, the wealthy landowners sought to change the designation of their estates so they could enforce their own covenants, conditions, and restrictions (CC&Rs), which would have restricted agricultural activities. The wealthy recognize the need for rules, so long as the rules do not get in their way. And forcing their neighbors to not farm is a rule that many of them support.

A basic issue in the narrative is: should development consider more than profits? This goes in several directions. Some see the plan and regulations as checks on harmful development. Others, including some developers, stated in planning meetings that developers themselves should consider more than just profits, and suggested that self-regulation was the best way forward. The question is: what types of restrictions, or incentives, should exist so the wealthy do not simply do whatever they want? In other words, the central issues are how to mitigate the impact of money, and what sorts of limits can be put in place, for whose benefit, and under whose jurisdiction. To put that differently: what, if anything, matters beyond money?

## PEOPLE MATTER

One of the fundamental keys to understanding the planning process is to consider who gets to participate and under what conditions. Some people may talk about the will of the people or the community's wishes, but who comprises "the people"? How are the "community's wishes" determined? The answers are not simple, in part because there is disagreement over who should participate and what status they should be given. Full-time residents, for instance, are easy to include because of their connection to the region. But that raises the question of ownership: does it matter whether full-time residents own their property? Should property owners who do not live in the area, or who have never been to Maui, be included? Should people who work full-time in the region be ignored because their bedroom is somewhere else?

Many categories of people are talked about: retirees, second-home owners, business owners, landlords, speculators, bureaucrats, lawyers, community leaders. At times, these people are also characterized in ways that either promote or undermine their status in the discussion—people talk of "greedy developers" or "local families" as a way of skewing the narrative of the plan in one direction or another. The cost of owning or renting property is also tied to the need for workers to commute, creating a situation in which parts of West Maui have become more like a theme park for the transient wealthy rather than a community.

In addition to individuals, various groups and organizations become part of the conversation. The Friends of Hāwea Point, for instance, challenged development plans at 6 Beach Drive. Community associations, and specifically community leaders, organize activities, publish statements, and create con-nections with sections of the community. Likewise, companies such as Maui Land & Pineapple have a key place in the conversation through their official representatives as well as the people they hire or encourage to support their positions. Hotel and hospitality companies, unions, and nonprofit groups also join the process.

The debates over community plans thus try to establish that certain types of people do or do not matter, and influence the direction of development accordingly. For instance, one policy option that has been discussed is whether there should be costs to owning property where someone does not live, and thus does not support the community. As with many places in Hawai'i and around the world, this issue has recently arisen in Kaka'ako on O'ahu, where many units in new buildings have been purchased by absentee owners and remain empty, making local businesses more difficult to sustain and leaving the community feeling like a ghost town. The land is owned, but no one is home.

## VALUES MATTER

The account of the debates provided in this book details how important values have been throughout the creation of the community plan. The goals are numerous, not always defined or explored, and not always consistent. There is, for instance, talk of the quality of life, of jobs, of the environment, of safety, of the quality of construction, of community, of livability, of walkability, of public health, of justice, of the right to private property, and of social services like schools and shelters. Some goals are less explicit, such as the desire to make more money. Of course, developers seldom say that greed is good or that they do not really care about the community. Even if those things are true, the goal of the public presentations is to offer the people in the audience positive feel-ings with the hopes that they do not pay attention to the details. Many of the values raised in public meetings do not have legal weight—and things that do have legal weight are the most dangerous for people trying to make money in development.

Changes to the land also impact sensitive spaces, such as ecologically fragile areas or places significant to Native Hawaiians. One person's garage lot may be another person's burial grounds. For those wanting to use money to make more money through development, history and nature are obstructions. A community plan will typically engage with these issues, or at least recognize that the issues exist and then leave actual decisions to someone else. The modern community plan becomes messy, in part, because it is no longer simply about expanding the tourism market or promoting luxury developments.

Debates over the community plan address broad issues connected to shared resources. Changes to the land, such as with building houses or hotels, have an impact on infrastructure: roads, water, sewage, parking, and a host of other considerations. If the goal is to make as much money as possible, then wealthy developers or landowners would rather not pay to support social resources. Let the county pay for the roads and the water. In economics, this is the strategy pursued by free riders.

The debate is not only about who pays for the infrastructure, but also what type of infrastructure is being created and who benefits from it, which connects to what kind of neighborhood, and what categories of people. Roads, parking, and water are well-worn issues, although even there the specifics can lead to considerable debates. Should the area be car-friendly? Could there be a vibrant public transportation system? Should there be electric vehicle charging stations? Where should the roads go? Should cul-de-sacs and gated communities be allowed or even encouraged? How should sewage be disposed of, and who should face any potential risks? Where should public parks be created? Should there be a surcharge on rental cars? Should there be homeless shelters? Or short-term rentals? Or businesses? There are also concerns for the health of the soil, the existence of forests, and, of course, beach access.

One way to categorize the varied positions is to distinguish having a grand vision and having an incrementalistic view. Goals and values also become debates over different visions of the future, of what is possible and desirable. The plan may simply be the groundwork for future developers to make more money. But other framing issues are also part of the debate, including climate change, shoreline retreat, the water supply, and the impact of population growth. As a way to limit the possibilities of the plan, some will claim the plan needs to be "realistic," and others will claim the future cannot be controlled. As with other facets of the planning process, it is important to step back and see who is saying what. For instance, when Amfac/JMB Hawaii Vice President Teney Takahashi said in 1995: "There's a misperception that growth can be controlled," the goal was likely to reduce government and community interference in large-scale developments. Some argue agricultural land should be converted to residential land to "accommodate projected growth," even if the projected growth is based on little more than a desire to build more residential developments. On the other hand, those advocating for slow growth are likely those with a stake in the community who see the downside of new projects. By and large, people advocate for their own interests, and use the community plan to support their interests over the interests of others, leaving others to live with the negative impacts of new projects.

The debates permeating the planning process all take place with language and visualizations: the future is imagined, groups are labeled. The plans, regulations, and legal challenges also pick up on the words that are used. Sometimes, older land-use designations, such as those that organized the sugar plantations, continue to be relevant, or at least supported by some. Should water that was used to grow sugar be available for new residential developments on the same land? The variety of possible land use designations is also important. There is a distinction between Agricultural, Residential, and Industrial, but other types and sub-types of land are also talked about and sometimes included in the plan, such as open space, Rural Residential, burial sites, and beach access. In every case, the terms are relevant at any point: from the debates, to the written documents, to the implementation. Finally, it is always possible to challenge what the words actually mean in practice. If they are not clearly defined and enforced, then they are much easier to ignore through loopholes, challenges, or general obfuscation. For those who want their money to be used freely, a confusing plan is almost better than no plan at all.

## HOUSING

While housing is a key element in recent Maui planning documents, there is no real discussion of large hotel developments. That theme fizzled out decades ago after most of the suitable land had already been developed. The basic question now is: what types of structures should be built and for whom? A plan that favors luxury housing will most likely make developers more money, but such a plan will also undermine the existing community. Cheap housing might help preserve the existing community, but developers will not make enough money, and those houses will quickly become either short-term rentals or too expensive to purchase once they are made available to the highest bidder. A beneficial plan for housing should include discussions about the realistic needs of the local community and not to simply create an entryway into the real estate market that allows quick profits through resale.

One thing to note here is the importance of the language used. What, for instance, does "affordable housing" mean? In a sense, all housing is affordable if you can afford it, and so while building affordable housing might have an emotional appeal to some people, it could also be used by developers to justify building luxury houses. Unless there are additional, specific rules involved, affordable housing is not very different from housing. What problem is "affordable housing" supposed to solve? As discussed earlier, the answer depends on who is talking. Generally, the idea is that affordable housing should be housing for the middle class: local workers such as hotel employees, teachers, and everyone else who supports the economic and social activities of the community. The structural problem, however, is that even if affordable housing is affordable to this group of people, it is also affordable to people with a lot more money, and even if the ownership begins with workers in the community, it quickly shifts to rentals, and even vacation rentals, owned by people with more money who may have no connection to the community. Once an "affordable" house is on the open market, only people with enough money can afford it.

In the debates summarized here, there is an interesting move away from using the term "affordable housing" and toward referring to "workforce housing." In this framework, the main question becomes how the house will be used, rather than about how much the house costs. The use of the property has little to do with its affordability. An affordable house can be the home for a working family, but it can also be a long-term rental, a vacation rental, or a gambling den. Workforce housing, on the other hand, speaks to the function of the property, and presumably carries with it limitations on ownership. For instance, some spoke of placing deed restrictions on workforce housing that would limit how the house could be resold so that the house would remain available to people in the workforce.

A key response to longstanding management of workforce housing is that it undermines private property and that it is at odds with what could be labeled as a vibrant housing market. Of course, these are the ideals of people with money who can afford private property and want to engage in the housing market without restrictions. For some, owning property is incidental to the larger game, which is about making more money. Whether workers can afford to live in their community is irrelevant. The workers, as with other members of the community, only become valuable as potential owners or renters—and in West Maui, they typically become commuters who have no place to make them relevant to the conversation.

In the planning debate, the opposite of affordable housing is the gentleman farm, where land previously devoted to growing sugarcane or other export crops is converted into large parcels where the wealthy can build self-indulgent houses. A primary point of reference in these debates here is Plantation Estates, where Brad Paulson proposed changing the designation from Agricultural to

Rural Residential, allowing expensive houses to be built on lots of a few acres. The change made some people a lot of money—especially the original land-owners, the developers, and the eventual owners of the subdivision. The change also reduced the amount of agricultural land in West Maui, diverted water to the lawns and pools of people who could afford multi-million-dollar properties, and had minimal positive impact on the surrounding community.

Terms such as "gentleman's estates" and "gentleman farms" were likely created by public relations firms. Gentleman farms are not real farms, and they are probably not owned by gentlemen. At best, they are upper-middle-class compounds with fruit trees, expensive lawns with shrubbery and a property tax break. Those who are interested should look at the properties on Plantation Club Drive currently for sale or being rented on real estate sites such as Zillow or Redfin. The debate revolves in part around what it means to be a farm, which is a vague enough concept that people can pretend to be farmers, enjoy the tax benefits and isolation, and secure enough water to fill their pool while actually doing little or no farming. As one person supporting the idea of gentleman farms claimed, the owners want the right to farm, "but they do not want the obligation to farm." Of course, if the property is zoned for farming, then there is a sense that farming should be taking place. Those who oppose gentleman's estates sometimes refer to "active agriculture" as opposed to fake farming. However, the wealthy owners do not want to be farmers, or even pay farmers to work the land. They did not buy farmland to become farmers—the return on investment is too low. The goal, instead, is to spend vacation days looking down on Lahaina.

## THE ONGOING FIGHT

If you are keeping score, the process that produces the community plan boils down to who is allowed to do what with the land and who pays for what is done. A park is great. If you are a developer, it is better to have a park right beside your new development and to have the county pay to create and maintain it. The plan is even better if the park is designed so people in your development can walk there, but people outside of the neighborhood have a hard time finding parking. These goals benefit the homeowners, and by implication the developer, but not the public, as the public resources are now converted to private goods.

Again, we can see the community plan is something fought over among people from very different positions with very different goals. Optimistically, the planning process provides the community with some control over the future of their shared spaces. Cynically, the process provides political cover to the developers by appearing to include the community while at the same time directing the discussion to a future that is more favorable for profit and wealthy outsiders. What the plan offers is a tool, or weapon, that can be used to either promote or discourage certain types of development. One result is that opposition to specific developments is funneled into what the plan allows and what the county bureaucracy is willing to enforce. Where outrage was once a viable response to unreasonable development, the range of allowable resistance to development is limited to the proper channels that allow only proper opposition. Input means outrage is no longer acceptable.

A typical development scenario begins with a minimum amount of information released about a project. Resistance can be turned into a "Save the" group, the group is dealt with through a combination of concessions and cash payments, and the plan goes ahead. Dealing with opposition is a cost of doing business, and a "good" compromise will leave the future open for developers or property owners to keep pushing against the opposition to establish the initial plan. A beach access point might be offered, but only at certain times of day or under conditions by which the owner can make it harder and harder for people to use. A developer might lose at one point, but there is always the next plan, always different procedures or tactics. One compromise sets the stage for another compromise that further increases the owner's control over space.

In other words, while developers play the game, they also avoid the rules whenever possible and try to create a game they are more likely to win. For the "Save the" group, the game is a single round. The game played by developers is much longer and expansive—plans can stretch out for decades and shift from one space to another. Developers will always want more opportunities, meaning the ability to change land to their profit, often to the detriment of others.

A basic, if implied, question concerning community planning is: why can't people with money just do what they want? If you live in a community long enough, or listen to those who have, you will likely hear stories of horrible developments. Every neighborhood probably has at least one: on Oʻahu, the Engelstad house in Lanikai and the array of overbuilt properties along Round Top come to mind. On Maui, the house Greg Brown has built in Napili could be added to the list. Each of these buildings involved community objections, fights with local governments, threats to sue, and lots of money. Rules were challenged or ignored. The buildings stand out now and for the foreseeable future, but not in a good way.

The community plan is thus both the result of, and a tool for, struggles between many groups, including residents, government, landowners, corporations, workers, and developers. The list of potential participants is extensive and fluid. Some participants are official and obvious; others are marginal, hidden, or even insidious. Often, the political conversation is distorted by lawyers and public relations firms, typically hired to assert the freedom of the wealthy in spite of community desires. In fact, sorting out what the real issues are, or how the language and rules will be used in the future, can often be difficult. Plans might try to resolve past problems or influence the current clusters of issues, but they are also a starting point for future debates. A chronicle of the current debates, as contained in this book, offers the reader an invaluable reference point for understanding not only where the plan came from, but how it might be implemented and how conversations over the next plan could take shape.

\* \* \*

The devastation caused by the Lahaina Fire of 2023 makes clear that the 2021 West Maui Community Plan is a failed document, not only because it failed to imagine possible threats, but also because the world the plan was created to respond to no longer exists. The situation has changed in fundamental ways: heritage buildings foundational to the plan, or which were in the way, are gone. The relied-upon infrastructure is gone. Hundreds of people are gone. The agreements and understandings that once created possibilities for development and for the community are no longer relevant, even if they might be appealed to for strategic reasons.

The 2021 West Maui Community Plan is a failed document in part because it was not a community plan. It offered certain adjustments in regulations and land designations, but as can even be seen in the discussions, there was little vision. The plan offered incremental changes, largely to the benefit of developers, but the future offered by the plan consisted of: more houses, more people, more tourists. Of course, the lack of vision is understandable. Visions are dangerous. Visions can undermine the assumptions, practices, and power of the present.

Now, after the Lahaina Fire, vision becomes possible. Unavoidable. The 1970s vision of Lahaina as a whaling town, or more accurately as a theme park, is no longer a given. This master narrative, largely based on fantasies of white colonization, was quaint for its time, but is now gone. The buildings are gone. The t-shirts are gone. The whale models are gone. What is left are memories, the ashes of the present, the bones of the ancestors, and potential for the future. Outrage has once again become viable.

There are many more questions that could be asked about how the future will be created, by whom and for whom. The default will be that the future is created by the highest bidder, and the devastation in Lahaina has created the possibility of holding a massive auction in which the people with longstanding ties to the area cannot afford to participate. More people are now aware of the impact of disaster capitalism as a way to lose control over local spaces. The actual future will depend on competing visions shared in a process where only some will be invited to play.

At this point the devastation is overwhelmed by the noise of blame and disinformation. It is easy to be cynical or feel helpless. But the game, more desperate now, continues—and there are opportunities to reimagine the future, reinvent how decisions are made, and reconsider who is allowed to take part.

There will probably be another plan, but only after major decisions have already been made. The discussions, instead, are being carried out in community centers, social media, press conferences, and government offices. Some wealthy people are helping the local community. Other people are trying to capture more land for development. Developers are trying to have rules suspended so buildings can be fast-tracked with little or no oversight. Water rights, which had begun to support local agriculture and Hawaiian communities, are being undermined. The list can be expanded. But each of these threats are also opportunities to engage.

## Back to the Future?

A formal planning process is likely years away, which means individual and group engagement is crucial now.

**Keep track of what is going on**—in the physical spaces, the discussions and the decisions! Good information is seldom the most vocal, and misinformation, whether conspiracy theories or plain public relations campaigns, is often used to confuse. There are many good sources, such as hearings, workshops, and demonstrations.

**Support places for the community to meet.** The physical spaces are important, in part because to change the community, its members must not be isolated.

**Support community groups.** There are a host of groups focused on key issues: the rights of tenants, the management of development, the right to water, the environment, workers' rights, and many more. These groups need help.

They need vocal support. They need their message broadcast widely. And they need to be encouraged to work together.

**Support the people in the community.** A key part of the process is the fight over who is included in the process in the first place. For some, money is key, even if the property was purchased a few weeks ago. For others, connection to the community is more important, even if the person has lived in a rental their entire life and could never purchase property.

**Engage with the government**, which includes not only the governor and the legislature, but also the county council and boards.

**Support legal actions.** Be aware that many of the decisions concerning land use arise from government decisions and regulations that need to be challenged through the courts.

**Support local businesses**, which includes attending cultural and social events that are helping the community to move beyond the devastation. The festivals will return.

**Support positive changes in all the physical spaces.** Much attention has been given to saving the Old Banyan Tree as a symbol of survival. Some attention has also been paid to restoring Moku'ula and the surrounding pond, Mokuhinia. What might be built around the Mokuhinia wetlands, if they are in fact restored, is an open question. Beyond that, however, will be a thousand other decisions over what is done with the land, with the use, with the design, and with the impact that specific buildings will have.

In other words, plan for different futures.

*'A'ole 'o ia mau nō.*

# Further Reading

Collins, Lance D., and Bianca K. Isaki. 2016. *Tourism Impacts West Maui*. Lahaina: North Beach-West Maui Benefit Fund, Inc.

Isaki, Bianca K., and Lance D. Collins, eds. 2019. *Social Change in West Maui*. Lahaina: North Beach-West Maui Benefit Fund, Inc.

Klieger, P. C. 1998. *Moku'ula: Maui's Sacred Island*. Honolulu: Bishop Museum Press.

# Appendix

**WEST MAUI
COMMUNITY PLAN
(1996)**

Maui County Council

# TABLE OF CONTENTS

# PART I

# INTRODUCTION OF THE WEST MAUI COMMUNITY PLAN

### A. Purpose of the West Maui Community Plan

The West Maui Community Plan, one of nine (9) community plans for Maui County, reflects current and anticipated conditions in West Maui and advances planning goals, objectives, policies and implementation considerations to guide decision-making in the region through the year 2010. The West Maui Community Plan provides specific recommendations to address the goals, objectives and policies contained in the General Plan, while recognizing the values and unique attributes of the region, in order to enhance the region's overall living environment.

The Maui County General Plan, first adopted in 1980, and updated in 1990, sets forth goals, directions and strategies for meeting the long-term social, economic, environmental and land use needs of the County. Similarly, the West Maui Community Plan, first adopted in 1982 as the Lahaina Community Plan, has been updated in 1992-93. As a part of the update, the plan was renamed the "West Maui" Community Plan in order to reinforce the regional nature of the plan.

### B. The Role of the Community Plan in the Planning Process

For Maui County, the General Plan and the community plans are strategic planning documents which guide government actions and decision-making. Both the General Plan and the community plans are part of a planning hierarchy which includes, as primary components, the Hawaii State Plan and State Functional Plans. (See Exhibit "A")

Mutually supporting goals, objectives, policies and implementing actions contained in the Hawaii State Plan, State Functional Plans, Maui County General Plan and the West Maui Community Plan provide for optimum planning effectiveness and benefits for the residents of the West Maui Community Plan region.

Implementation of the goals, objectives and policies contained in the Community Plan are defined through specific implementing actions, also set forth in each community plan. Implementing actions as well as broader policy recommendations are effectuated through various processes, including zoning, capital improvements program, and the County budgeting process.

1

## C. The 1992 Community Plan Update

The update process was driven by the work of the Lahaina Citizens Advisory Committee (CAC). This 14 member panel met a total of 17 times during a 225-day deliberation process to identify, formulate and recommend appropriate revisions to the then Lahaina Community Plan. The CAC carefully reviewed the 1982 version of the Community Plan, reshaping the plan to create a viable document which will serve the West Maui region through the turn of the century.

The update process incorporated technical studies and assessments. The results of these four studies were used by the Department of Planning and CAC to understand possible future conditions and needs. The technical studies consisted of the following:

1.  A *Socio-Economic Forecast* which projects population, employment and housing characteristics through the year 2010 for each community plan region;

2.  A *Land Use Forecast* which provides a measure of existing and future vacant and undeveloped lands (by community plan land use designation) for each community plan region;

3.  An *Infrastructure Assessment* which identifies infrastructure (e.g., roadways, drainage, water, wastewater, telephone and electrical systems) limits and opportunities in high-growth community plan regions; and

4.  A *Public Facilities and Service Assessment* which identifies public facilities and services (e.g., schools, parks, police and fire protection, hospital and solid waste disposal services), and their limits and opportunities in high-growth community plan regions.

Following the 225-day CAC, process, the CAC's recommendations were submitted to the Department of Planning. The Department of Planning prepared the revised Community Plan, based on the work of the CAC. The revised Community Plan was forwarded to the Maui Planning Commission for public hearing and review, and then sent to the County Council for further review and adoption by ordinance. This process is summarized graphically in Exhibit "B".

2

Exhibit "A"

County Planning Hierarchy

3

Exhibit "B"

Community Plan Review Process

4

# PART II

# DESCRIPTION OF THE REGION AND ITS PROBLEMS AND OPPORTUNITIES

---

A.  **Planning Area Description**

   1.  **General Description of Region and Existing Community Plan Boundary**

   The West Maui Community Plan covers the entire Lahaina Judicial District located on the western slopes and coastal plain of West Maui. Its common boundary with the Wailuku Judicial District begins at the southern shore of West Maui about 3/4 of a mile west of Papawai Point. Beginning at this point, the West Maui region's boundary runs mauka along the centerline of the Manawainui Gulch to the ridge line of the West Maui Mountains. The boundary then continues along the ridgelines in a northerly direction to Eke Crater, and then due north along Poelua Gulch to the northern shoreline of West Maui.

   Existing population and urban settlements in the region are located at Olowalu, at Lahaina and in a band along the shoreline between the northern end of Lahaina and Kapalua. In some areas, existing urban development extends mauka. At Lahaina town, settlement patterns extend mauka at Wahikuli and along Lahainaluna Road. This development pattern is set against a dramatic backdrop of rolling sugar cane and pineapple fields and the West Maui Mountains.

   The region has seen significant growth in virtually all aspects of the community. Resident population has increased from 5,524 in 1970, to 10,284 in 1980, to 14,574 in the most recent census (1990). More dramatic are the increases in visitor units over the same period, from 1,826 units in 1970, to 5,357 units in 1980, to 9,285 units in 1990.

   Development, for the most part, reflects the region's visitor and agricultural industries. Visitor accommodations are located along the shoreline with necessary support facilities and residential communities. These activity centers include the Lahaina town, Kaanapali, Honokowai, Napili and Kapalua communities. Kaanapali and Kapalua are important visitor

5

destination anchors, while the old Lahaina town with its historic character and charm serves as the region's visitor, service, commercial and residential center. Small plantation camps and agricultural communities are located further inland. (See Exhibit "C".)

2. **Historic and Environmental Context of the Region**

The West Maui Community Plan region includes two major historical land divisions, the Lahaina and the Ka`anapali districts. The region historically has been a significant agricultural area from prior to western contact. The town of Lahaina was for a period of time the capital of the Hawaiian Kingdom and a major port of call for the Pacific whaling fleet in the mid-19th century. The region was known for the Hono-a-Pi`ilani, the bays of Pi`ilani, for which the major highway through the region is named.

The traditional district of Lahaina included the leeward half of West Maui from Honokowai to Maalaea (the southern portion of this area is not within the West Maui Community Plan region). The Lahaina District is comprised of 21 *ahupua`a*, most of which were small and concentrated around the population center in Lahaina. Lahaina town once contained numerous brackish ponds and springs, and was a very productive taro growing area. The first lighthouse was erected at Lahaina and the town became an important center of commerce and trade in the 19th century. For a time, Lahaina served as the capital of the Hawaiian Kingdom and Hawaiian royalty established a number of important sites there, including the sacred island of Moku`ula, located at the site of the present Malu-ulu-olele Park.

The influx of westerners was greater in Lahaina than elsewhere on Maui, and it served as the primary base for missionary expansion. The area also served as a major port of call for the Pacific whaling fleet during the mid-19th century. Many historic sites and structures date from these early western influences, including the Baldwin House, Hale Pa`i (and Lahainaluna School), and the Seaman's Hospital. As in the rest of Hawai`i, the late 19th century witnessed the coming of the plantation era. This brought along with it the architecture and cultural diversity of this period as can be seen in the Pioneer Inn, the Wo Hing Society Building, and various other structures and buildings.

To the south of Lahaina are the three large *ahupua`a* of Launiupoko, Olowalu and Ukumehame. These lands still contain evidence of Hawaiian agricultural terraces above the canefields and in undisturbed areas. *Heiau* sites, complexes of temporary habitation, petroglyphs and small shrines are also present in each of these *ahupua`a*. Post-contact sites include the Lahaina Pali trail (being developed for public access by the Na Ala Hele Trails and Access program) and the Olowalu church ruins.

6

North of Lahaina is the Ka`anapali district, from Honokowai to Hulu island, which contains 15 *ahupua`a* and the *kalana* of Kahakuloa. Again, the extreme portion of this traditional district (in the area around Kahakuloa) is not within the current West Maui Community Plan region. Within this district are five of the famed Hono-a-Pi`ilani, the bays of King Pi`ilani, including Honokohau, Honolua, Honokahua, Honokeana and Honokowai. Four of these areas contained perennial streams that, along with Kahana Stream, were extensively used for irrigated taro cultivation. Honokohau Valley still supports taro cultivation and vestiges of historic agricultural complexes can be found within the undeveloped portions of the other valleys. *Heiau* sites are still present along the coastal ridges in Honokohau and Honolua. An extensive pre-contact sand dune burial site was discovered at Honokahua (within the Kapalua Resort) and is being preserved.

One of Maui's first coffee plantations was started in Honokohau and Honolua and later became Honolua Ranch. In 1915, H. P. Baldwin moved the ranch headquarters to Honokahua, and the village which grew around it was called Honolua (the Honolua Store, which also moved to this site in 1915, is still in operation).

7

Exhibit "C"

8

## B.    Identification of Major Problems and Opportunities of the Region

This description of key problems and opportunities as formulated by the Lahaina CAC provides the underlying basis for the planning goals, objectives and policies which are described in the Community Plan.

### 1.    Problems

*THREATS TO THE ENVIRONMENT AND THE POTENTIAL LOSS OF OPEN SPACE.*  The natural environment is an important aspect of the region's economy, lifestyle and recreational needs.  Therefore, potential threats to the environment are seen as major problems.  This includes any developments or projects that may have potential adverse impacts on water quality, whether it be potable water or nearshore and offshore waters.  Strong programs should be established and pursued in order to prevent degradation of the environment.

As the region develops, the importance of open space, especially along the shoreline, increases.  Existing areas of open space, including agricultural lands and gulches, should be viewed as a resource which should be protected and enhanced.  There is also a need to protect view corridors and scenic vistas and design landscape buffers along the major roadways in such a manner as to provide periodic views of the mountains and ocean.

*LAND    USE    CONTROLS    AND    COMMUNITY    PLAN IMPLEMENTATION.*  The integrity of the Community Plan and the existing system of land use controls must be preserved and enhanced in order to ensure sensible levels of development and growth in the region.  The implementation of the Community Plan has been lacking and community input should be actively solicited prior to each proposed amendment to the Community Plan.  Projects have been permitted that were inconsistent with the Community Plan and agriculturally designated lands are being used for other than agricultural purposes.  Other specific problem areas include the inconsistency of zoning and that development has preceded infrastructural improvements.

*INFRASTRUCTURE.*  Inadequate infrastructure and the failure of existing infrastructural systems are seen as major problems for the region.  Infrastructural improvements need to be constructed prior to the issuance of building permits in order to prevent the lag time needed for infrastructure to catch up with  development.  Water resources should be conserved and new sources need to be developed.  The closing of the region's only landfill presents a potential challenge to efficient solid waste management.  There is

9

a need to develop a public transportation system and to support the development of more bikeways.

***GROWTH***. Unconstrained growth places severe stress on infrastructure systems, the availability of housing, environmental and natural resources in the region and the social fabric of the community. The region's de facto population is made up of three major components: the residents who live here, the tourists who stay here and the commuters who travel back and forth to jobs in the region. Unconstrained growth of any of these groups adversely affects the quality of life within the region. The plan needs to address resident and de facto population levels, density and distribution.

The following other areas of importance were also identified:

- LONG TERM STABILIZATION OF THE ECONOMY. The tourist industry provides a strong economic base. Yet, the industry is subject to seasonal fluctuations, increasing competition and uncertainties in national and international economic conditions. There is a need to stabilize the economy of the region and to protect and improve the visitor experience. A stable economy also involves the need to actively promote a diversification of the region's economic base. There is a need to provide more light industrial lands.

- AFFORDABLE HOUSING. There is an ongoing need to provide affordable housing in the region. However, care should be taken not to repeat mistakes made in the past. It is also important to provide a wider range of affordable housing choices in order to serve the full spectrum of residents (from single persons to large families) and to seek to address the problem of homelessness.

- SOCIAL CONDITIONS. There is a need to control the increased crime rate, to address the problems of youth at risk, to promote activities for better use of spare time, and to create a wider range of educational opportunities. There is a need to increase the level of health and social services provided in the region.

  There is also the need to preserve and protect the cultural diversity and remaining rural lifestyles within the region. Archaeological, cultural and historic resources need to be preserved and interpreted to maintain a link with the past as the region moves into the future.

2.  **Opportunities**

**NATURAL ENVIRONMENT.** The natural environment is a major asset of the region -- the open spaces and stretches of shoreline between the south boundary of the district and Puamana and from Kapalua to Nakalele Point, the expansive landscape of agricultural and natural open space areas against the backdrop of the West Maui Mountains, the warm climate, abundant water resources, nice sandy beaches, and clean ocean environment. The natural environment of the Lahaina region characterizes much of what is special about West Maui as a place to live and to visit.

The marine and nearshore environment and open space areas are important assets of the region that should be protected and preserved for the long-term. Also reuse of treated effluent and the reduction in sedimentation of nearshore waters must be pursued to protect and enhance the region's land, water and marine environments.

**STABILITY OF THE ECONOMIC BASE.** The success of an urban community relates to the stability of its economy. In West Maui, sugar, pineapple and tourism are the primary industries. With the dependence on the visitor industry and the ever-present uncertainties facing agriculture, it is recognized that the economic base is potentially vulnerable and must be nurtured in a responsible manner to insure stable employment opportunities for residents and their descendants.

It is therefore important to maintain a stable economic base by encouraging the upgrading of existing visitor facilities; pursuing diversified economic opportunities; insuring responsible and sustainable growth to provide a range of job opportunities so that the young people can remain in or return to the community; encouraging alternate energy production (i.e. solar, wind and biomass); identifying potential uses of federal, state and county lands to benefit the community; and in general, creating opportunities for more self-sufficiency.

**HISTORY OF THE LAHAINA REGION.** History tells us much about a community -- what it is and where it has come from. Lahaina has a rich history dating back to the times of pre-contact Hawaii, the Hawaiian Monarchy, the missionaries, the whaling industry and the sugar and pineapple plantations. Each successive passage of an era has added to the cultural richness of the community. And through the tireless efforts of numerous organizations and individuals in the community, much has been done to restore historic sites and to preserve the historic character of Lahaina town.

11

It is important to preserve and protect the region's cultural resources and traditional lifestyles, including the agricultural pursuits of Native Hawaiians in Honokohau Valley.

**_SYSTEM OF LAND USE CONTROLS_**. The implementation of a community plan is guided by a system of land use controls and regulations. There are opportunities to improve this regulatory system, in terms of procedures and programs implementing policies for beach access, preservation of open space, use of agricultural lands, and zoning consistent with the Community Plan's land use map.

C.   **Interregional Issues**

In the consideration of possible amendments to the Lahaina Community Plan, there were several issues brought up by the CAC which affect other regions or require a county- or island-wide analysis. This section lists these issues which suggest interregional, county-wide or island-wide analysis.

1.   The need for "balanced" island-wide growth;
2.   The need for expanded boating and harbor facilities, especially along the leeward coast of Maui; and
3.   The responsible use of the county's natural resources.

# PART III

# POLICY RECOMMENDATIONS, IMPLEMENTING ACTIONS, AND STANDARDS FOR THE WEST MAUI REGION

## A. Intended Effects of the West Maui Community Plan

Policy recommendations contained herein express the long-term visions for the West Maui community. They will be used in formulating and prioritizing programs. Most significantly, the recommendations establish a long-range land use pattern for the region.

For these reasons, the West Maui Community Plan will play a key role in directing economic growth and stabilization for the West Maui region. Accordingly, the population of West Maui will, to a large degree, be affected by the policy recommendations contained in the Community Plan.

Population projections, while subject to a host of variables and external factors, provide a useful benchmark for conceptualizing growth in a region and providing a measure of the effectiveness of the West Maui Community Plan and future strategies to direct and manage growth. Population forecasts were utilized to provide some insight into long-term trends and likely future land use demands.

For the year 2010, the population forecasts projected a West Maui resident population of 22,633 if growth is unconstrained, and a resident population of 21,149 if growth is constrained. Additionally, the forecasts projected an average visitor census of 37,734 if growth is unconstrained, and a visitor census of 31,775 if growth is constrained. For the purposes of this plan, the "constrained" forecasts shall serve as the guidelines in determining future land uses and community development needs in the West Maui region.

As with population, the policy recommendations of the West Maui Community Plan and any future amendments to the plan will have a direct effect on the sequence and pattern of growth in the region. The plan recognizes Lahaina town as the regional center of West Maui and strives to balance future growth with the protection of the environment. The quality of the region's natural and marine environment is an inherent aspect of what West Maui represents to its residents and visitors alike. Accommodating a sufficient supply of land for affordable housing and parks is another objective of this Community Plan. The plan also recognizes the need to protect and preserve historic, archaeological and cultural resources for present and future generations.

Any interpretation of the policies of this plan or any amendment proposed to this plan shall be based in large part to the specified intended effects of this plan. These are:

1. Allocate adequate open space for public recreational activities, especially within the urbanized areas of the region and along the shoreline.

2. Slow the rate of growth and stabilize the economy.

3. Protect the natural resources of the region and promote environmentally sound uses and activities.

4. Exert more control on the timing and patterns of development within the region through the community plan, zoning, and the permitting process.

5. Encourage infill in order to protect agriculture and mauka open spaces.

B. **Goals, Objectives, Policies and Implementing Actions**

The West Maui Community Plan sets forth goals which are statements identifying preferred future conditions. The objectives and policies specify steps and measures to be taken to achieve the goals. Implementing actions identify specific program or project requirements to conduct tasks necessary for the successful implementation of the plan. The pattern and mix of land uses provided for within this Community Plan shall be identified on the "Land Use Map".

## LAND USE

### Goal

An attractive, well-planned community with a mixture of compatible land uses in appropriate areas to accommodate the future needs of residents and visitors in a manner that provides for the stable social and economic well-being of residents and the preservation and enhancement of the region's open space areas and natural environmental resources.

### Objectives and Policies for the West Maui Region in General

1. Protect and enhance the quality of the marine environment.

2.  Preserve and enhance the mountain and coastal scenic vistas and the open space areas of the region.

3.  Ensure that appropriate lands are available to support the region's present and future agricultural activities.

4.  Establish an appropriate supply of urban land within the region to meet the needs of the community over the next 20 years. The Community Plan and its map shall define the urban growth limits for the region and all zoning requests and/or proposed land uses and developments shall be consistent with the West Maui Community Plan and its land use map.

5.  Preserve the current State Conservation District and the current State Agriculture District boundaries in the planning region, in accordance with this Community Plan and its land use map. Lands north of Kapalua and south of Puamana to' the region's district boundaries should ensure the preservation of traditional lifestyles, historic sites, agriculture, recreational activities and open space.

6.  Special Permits in the State Agricultural Districts may be allowed only: (1) to accommodate public and quasi-public uses; (2) public facility uses such as utility installation, landfills and sewer treatment plants whose location is determined by technical considerations; (3) uses which are clearly accessory and subordinate to a principal agricultural use on the property; and (4) extractive industries, such as quarrying, where the operation does not adversely affect the environment or nearby agricultural uses.

7.  Provide for specific criteria for the subdivision of lands designated for agricultural use in order to control the potential loss of productive agricultural lands and the open space resource.

8.  Where possible, relocate the Honoapiilani Highway south of Puamana in order to reduce potential inundation and disruption of service due to storm-generated wave action. Where the highway is relocated for the purpose stated, lands makai of the new alignment shall be designated Open Space (OS) or Park (PK) to provide for ocean-related recreational use. Notwithstanding the foregoing, continued agriculture use shall be allowed within these areas.

9.  Preserve the existing domestic, small farm, business, youth care, and recreational uses from Honokahua Bay to the district's north boundary and from Puamana to the district's south boundary. Support

15

continuation of the traditional agriculture activities in Honokohau Valley by recognizing Native Hawaiian water rights protected by Article XII, Section 7, of the State Constitution, and Section 1.1, Hawaii Revised Statutes.

10.   Provide and maintain parks and beach access for the present and future needs of residents and visitors. For the areas outside Lahaina town, establish or expand parks and public shoreline areas to include but not limited to the following:

    a.   The proposed Napili regional park between the Honoapiilani Highway and the Lower Honoapiilani Road and adjacent to the Kapalua Bay Golf Course comprising an area of approximately 50 acres.

    b.   The development of a public beach park at Olowalu near Camp Pecusa for camping and ocean-related recreational and educational activities. The final boundaries of this park shall be determined in consultation with the landowner. However, if agriculture in the area is decreased by 50 percent, 20 acres of park land shall be considered for addition to the 10 acres of park land currently designated in the Land Use Map.

    c.   The proposed Mahinahina regional park on approximately 50 acres of land below the Kapalua/West Maui Airport.

11.   Recognize the following approved major masterplanned affordable housing developments. Approvals of these projects provide that no less than 60 percent of the housing units will be in the affordable price range. Lands makai of the proposed Lahaina Bypass Highway shall be developed prior to those lands mauka of the bypass. The land use designation of Agriculture (AG) shall apply to all portions of the following projects not fully developed under and pursuant to Hawaii Revised Statutes Act 15, Session Laws of Hawaii, 1988.

    a.   Villages of Leiali`i--This project is planned by the State Housing Finance Development Corporation and situated mauka of Honoapiilani Highway in the vicinity of the Lahaina Civic Center and Wahikuli Terrace comprising an area of approximately 1,120 acres. The planned residential community will include approximately 4,813 housing units to be developed in phases, an 18-hole golf course, two elementary school sites, neighborhood business commercial uses, church, child care, recreational/park uses, and other public uses.

16

b.    Puukolii Village--This project is proposed by AMFAC/JMB, a Hawaii Corporation, in the vicinity of the former Puukolii Village and comprises an area of approximately 299 acres. The proposed residential community is to include approximately 1,700 housing units to be developed in phases as well as sites for neighborhood commercial uses, hospital/emergency medical facilities, child care center, church, elderly housing, elementary school, and a community park.

12.    Designate 10 acres of land mauka of Honoapiilani Highway near the Civic Center for Public/Quasi-public use as a site for future public parking.

13.    Maintain the current size, scale and level of services at the airstrip in Mahinahina through appropriate zoning conditions.

### *Objectives and Policies for Lahaina Town*

1.    The area bounded by Honoapiilani Highway and Front Street define Lahaina town. Within this core, allow higher density commercial and civic activities with lower density residential uses on the periphery to emphasize the importance of Lahaina town as the regional service center and an attraction to residents and visitors alike.

2.    Emphasize visitor amenities, regional commercial activities and facilities which convey community identity along Front Street between Baker and Prison Streets.

3.    Provide resident-oriented commercial uses along Wainee Street from Baker to Dickenson Streets.

4.    Concentrate multifamily dwelling units around the central commercial district in the following locations:

   a.    At the north end of Lahaina town between Front Street and Honoapiilani Highway, from Kahoma Stream to Baker Street.

   b.    Toward the south end of Lahaina town along Wainee Street, generally from Lahainaluna Road to Shaw Street.

5.    Provide for a mixture of residential and commercial uses along the makai side of Wainee Street, between Dickenson and Prison Streets.

17

6.  Preserve the two-story height limit on all buildings in the approximately 8.6 acres that are now the site of the Maui Islander.

7.  Provide for commercial uses in the following areas:

    a.  At the north end of Lahaina town makai of Front Street from Kahoma Stream to Kapunakea Street.

    b.  In the vicinity of Panaewa Street and bounded by Wainee Street, Lahainaluna Road, Luakini Street and Dickenson Street.

    c.  Along Dickenson Street between Mill Street and Front Street.

8.  Preserve the area makai of Front Street between Market and Papelekane Streets for the continued location of the library and open space.

9.  Preserve the area bounded by Prison, Front, Shaw and Wainee Streets for residential, park and public/quasi-public uses.

10. Preserve the remaining single family residential uses north of Kapunakea Street; between Ala Moana and Papalaua Streets and south of Shaw Street.

11. Establish, expand and maintain parks, public and private open spaces, public facilities, cemeteries, and public shoreline areas within Lahaina town.  Major park spaces to be maintained, expanded, or established are:

    a.  A marine-oriented park at Mala Wharf along the south side of Kahoma Stream with provision for a second boat launch ramp.

    b.  A new community-oriented park along the south bank of Kahoma Stream and between Front Street and Honoapiilani Highway.

    c.  A shoreline park at Puunoa Point adjacent to the Jodo Mission, provided that the cemetery is appropriately relocated.

    d.  An urban park along the south side of Dickenson Street, between Luakini and Front Streets, maintaining the historic character of structures and landscaping.

18

e.   The park space behind the existing small boat harbor, containing the Banyan Court and Kamehameha III School.

f.   Restoration of and improvements to Malu-ulu-olele Park and Moku`ula Island at the corner of Front and Shaw Streets.

g.   Maintain Armory Park without sacrificing additional land for parking.

h.   The continued development and expansion of the park at Wainee into a regional recreational and sports facility.

i.   The development of a "gateway" park mauka of Honoapiilani Highway near the southern end of the Lahaina Watershed Drainage Improvement Project.

12.  Provide parking that is adequately marked or assigned and conveniently located in retail commercial shopping areas, at public parking sites and at major commercial complexes. Where appropriate, multi-decked parking structures may be allowed. Principal parking locations include:

a.   Expanded public parking south of Prison Street between Front and Luakini Streets.

b.   Public parking north of Dickenson Street between Luakini and Wainee Streets.

c.   Parking at the shopping complex within Baker, Front, Papalaua, and Wainee Streets.

## Implementing Actions

1.   Plan, design and construct a regional recreational and sports complex, including all-weather track and community meeting facilities, in the Wainee area near the existing swimming pool and youth center complexes.

2.   Identify and inventory exceptional open space resources and viewsheds for protection via covenants, easements, and other planning tools.

3.   Develop and implement a directed and managed growth plan and strategies to guide and coordinate future development.

19

4. Install signs clearly identifying public parking in Lahaina town.

5. Establish and enforce agricultural subdivision criteria.

6. Establish a "Watershed Protection Overlay Plan" for West Maui and propose and adopt appropriate ordinances to implement the plan. The purpose of the overlay plan is to insure the protection of (1) the quantity and quality of drinking water supplies; (2) the quality of coastal waters and marine resources; and (3) the long term economic viability of the community. The overlay plan should include specifications for drainage, erosion control, water conservation, wastewater reuse, and shoreline setbacks as needed to supplement existing policies and rules.

7. Continue to study the feasibility of a West Maui multi-purpose facility designed for public, educational, cultural, and convention uses.

## ENVIRONMENT

### Goal

A clean and attractive physical, natural and marine environment in which man-made developments on or alterations to the natural and marine environment are based on sound environmental and ecological practices, and important scenic and open space resources are preserved and protected for public use and enjoyment.

### Objectives and Policies

1. Protect all waters and wetland resources. Such resources provide open space and habitat for plant and animal life in the aquatic environment. They are also important for flood control and natural landscape.

2. Preserve agricultural lands and open space with particular emphasis on natural coastal areas along major highways.

3. Protect the quality of nearshore and offshore waters. Monitor outfall systems, streams and drainage ways and maintain water quality standards. Continue to investigate, and implement appropriate measures to mitigate, excessive growth and proliferation of algae in nearshore and offshore waters.

4.  Emphasize land management techniques such as natural landscaping, regular maintenance of streams and drainage ways and siltation basins, avoidance of development in flood-prone areas, and other measures that maintain stream water quality. Wherever feasible, such management techniques should be used instead of structural solutions, such as building artificial stream channels or diversion of existing natural streams.

5.  Encourage soil erosion prevention measures and the installation of siltation basins to minimize downstream sedimentation and degradation of nearshore and offshore water quality.

6.  Integrate stream channels, gulches and other areas deemed unsuitable for development into the region's open space system for the purposes of safety, open space relief, greenways for public use and visual separation. Existing development of these stream channels, gulches and other areas shall be maintained and shall not be expanded. Drainage channels and siltation basins should not be considered for building sites, but used, rather, for public open space.

The following major streams and gulches, as named on the United States Geologic Survey topographic maps (Lahaina and Honolua, Hawaii, 7.5 minute series, 1:24,000 scale), are to be kept as open space:

a.  Kahoma Stream
b.  Wahikuli/Hahakea Gulch
c.  Honokowai Stream
d.  Mahinahina Stream
e.  Kahana Stream
f.  Kaopala Gulch
g.  Honokeana Stream
h.  Napili Stream (2-3)
i.  Napili Stream (4-5)
j.  Honokahua Stream
k.  Mokupea Gulch
l.  Honolua Stream
m.  Papua Gulch
n.  Kauaula Stream

For other natural drainageways that discharge to the ocean during part of the year, their natural filter functions shall be preserved. The preservation of these natural filter functions may be accomplished by the use of structural controls or solutions in accord with accepted

21

engineering standards or rules as may be adopted by the Department of Public Works and Waste Management, and includes the use of best management practices such as desilting basins, moderation of flow velocity, subsurface infiltration systems, and baffles.

7. Preserve, protect and/or nourish the shoreline sand dune formations throughout the planning region. These topographic features are essential to beach preservation and a significant element of the natural setting that should be protected.

8. Promote public/private initiatives in the maintenance, and, where appropriate, landscaping of drainage ways.

9. Promote recycling programs to reduce solid waste disposal in landfills.

10. Encourage park, golf course, landscape and agricultural uses of treated effluent. Plan for wastewater reuse in the design of new parks, golf courses, and open spaces.

11. Prohibit the construction of vertical seawalls and revetments except as may be permitted by rules adopted by the Maui Planning Commission governing the issuance of Shoreline Management Area (SMA) emergency permits, and encourage beach nourishment by building dunes and adding sand as a sustainable alternative.

12. Prohibit the dumping of heavy metals, oil and untreated sewage on land and in the nearshore waters and provide accessible and safe disposal for hazardous materials.

13. Promote the planting of trees and other landscape planting to enhance streetscapes and the built environment.

14. Protect the shoreline and beaches by preserving waterfront land as open space wherever possible. This protection shall be based on a study and analysis of the rate of shoreline retreat plus a coastal hazard buffer zone. Where new major waterfront structures or developments are to be approved, preservation should be assured for 50-100 years by employing a shoreline setback based on the rate established by the appropriate study.

15. Promote drainage and stormwater management practices that prevent flooding and protect coastal water quality.

16. Create a coastal improvement district emphasizing the equal preservation of both coastal lands and beaches through the adoption of zoning and land use controls that encourage compatible development in safe areas, provide for the long-term economic needs of beach and dune nourishment and maintenance, and enable strategic retreat from the coast wherever feasible through a program of land acquisition, economic incentives, and specific construction guidelines.

### Implementing Actions

1. Develop and maintain a program to identify and preserve the district's environmentally sensitive areas.

2. Establish and maintain programs which control invasive alien plant and animal species.

3. Periodically maintain and monitor outfall systems, streams and drainage ways for compliance with water quality standards.

4. Continue to investigate and monitor algae bloom conditions in West Maui's offshore waters and implement appropriate mitigative measures.

5. Plan, design, construct and regularly maintain siltation basins within major drainage ways and subdivision developments in order to enhance stream and offshore water quality.

6. Study the desirability of a National Seashore designation for West Maui.

7. Assess the need for standards for the siting of large-scale energy generation systems, including alternative energy systems such as wind turbine and photovoltaic arrays, in order to mitigate environmental and visual impacts.

## ECONOMIC ACTIVITY

### Goal

A diversified economy that provides a range of stable employment opportunities for residents, allows for desired commercial services for the community, and supports the existing visitor and agricultural industries, all in a manner that will enhance both the community's quality of life and the environment.

## Objectives and Policies

1. Promote a diversified economic base which offers long term employment to West Maui residents, and maintains overall stability in economic activity in the areas of:

   a. Visitor accommodations.
   b. Visitor-related service/commercial services.
   c. Recreation-related service/commercial services.
   d. Resident-related service/commercial services.
   e. Light industrial activities, including diversification into "clean" industries.
   f. Agriculture.

2. Provide for the preservation and enhancement of agriculture.

   a. Maintain the land acreage required to sustain present and future agricultural operations and open space.
   b. Prevent urbanization of agricultural lands to the greatest extent possible.
   c. Encourage maintenance and development of water sources for agricultural activities which do not conflict with domestic demand for potable water.
   d. Discourage use of agricultural lands for non-agricultural purposes.
   e. Adopt ordinances to establish appropriate standards for agricultural lands.

3. Expand light industrial and service commercial activities in appropriate locations to accommodate the region's needs.

   a. Enhance Lahaina town's role as the regional center for resident-related commercial and professional services.
   b. Encourage neighborhood commercial activities and professional services to serve existing and future residents.
   c. Encourage a diversity of visitor-oriented commercial offerings at the resort destinations and as a major component of Lahaina town.
   d. Encourage the development of marine-related light industrial businesses to service the boating community.

24

e. Encourage strict compliance with the Lahaina Historic District Ordinance in order to preserve and enhance the visitor experience thus maintaining economic stability within the region.

4. Maintain a stable and viable visitor industry.

   a. Limit visitor facilities to the existing planned resorts of Kaanapali and Kapalua as designated on the land use map and coordinate future growth with development of adequate infrastructure capacity and housing for employees.

   b. Encourage the renovation and improvement of existing visitor facilities without a substantial increase in the room count. Promote activities and industries that compliment and support the use of existing visitor industry facilities, such as sporting events, eco-tourism and conferences.

5. Promote the use of local products, and encourage the employment of local residents.

   a. Encourage local industries, businesses and consumers to purchase products grown or made in the region.
   b. Support programs that encourage visitors to purchase local products.
   c. Urge the adoption of a program to promote the employment of local residents.

### Implementing Actions

1. Evaluate, formulate and implement strategies for economic diversification in West Maui.

2. Quantify the economic value of agricultural lands and open space as a factor in resident and visitor satisfaction and as appropriate, incorporate this data in regional socio-economic assessments.

## CULTURAL RESOURCES

### Goal

To preserve, protect and restore those cultural resources and sites that best represent and exemplify the Lahaina region's pre-contact, Hawaiian Monarchy, missionary and plantation history.

*Objectives and Policies*

1.  Preserve and protect significant archaeological, historical and cultural resources that are unique in the State of Hawaii and Island of Maui.

2.  Foster an awareness of the diversity and importance of cultural resources and of the history of Lahaina.

3.  Encourage and protect traditional shoreline and mountain access, cultural practices and rural/agricultural lifestyles. Ensure adequate access to our public shoreline areas for public recreation, including lateral continuity.

4.  Establish programs to restore, maintain and interpret significant cultural districts, sites and artifacts in both natural and museum settings.

5.  Promote distinct cultural resources as an identifying characteristic of the region.

6.  Ensure that new projects or developments address potential impacts on archaeological, historical, and cultural resources and identify all cultural resources located within the project area as part of initial project studies. Further require that all proposed activity adequately mitigate potential adverse impacts on cultural resources.

7.  Encourage the ongoing state and national register nomination process, by government and private property owners, to increase awareness and protection of sites and districts.

8.  Support public and private efforts to inventory, evaluate and register historic and archaeological sites to expand the public's knowledge of the region's cultural resources.

9.  Protect and preserve Honokohau Valley's historic and traditional use for domestic and agricultural activities. Ensure the availability of sufficient quantities and quality of water for these activities by recognizing Native Hawaiian water rights and traditional access protected by Article XII, Section 7, of the State Constitution, and Section 1.1, Hawaii Revised Statutes.

10. Ensure that site identification and interpretation is not damaging to any historical or archaeological sites.

11. Recognize the importance of buffer areas to enhance and protect historical or archaeological sites.

12. Recognize areas of historic vegetation and significant native vegetation zones as cultural resources.

13. Encourage community stewardship of historic sites.

14. Encourage the development of "cultural parks" for visitation and education.

15. Encourage cultural and educational programs to perpetuate Hawaiian and other ethnic heritages.

16. General site types and areas that should be flagged for possible preservation include the following:

    a. Ancient trails/old government roads
    b. Fishponds
    c. Landings
    d. Nearshore marine cultural resources
    e. Stream valley areas
       1) habitation complexes (shoreline and interior)
       2) lo`i and `auwai
       3) terraces
    f. Significant native vegetation zones
    g. Plantation ditch systems
    h. Religious structures (shrines, churches and heiau)
    i. Old bridges
    j. Plantation camps
    k. Plantation era structures and homes
    l. Petroglyphs
    m. Burials

17. Important site types and areas in the West Maui region include but are not limited to the following:

    a. Lahaina Pali trail
    b. Olowalu Church ruins
    c. Olowalu heiau
    d. Stream valley sites
    e. Plantation ditch system
    f. Sites and structures within the National Historic District

27

g.   Plantation buildings
h.   Lo`i terraces and `auwai
i.   Ukumehame complex
j.   Launiupoko complex
k.   Moku`ula Island
l.   Camp Pecusa
m.   Honolua archaeological district
n.   Honokohau Valley
o.   Olowalu petroglyphs
p.   Pioneer Mill
q.   Lahainaluna High School
r.   Olowalu Landing
s.   Mala pre-contact burials

*Implementing Actions*

1.   Develop cultural parks appropriate for public visitation and educational programs in various areas of the region.

2.   Enforce the provisions of the Lahaina Historic District in order to preserve the cultural integrity of Lahaina town. Expand the Lahaina Historic District to include both sides of Wainee Street between Lahainaluna Road and Shaw Street and both sides of Front Street from Shaw Street to Puamana.

3.   Identify specific historical or archaeological sites for protection and interpretation.

4.   Update the County Cultural Resource Management Plan to further identify specific and significant cultural resources in the region and provide strategies for preservation and enhancement.

5.   Formulate and adopt rural and historic district roadway standards to promote the maintenance of historic landscapes and streetscapes in character with the region, and, where appropriate within the context of the town's historic character, allow for narrower lanes, curbs, gutters and sidewalks, smaller corner radius, and deletion of sidewalk requirements on two sides of the street.

6.   Revise the Lahaina Historic District Ordinance to include an overlay mechanism, a historic landmark (isolated property with buffers) provision, and updated restrictions on uses and buildings in the Lahaina District.

28

7.   Provide information and assistance to homeowners seeking to preserve historic structures through registration, tax incentives and code waivers.

8.   Implement a County historical marker program to identify the former plantation camps, landings and other significant historical and legendary sites that are appropriate for public interpretation.

9.   Modify restrictive building code requirements to allow new buildings and renovations to be consistent with historic designs, such as balconies and canopies that protrude over the sidewalk.

10.  Pursue restoration of the Lahaina Courthouse as an interpretive center and museum.

## HOUSING

### Goal

A sufficient supply and choice of attractive, sanitary and affordable housing accommodations for a broad cross section of residents.

### Objectives and Policies

1.   Accommodate the 20-year housing needs of the planning region.

2.   Provide a variety of affordable housing opportunities, including improved lots and self-help projects and special needs housing for the elderly, single parent families, homeless and disabled.

3.   Coordinate the planning, design and construction of public infrastructure improvements with major residential projects that have an affordable housing component.

4.   Plan, design and construct off-site public infrastructure improvements (i.e., water, roads, sewer, drainage, police and fire protection, and solid waste) in anticipation of residential developments defined in the Community Plan and consistent with the directed and managed growth plan required by the County General Plan.

5.   Encourage public sector projects, government assistance programs, anti-speculation provisions, joint public-private efforts, and other housing assistance programs to reduce costs and increase housing

availability. Such programs should be aimed at expanding housing choices with wide price variety.

6. Promote efficient housing designs in order to reduce residential home energy consumption.

7. Maintain acceptable standards for affordable housing projects, including but not limited to, the installation of sidewalks and provision of adequate off-street parking.

8. Support efforts to develop housing for the elderly and for the homeless.

### Implementing Actions

1. Develop a comprehensive plan for housing assistance programs which coordinates all available public and private financial resources and incorporates appropriate regulatory measures.

2. Establish a housing rehabilitation program, including loans, grants and/or technical assistance, and community outreach.

3. Adopt standards for housing design and construction to reduce energy and water consumption.

4. Formulate or amend functional plans and studies to further implement recommendations of the Community Plan. These would include police and fire protection, water development, housing, local and regional circulation, drainage, solid waste, sewage disposal and treatment and other special plans and studies as required.

## URBAN DESIGN

### Goal

An attractive and functionally integrated urban environment that enhances neighborhood character, promotes quality design at the resort destinations of Kaanapali and Kapalua, defines a unified landscape planting and beautification theme along major public roads and highways, watercourses, and at major public facilities, and recognizes the historic importance and traditions of the region.

### Objectives and Policies for the West Maui Region in General

1. Enhance the appearance of major public roads and highways in the region.

2. Maintain a high level of design quality for West Maui resort destination areas.

3. Improve pedestrian and bicycle access within the region.

4. Establish, expand and maintain parks, public facilities and public shoreline areas outside of Lahaina town.

5. Integrate stream channels and gulches into the region's open space system for the purposes of safety, open space relief, greenways for public use and visual separation. Drainage channels and siltation basins should not be used for building sites, but, rather, for public open space. Drainage channel rights-of-way and easements may also be used for pedestrian walkways and bikeway facilities.

6. Promote a unified street tree planting scheme along major highways and streets. Hedge planting should be spaced and limited in height, in order to provide vistas to the shoreline and mountains.

7. Buffer public and quasi-public facilities and light-heavy industrial/commercial type facilities from adjacent uses with appropriate landscape planting.

8. Maintain shrubs and trees at street intersections for adequate sight distance.

9. Save and incorporate healthy mature trees in the landscape planting plans of subdivisions, roads or any other construction or development.

10. Incorporate drought-tolerant plant species in future landscape planting.

11. Use native plants for landscape planting in public projects to the extent practicable.

12. Existing and future public rights-of-way along roads and parks shall be planted with appropriate trees, turfgrass and ground covers.

13. Encourage neighborhoods and community organizations to upgrade and maintain streets and parks in accordance with the Maui County Planting Plan.

14. Require all future subdivisions, construction projects and developments to comply with the Maui County Planting Plan.

15. Emphasize contrasting earth-tone color schemes for buildings and avoid bright or garish colors.

16. Encourage the review of architectural and landscape architectural plans for all public projects by the County's Urban Design Review Board.

## Objectives and Policies for Lahaina Town

1. Maintain the scale, building massing and architectural character of historic Lahaina town.

2. Improve pedestrian and bicycle access within the town core.

3. Generally locate additional off-street parking facilities near commercial areas.

4. Establish, expand and maintain parks, public and private open spaces, public facilities, cemeteries, and public shoreline areas within Lahaina town.

5. Preserve the area makai of Front Street between Market and Papelekane Streets for the continued location of the library and open space.

6. Circulation and Parking:

    a. Kapunakea, Papalaua, Lahainaluna, and Shaw Streets should serve as the major mauka-makai cross streets at Honoapiilani Highway.

    b. Consolidate public and private off-street parking at locations within convenient walking distance to the Front Street shopping districts. Access to parking areas should be from interior streets and clearly identified with directional signs.

    c. Enforce existing parking regulations.

    d. Support double-decked parking structures in appropriate locations.

32

e.    Provide for mid-block pedestrian crossings and connections.

7.    Landscape Character:

a.    Open off-street parking facilities should be landscaped and maintained with canopy trees for shade. Parking facility perimeters should be landscaped and maintained with shrubbery to soften the parking edge when viewed from the street. Existing non-conforming parking lots should be made to conform with the current off-street parking ordinance as a prerequisite to future building permits.

b.    The new park along the south edge of Kahoma Stream, Malu-ulu-olele Park, the pool/park and the park space behind the existing boat harbor should be recognized as major entry features to Lahaina town with appropriate landscape planting treatment.

c.    Front Street landscape planting should provide canopy shade trees, compatible in scale and subordinated to adjacent buildings. These trees should not obscure the continuous facades of the commercial district; they should allow views of storefronts and the ocean.

d.    Landscaping along Wainee Street and other interior streets should be designed to soften the effects of the built environment and to provide buffers for parking areas.

e.    The south-side of the Kahoma Stream channel should incorporate a 20-foot-wide landscaped linear park or greenway, including pedestrian and bike ways, to provide visual and open space continuity between Front Street and the Honoapiilani Highway.

8.    Building Character:

a.    New building and renovation of existing buildings in Lahaina town should respect the scale, texture, materials, and facades of existing structures in the Lahaina Historic District.

b.    Building heights should reflect the context of existing building heights and massing in the Lahaina Historic District. The maximum building heights shall be two stories or 35 feet with a mixture of one- to two-story building heights encouraged.

c. Building design should complement the pedestrian character of Lahaina town. Restraint and harmonious relationships with natural and man-made surroundings should characterize building form; harsh forms or shapes should be avoided; sloped roofs should be encouraged. Design elements which relate to human scale should be emphasized. Design features should reflect prevalent town themes through traditional or contemporary means. Such themes may include:

1) First story awnings or covered walkways.
2) Transom openings above windows and doorways.
3) Multiple panes in storefront windows.
4) Second story balconies.

d. Encourage the use of natural materials in existing or new buildings.

e. Emphasize contrasting earth-tone color schemes for buildings.

f. Design of signs should be restrained and in keeping with requirements of the Lahaina Historic District.

g. Emphasize pedestrian amenities for commercial and public facility projects. Covered, landscaped pedestrian walkways integrated within the building organization should be encouraged. Larger new complexes should include interior pedestrian circulation with shaded areas for resting and gathering.

h. Encourage the maintenance of landscaped setbacks and common open spaces adjacent to residential areas.

i. Encourage underground installation of utilities in Lahaina town and in all new residential communities to enhance streetscape environments with the possible exception of the commercial section of Front Street to retain the flavor of old Lahaina.

*Implementing Actions*

34

1. Implement related actions specified in the Transportation section of the Community Plan related to roadway, pedestrian, bikeway improvements for Lahaina town and the region.

2. Formulate a unified landscape planting scheme for major public highways and roads in the region.

## INFRASTRUCTURE

### Goal

Timely and environmentally sound planning, development, and maintenance of infrastructure systems which serve to protect and preserve the safety and health of the region's residents, commuters, and visitors through the provision of clean water, effective waste disposal and efficient transportation systems which meets the needs of the community.

### Transportation

### Objectives and Policies

1. Support construction of the planned Lahaina Bypass Road in such a way as to promote safe, efficient travel across the region without encouraging further urbanization or impeding agricultural operations.

2. Support the provision of an alternate route between West Maui and Central Maui.

3. Support improvements for the safe and convenient movement of people and goods, pedestrians and bicyclists in the Lahaina region particularly along Honoapiilani Highway, Front Street and Lower Honoapiilani Road and seek to establish a regional network of bikeways and pedestrian paths.

4. Support ridesharing, programs to promote safe bicycle and pedestrian travel, alternative work schedules, traffic signal synchronization, and other transportation demand management strategies.

5. Promote residential communities that provide convenient pedestrian and bicycle access between residences and neighborhood commercial areas, parks and public facilities, in order to minimize use of the automobile.

35

6. Provide landscaping along major local streets in Lahaina town to enhance the street level walking and driving experience, to aid in orientation, and to emphasize mauka-makai views. Particular attention should be given to Wainee Street and to the five mauka-makai streets giving access to Honoapiilani Highway. Landscaping should soften the effects of the built environment, provide a sense of place within town, and establish a hierarchy of streets.

7. Establish Front Street and Wainee Street as local roads within Lahaina Town with an emphasis on enhancing pedestrian and bicycle amenities through (a) reduction of on-street parking; and (b) improvements to pedestrian circulation.

8. Eliminate bus traffic on Front Street north of Dickenson Street.

9. Encourage the development of public or private off-street parking that provides convenient access to shops at Front Street and Wainee Street.

10. Provide adequate facilities for marine-related light industrial activities.

11. Maintain a community airstrip in the Mahinahina area and limit the current size, scale and level of services at the airstrip through conditional zoning.

12. Create a direct control overlay district in and around the Kapalua/West Maui Airport generally defined by the 60 LDN isoline of the FAA approved noise contour map for the airport. The intent of the district shall be to establish specific guidelines for noise attenuation standards within the district.

*Implementing Actions*

1. Improve the existing highway through Lahaina town and Kaanapali by establishing or further improving turning lanes and coordinated traffic signals at the following key intersections:

   a. Southern portion of Front Street (Puamana)
   b. Kekaa Drive
   c. Lower Honoapiilani Road
   d. Akahele Street
   e. Napilihau Road
   f. Office Road

36

2. Construct left turn lanes on the Lahainaluna Road at its intersection with Honoapiilani Highway.

3. Widen the existing highway to four lanes from the pali to Lahaina town and from Kaanapali Parkway to Office Road.

4. Establish public parking areas and publicly available and privately supplied parking facilities within Lahaina town commercial centers. Parking should provide convenient access to Front and Wainee Street shops.

5. Establish major recreation ways for pedestrians and bicycles from the pali to Lahaina town and to Kapalua along the coastal highways, including Honoapiilani Highway and Lower Honoapiilani Road, and along the southern side of Kahoma Stream and other major drainage channels.

6. Redesign mauka-makai streets in Lahaina town to enhance pedestrian and bicycle movement to include enhanced sidewalk/mall facilities, bicycle lanes, and street furniture with particular attention to Lahainaluna Road.

7. Study the feasibility for a new small boat harbor between Mala Wharf and Kapunakea Street. New technologies, such as floating breakwaters and other environmentally sensitive forms of wave and surge attenuation may make this project feasible, while still protecting the ocean and nearshore environment.

8. Reduce bus traffic on Front Street by designating drop-off points and enforcing parking regulations for businesses. Prohibit bus traffic on Front Street north of Dickenson Street.

9. Discourage at-grade intersections along the planned Lahaina Bypass Road, in order to maintain safe and efficient traffic flow without traffic signals. When and where appropriate, provide for the safe under passage of agricultural equipment and vehicles, such as via stream crossings.

10. Provide a landscaped buffer area along Honoapiilani Highway to enhance both pedestrian and vehicular circulation, as well as to soften the effects of the built environment.

11. Modify Front Street and Wainee Street between Prison and Papalaua Streets for pedestrian/bicycle emphasis. Pedestrian connections through block interiors should be encouraged as part of larger development projects.

12. Study, design and implement measures for safe pedestrian access connecting Lahaina town with its mauka pool and park, including consideration of pedestrian overpasses.

13. Provide marked pedestrian crossings and other safety improvements or measures along Lower Honoapiilani Road in the vicinity of commercial developments.

14. Provide a roadway for ingress and egress between Kelawea Mauka and Honopiilani Highway, located in the vicinity of Kuhua Street and Hinau Street.

Water and Utilities

*Objectives and Policies*

1. Protect ground water resources in the region.

2. Improve the quality of domestic water.

3. Reduce potable water consumption outside urban areas.

4. Coordinate the construction of all water and public utility improvements to minimize construction impacts.

5. Study the feasibility of integrating all regional water systems into a public water system to be managed and operated by the County.

6. Improve and expand the West Maui water development program projected by the County to meet future residential expansion needs and establish water treatment facilities where necessary.

7. Coordinate expansion of and improvements to water system to coincide with the development of residential expansion areas.

8. Promote water conservation and education programs.

9. Promote conservation of potable water through the use of treated wastewater effluent for irrigation.

38

10. Encourage the installation of underground electrical, telephone and cable television lines.

11. Encourage reasonable rates for water and public utility services.

*Implementing Actions*

1. Update the County's Water Use and Development Plan and estimated water use for the West Maui region.

2. Develop a plan for the eventual acquisition by the County of Maui of all private water systems within the region.

Liquid and Solid Waste

*Objectives and Policies*

1. Reuse the treated effluent from the County's wastewater treatment system for irrigation and other suitable purposes in a manner that is environmentally sound.

2. Reduce the disposal of solid waste in landfills through expanded recycling programs and the provision of convenient drop-off facilities.

3. Improve sewage treatment services for Lahaina and provide services to residential expansion areas in the following manner:

    a. Improve facilities, operations and processing at the existing plant to reduce odors and leakage.

    b. Recycle wastewater.

    c. Provide landscaped buffer areas around the periphery of the existing plant.

    d. Extend sewage treatment service to populated areas not currently serviced.

4. Provide adequate sewage disposal facilities for boats at the Lahaina Small Boat Harbor and at Mala Wharf.

*Implementing Actions*

1.  Develop and implement a comprehensive waste management and recycling plan for the region.

2.  Design and construct improvements to expand the capacity of the Lahaina Wastewater Treatment Plant consistent with the West Maui Community Plan.

Drainage

*Objectives and Policies*

1.  Construct and maintain, as needed, desilting basins along major drainage channels.

2.  Construct necessary drainage improvements in flood-prone areas, incorporating landscaped swales and unlined channels to provide open space continuity. Urge the use of landscaped/green belt drainage channels as opposed to concrete-lined channels or culverts.

3.  Insure that new developments will not result in adverse flooding conditions for downstream properties by requiring onsite retention facilities for stormwater run-off generated by the development.

4.  Support the implementation of flood control projects and siltation basins mauka of Honoapiilani Highway to address present problem areas.

*Implementing Actions*

1.  Formulate or update a drainage master plan.

2.  Establish a comprehensive program of improvements to the storm drain system, implement a maintenance program, and ensure that safety, property loss and the need for comprehensive planning be considered.

3.  Construct Drain Line F situated makai of the Lahaina Aquatic Center and Honoapiilani Highway.

4.  Support the construction of the Lahaina Watershed Drainage Improvement Project above Wainee Village and desilting basins, as shown on the Land Use Map.

5.  Investigate the need to improve and, if necessary, extend the drainage channel just north of the Lahaina Civic Center to handle potential increases in runoff generated by new development mauka of Wahikuli and Hanakaoo.

Energy

*Objectives and Policies*

1.  Promote energy efficiency as the energy resource of first choice and seek to increase energy efficiency in all sectors in the community.

2.  Interface county planning with the energy utilities' integrated resource planning programs.

3.  Promote the environmentally sensitive use of renewable energy resources, such as biomass, wind, and solar.

4.  Promote energy conservation and education programs.

5.  Support energy efficient technologies in conjunction with new urban development and encourage energy efficient building design and site development practices.

6.  Increase the energy security of community "lifeline" facilities and improve energy emergency response capabilities.

*Implementing Actions*

1.  Develop incentives and requirements for energy-efficient building design and site development practices, including modifications to building, zoning, and subdivision codes.

2.  Develop, compile, and disseminate information on new energy technologies, policies, and programs.

3.  Develop and implement an integrated County energy resource plan.

## SOCIAL INFRASTRUCTURE

### Goal

Develop and maintain an efficient and responsive system of public services which promotes a safe, healthy, and enjoyable lifestyle, and offers opportunities for self improvement and community well being.

### Recreation and Open Space

### Objectives and Policies

1.  Provide adequate community-oriented park facilities including facilities for field and court games, children's play, and picnicking within, or adjacent to, existing and future residential areas at the following existing or planned park sites:

    a.  Wainee area near the existing swimming pool and youth center.
    b.  Major residential projects.
    c.  Napili.

2.  Provide urban park space for passive activities which allow respite from shopping and sightseeing activities within Lahaina town.

3.  Provide resource-oriented regional park facilities and public access along the shoreline for picnicking, camping, informal play, swimming, sunbathing, and other coastal-related activities along coastal lands makai of the existing or future realigned coastal highways from Honokahua Bay to the district's north boundary and from Puamana to the district's south boundary, except for the agriculture designated lands makai of the highway at Olowalu.

4.  Establish adequate public access to suitable mauka recreational areas for hiking, hunting, camping, nature study, and other back country, leisure time activities, based on a mountain access study.

5.  Provide public camping areas along the shoreline of the region, such as at Olowalu near Camp Pecusa.

6.  Support programs to enhance youth-oriented recreational opportunities such as Malu-ulu-olele Park, and the West Maui Youth Center.

42

7. Ensure adequate public access to shoreline areas, including lateral access to establish the continuity of public shorelines.

8. Establish park areas appropriate for nature study.

9. Support a study for additional boat launching ramps along the West Maui coast including but not limited to, Kahana and Olowalu.

### Implementing Actions

1. Develop a long-range land acquisition program for public uses.

2. Undertake a mountain access study and support the continuation of the State's Na Ala Hele Trail and Access Program.

3. Appropriate adequate funds for park acquisition and expansion consistent with the Community Plan, County's beach access plan and other State and County recreational master plans.

4. Develop a long-range beach park acquisition and development program involving residents, landowners, businesses, government, and public interest organizations.

5. Adopt a beach/mountain access dedication ordinance pursuant to Chapter 46, H.R.S., and acquire accesses through purchase, dedication, condemnation or land exchange.

6. Implement a program to acquire and develop sites for future park use, consistent with the Community Plan.

7. Plan, design and construct a regional park at Napili.

### Health and Public Safety

### Objectives and Policies

1. Support the appropriate level of police services in consideration of the region's resident and visitor population.

2. Establish an emergency medical care facility in West Maui.

3. Enhance fire protection for multi-story buildings.

4. Continue to increase the visibility of police services in the region.

5.   Encourage the expansion of community and social service facilities and programs in West Maui in convenient and accessible locations through public and private partnerships.

6.   Support the expansion of child care facilities in West Maui.

*Implementing Actions*

1.   Determine the needs and feasibility for an emergency medical care facility for the West Maui region.

2.   Expand the fire-fighting capabilities at the existing fire station by providing ladder company equipment for multi-story fire fighting.

3.   Provide resources to assist residential areas in implementing Neighborhood Watch programs.

4.   Expand police patrols.

5.   Determine the needs and the facility and operational requirements for community and social service agencies in West Maui.

Education

*Objectives and Policies*

1.   Ensure adequate school facilities and educational opportunities within the region.

2.   Support the improvement and maintenance of existing school facilities.

3.   Encourage the construction of permanent classroom facilities in place of portable facilities.

4.   Support school/community-based management programs and innovative educational programs.

5.   Encourage the development of child care and pre-school facilities, in conjunction with major centers of employment.

6.   Provide for additional elementary schools at Napilihau and in conjunction with major residential developments.

7. Urge the Board of Education and the State Library system to retain and expand the Lahaina Public Library at its current location.

8. Encourage the public educational system to foster student understanding of the State and County planning process; the environment and ecosystems; the Hawaiian and other ethnic cultures; and the effects of alien species on the environment and agriculture.

### Implementing Actions

1. Monitor needs for expanded intermediate and high school facilities and programs to ensure that facilities and services are in place.

2. Coordinate with the State Department of Education plans for future residential development, so that facilities are planned and constructed in a timely manner.

3. Monitor and, when necessary, upgrade existing school facilities.

## GOVERNMENT

### Goal

Government that demonstrates the highest standards of fairness, responsiveness to the needs of the community, fiscal integrity, effectiveness in planning and implementing programs and projects to accommodate a stable social and economic well-being for residents, a fair and equitable approach to taxation, and efficient and results-oriented management.

### Objectives and Policies

1. Coordinate and direct future public and private development, including capital improvement projects, consistent with the Community Plan and the island-wide directed and managed growth plan required by the General Plan.

2. Monitor the implementation of and compliance with the Community Plan.

3. Remove unnecessary delays in the permit process through means such as consolidated public hearings and concurrent processing of applications.

4. Expedite the review and approval process for projects, which will result in public benefit by "fast-tracking."

5. Use the County's budgeting process as a means of carrying out the policies and priorities of the Community Plan by targeting important projects designated by the plan for funding.

6. Support a program of incentives, rebates or credits for voluntary energy conservation and the installation of related improvements, such as solar heating, photovoltaic electrical systems and low flow fixtures.

7. Insure that adequate infrastructure is or will be available to accommodate planned development.

8. Support public and private partnerships to fund the planning and construction of infrastructure, subject to advanced public notification.

9. Improve the availability of government services to the community.

*Implementing Actions*

1. Formulate special plans and studies to implement recommendations of the Community Plan. These would include water development, housing, local and regional circulation, drainage, solid waste, sewage disposal and treatment, human services, recreation, public safety and other special plans and studies as required.

2. Adopt a beach-mountain access dedication ordinance pursuant to Chapter 46 H.R.S. as part of an island-wide comprehensive mountain and beach access study.

3. Review and amend building and subdivision codes and zoning standards such as minimum lot sizes, and compact parking ratios as a way to reduce the cost of development.

4. Prepare a progress report five years after the adoption of this plan for review by the public and Maui County Council describing the status of general and community plan implementation and actions taken to comply with same.

5. Formulate and implement a directed and managed growth program, consistent with the adopted community plans and sustainable carrying capacity.

46

6. Continue to fund and operate mobile/satellite government facilities.

7. Adopt ordinances to establish appropriate standards to insure that agricultural lands will be used for agricultural purposes or remain available for future agricultural uses.

## INDIGENOUS ARCHITECTURE

### Goal

Reserving for future implementation Indigenous Architecture, as may be adopted from time to time by the County Council or the Maui County Cultural Resources Commission.

### Objectives and Policies

1. To legitimatize Indigenous Architecture as viable spaces for living, work and recreation.

### Implementing Actions

1. Develop a County ordinance for Indigenous Architecture.

2. Adopt standards for Indigenous Architecture.

## C.   Planning Standards

The following planning standards are specific guidelines or measures for development and design. These standards are essential in clarifying the intent of the land use and town design objectives and policies and the "Land Use Map".

### 1.   LAND USE STANDARDS

a. All zoning and land use approvals shall be consistent with the West Maui Community Plan and its land use policies.

b. Limit multifamily and single-family residential, business commercial, and industrial uses to areas designated for such purposes on the Community Plan Land Use Map.

c. Special Permits in the State Agricultural District may be allowed only: (1) to accommodate public and quasi-public uses; (2) for public facility uses such as utility installation, landfills and sewer treatment

47

plants whose location is determined by technical considerations; (3) for uses which are clearly accessory and subordinate to a principal agricultural use on the property; and (4) for extractive industries, such as quarrying, where the operation does not adversely affect the environment or nearby agricultural uses.

d.  Maintain acceptable standards for affordable housing projects, including but not limited to, the installation of sidewalks and provision of adequate off-street parking.

e.  For the purposes of regulating and appropriately managing the provisions of the Community Plan and properly timing the phases and patterns of development throughout its twenty year horizon, the use of the "Urban Reserve Zoning District" shall be deemed consistent with the intent of this plan.

f.  Development of the rural areas in the Mailepai Subdivision shall be restricted to lot sizes of one acre or larger.

g.  Due to an adjacent senior citizen housing, business/commercial use of the parcel identified as TMK: 4-5-07:04, Lahaina, Maui, Hawaii, shall be restricted to office type uses during daylight hours.

2.  PROJECT DISTRICT STANDARDS

The implementation procedure for several areas within the planning region is to utilize the project district development approach. This provides for a flexible and creative planning approach rather than specific land use designations. This planning approach establishes continuity in land uses and designs while providing for orderly growth of the community, as well as comprehensive and concurrent provision of infrastructural facilities and systems.

Because of the variety of conditions and constraints related to the different project districts, each project district will be implemented through a separate ordinance. Each project district ordinance will specify the permitted uses, densities, design guidelines and other information necessary to attain each project district's objective and the objectives of the West Maui Community Plan.

PROJECT DISTRICT 1     (Kapalua)     approximately 220 acres

This project district is within the Kapalua Resort makai of Honoapiilani Highway between the proposed Napili Regional Park

48

and Lower Honoapiilani Highway at Honokahua Bay, as identified on the West Maui Community Plan Land Use Map. The project district is intended to provide a mixture of visitor-oriented facilities, including hotel accommodations, single-family and multi-family residences, and supporting commercial services within an open-space setting organized around a central village core. This central core should function as a town center, containing public spaces, public uses and facilities, commercial services, and residential areas.

Visitor accommodations should not exceed 1050 rooms. The residential component should be limited to 900 units in a mixture of single-family and multi-family densities. The golf course and open space system should continue the open space theme established within the existing portions of the resort.

PROJECT DISTRICT 2     (Kapalua-Mauka)     approximately 450 acres

This project district is generally defined by Honokahua Stream to the east, State of Hawaii lands to the west and various topographical features as identified on the West Maui Community Plan Land Use Map. This project district is intended to provide, within the context of the Kapalua Resort, a mix of recreational activities including an existing golf course (with possible expansion to 27 holes), a clubhouse, pro shop, restaurants and bars, tennis courts, swimming pool and other related recreational amenities and commercial services. The project district also includes 750 residential units (with an overall average density of 5 units/acre) in a mixture of single-family and multi-family uses integrated with and complementary to the recreational facilities mentioned above. Spatial allocations are as follows:

Golf Course, Open Space and Roadways ..............................261 acres
Commercial ................................................................................5 acres
Residential..............................................................................144 acres
Parks, open space, and buffer zones ........................................ 34 acres
Elementary School.......................................................................6 acres

PROJECT DISTRICT 3 (Kaanapali-North Beach Mauka) approximately 310 acres

The North Beach Mauka project district involves land at the northern extension of the Kaanapali Resort mauka of Honoapiilani Highway, as identified on the West Maui Community Plan Land Use Map. This project is intended to provide, within the context of the Kaanapali

49

Resort, a mixture of resident and visitor-oriented residential, commercial and recreational uses. The character of the project district will be defined by a village core which will utilize elements of Lahaina architecture and other traditional Hawaiian architecture and urban design forms. The central area of the core will feature a visitor-oriented commercial center. The project district's 1200 residential units will be characterized by a variety of single-family and multi-family product types. Amenities such as parks, gardens, golf activities, and other recreational activities or attractions will be included to provide open space within the project district.

PROJECT DISTRICT 4    (Weinberg Property) approximately 24 acres

This project district involves approximately 24 acres bounded by Kahoma Stream, Front Street, Kenui Street, and Honoapiilani Highway. The project district is intended to provide a mixture of commercial/business and multi-family and senior citizen residential uses. There shall also be 6 acres of park land within the project district, including a linear park or greenway adjacent to the south bank of Kahoma Stream, from Honoapiilani Highway to Front Street, at least 60 feet wide and approximately 1.5 acres in size. The extension of Wainee Street from its present terminus at Kenui Street to Front Street, as well as the realignment of Kenui Street shall also be considered. Said roadway improvements should be developed and funded in conjunction with appropriate government agencies. The remaining acres in the project district shall be evenly divided between the commercial/business uses, and the multi-family and senior citizen residential uses, to the greatest extent practicable.

3.    BUILDING STANDARDS

    a.    Insure that new buildings and renovations in areas within or adjacent to the Historic District respect the massing, scale, texture and appearance of old Lahaina and a maximum building height of two stories or 35 feet.

    b.    Review projects for consistency with the design guidelines specified in the Community Plan or as otherwise may be adopted.

4.    LANDSCAPE PLANTING STANDARDS

    a.    Buffer public and quasi-public facilities and light-heavy industrial/commercial type facilities from adjacent uses with appropriate landscape planting.

b.  Save and incorporate healthy mature trees in the landscape planting plans of subdivisions, roads or any other construction or development.

c.  Incorporate the use of drought-tolerant plant species in future landscape planting.

d.  Require all future subdivisions, construction projects and developments to comply with the Maui County Planting Plan.

5.  CULTURAL RESOURCES

a.  Ensure that site identification and interpretation is not damaging to any sites.

b.  Recognize the importance of buffer areas to enhance and protect sites.

c.  Support the preservation of sites and site types identified earlier within the Policies and Objectives section related to Cultural Resources.

d.  Recognize areas of historic vegetation and significant native vegetation zones as cultural resources.

6.  ENVIRONMENTAL ASPECTS

a.  Preserve the shoreline sand dune formations throughout the planning region. These topographic features are a significant element of the natural setting and should be protected from any actions which would detract from their scenic value.

b.  Promote the planting of trees and other landscape planting to enhance streetscapes and the built-environment.

c.  Prohibit the construction of vertical seawalls, except as approved by the planning commissions of the County of Maui.

d.  Insure that new developments will not result in adverse soil erosion or flooding conditions for downstream properties.

# PART IV

## IMPLEMENTATION CONSIDERATIONS

To facilitate the implementation of the West Maui Community Plan, the implementing actions shall be considered by County and State agencies in their planning, programming and budgeting. In this regard, respective County agencies shall review and consider applicable implementing actions, as well as the broader statements of goals, objectives and policies contained in the West Maui Community Plan as follows:

1.  Annual budget requests shall address requirements identified by implementing actions contained in the West Maui Community Plan;

2.  Capital improvements programming undertaken by each agency shall incorporate, as appropriate, specific projects listed in the West Maui Community Plan;

3.  Priority listings of capital improvement projects shall consider implementing actions contained in the West Maui Community Plan;

4.  Agency master plans shall address project, program and policy actions advanced in the West Maui Community Plan;

5.  Agency program and policy formulation processes shall consider, and where appropriate, incorporate implementing actions set forth in the West Maui Community Plan; and

6.  Agency reviews of and recommendations on individual projects being processed for approval shall consider the relationship of the proposed action to implementing provisions contained in the West Maui Community Plan.

The following table summarizes and categorizes each action as either a program, policy or project-related implementing action to further facilitate agency review, consideration and action on applicable implementing provisions.

**Table 1**

**West Maui Community Plan Region**
**Implementation Responsibilities**

| DEPARTMENT: Department of Planning | | | |
|---|---|---|---|
| **Action Category** | | **Implementing Action** | **Planning Category** |
| **Program** | 1. | Develop and implement a directed and managed growth plan and strategies to guide and coordinate future development. | Land Use |
| | 2. | Update and publicize the County's socio-economic forecast to provide an on-going basis for evaluating socio-economic issues and conditions in the West Maui Community Plan region. | Economic Activity |
| | 3. | Present recommendations for the designation of "Exceptional Trees" to the Maui County Arborist Committee, including all trees, or groves of trees, that have historic or cultural value, represent an important community resource, or are exceptional by reason of age, rarity, location, size, aesthetic quality or are endemic. | Urban Design |
| | 4. | Develop and maintain a program to identify and preserve the district's environmentally sensitive areas. | Environment |
| | 5. | Establish public parking areas and publicly available and privately supplied parking facilities within Lahaina town commercial centers. Parking should provide convenient access to Front and Wainee Street shops. | Transportation |
| | 6. | Coordinate with the State Department of Education plans for future residential development, so that facilities are planned and constructed in a timely manner. | Education |
| | 7. | Prepare a five-year report for review by the public and Maui County Council describing the status of general and community plan implementation and actions taken to comply with same. | Government |
| **Policy** | 1. | Discourage at-grade intersections along the planned Lahaina Bypass Road, in order to maintain safe and efficient traffic flow. | Transportation |
| **Project** | 1. | Identify and inventory exceptional open space resources and viewsheds for protection via covenants, easements, and other planning tools. | Land Use |
| | 2. | Establish a new zoning classification to implement the land use designations in the Community Plan, including but not limited to Business/Multi-Family. | Land Use |
| | 3. | Identify specific historic, cultural and archaeological sites for protection and interpretation. | Cultural Resources |
| | 4. | Update the County Cultural Resource Management Plan to further identify specific and significant cultural resources in the region and provide strategies for preservation and enhancement. | Cultural Resources |

53

| Action Category | Implementing Action | Planning Category |
| --- | --- | --- |
| | 5. Formulate and adopt rural and historic district roadway standards to promote the maintenance of historic landscapes and streetscapes in character with the region. | Cultural Resources |
| **DEPARTMENT: Department of Planning (Con't.)** | | |
| Project (Con't.) | 6. Implement alternative roadway improvement standards for the Historic District such as narrower lanes, curbs, gutters and sidewalks, smaller corner radius, and deletion of sidewalk requirements on two sides of the street. | Cultural Resources |
| | 7. Revise the Lahaina Historic District Ordinance to include an overlay mechanism, a historic landmark (isolated property with buffers) provision, and updated restrictions on uses and buildings in the Lahaina District. | Cultural Resources |
| | 8. Formulate a unified landscape planting scheme for major public highways and roads in the region. | Urban Design |
| | 9. Study the desirability of a National Seashore designation for West Maui. | Environment |
| | 10. Assess the need for standards for the siting of large-scale energy generation systems in order to mitigate environmental and visual impacts. | Environment |
| | 11. Redesign mauka-makai streets in Lahaina town to enhance pedestrian and bicycle movement to include enhanced sidewalk/mall facilities, bicycle lanes, and street furniture with particular attention on Lahainaluna Road. | Transportation |
| | 12. Develop incentives and requirements for energy efficient building design and site development practices, including modifications to building, zoning, and subdivision codes. | Energy |
| | 13. Develop and implement an integrated County energy resource plan. Develop, compile, and disseminate information on new energy technologies, policies, and programs. | Energy |
| | 14. Adopt a beach/mountain access dedication ordinance pursuant to Chapter 46, H.R.S., and acquire accesses through purchase, dedication, condemnation or land exchange. | Recreation and Open Space; Government |
| | 15. Undertake a study to identify suitable shoreline areas for public camping. | Recreation and Open Space |
| | 16. Determine the needs and the facility and operational requirements for community and social service agencies in West Maui. | Health and Public Safety |
| | 17. Adopt ordinances to establish appropriate standards to insure that agricultural lands will be used for agricultural purposes or remain available for future agricultural uses. | Government |

**West Maui Community Plan Region**
**Implementation Responsibilities**

| Action Category | | Implementing Action | Planning Category |
|---|---|---|---|
| **DEPARTMENT: State Department of Land and Natural Resources** | | | |
| Program | 1. | Provide information and assistance to homeowners seeking to preserve historic structures through registration, tax incentives and code waivers. | Cultural Resources |
| | 2. | Undertake a mountain access study and support the continuation of the State's Na Ala Hele Trail and Access Program. | Recreation and Open Space |
| Project | 1. | Study the feasibility for a new small boat harbor between Mala Wharf and Kapunakea Street. New technologies, such as floating breakwaters and other environmentally sensitive forms of wave and surge attenuation may make this project feasible, while still protecting the nearshore environment. | Transportation |
| **DEPARTMENT: Department of Parks and Recreation** | | | |
| Program | 1. | Develop cultural parks appropriate for public visitation and educational programs in various areas of the region. | Cultural Resources |
| | 2. | Establish major recreation ways for pedestrians and bicycles from the pali to Lahaina town and to Kapalua along the coastal highways, including Honoapiilani Highway and Lower Honoapiilani Road, and along the southern side of Kahoma Stream and other major drainage channels. | Transportation |
| | 3. | Develop a long-range land acquisition program for public uses. | Recreation and Open Space |
| | 4. | Develop a long-range beach park acquisition and development program involving residents, landowners, businesses, government, and public interest organizations. | Recreation and Open Space |
| | 5. | Implement a program to acquire and develop sites for future park use, consistent with the Community Plan. | Recreation and Open Space |
| Policy | 1. | Maintain Armory Park without sacrificing additional land for parking. | Cultural Resources |
| Project | 1. | Plan, design and construct a regional sports community complex, including all-weather track and community meeting facilities in the Wainee area and near the existing swimming pool and youth center complexes. | Land Use |
| | 2. | Implement a County historical marker program to identify the former plantation camps, landings and other significant historical and legendary sites that are appropriate for public interpretation. | Cultural Resources |

## West Maui Community Plan Region
### Implementation Responsibilities

**DEPARTMENT: Department of Parks and Recreation (Con't.)**

| Action Category | | Implementing Action | Planning Category |
|---|---|---|---|
| **Project (Con't.)** | 3. | Reconstruct Mokuhinia Pond and Moku'ula Royal Compound at Malu-ulu-olele Park, provided that an alternative park location can be acquired and developed, and sufficient funds committed to maintain the historical feature as an attractive asset to Lahaina town. | Cultural Resources |
| | 4. | Study, design and implement measures for safe pedestrian access connecting Lahaina town with its mauka pool and park, including consideration of pedestrian overpasses. | Transportation |
| | 5. | Plan, design and construct a regional park at Napili. | Recreation and Open Space |
| | 6. | In conjunction with the plan to restore Malu-ulu-olele Park, plan, design and construct park facilities at the proposed Wainee site for active and passive recreational uses with particular emphasis on those facilities or uses that may be displaced by the restoration of cultural sites. | Recreation and Open Space |

**DEPARTMENT: Department of Public Works and Waste Management**

| Action Category | | Implementing Action | Planning Category |
|---|---|---|---|
| **Program** | 1. | Install pedestrian crossings and other safety improvements or measures along Lower Honoapiilani Road in the vicinity of commercial developments. | Transportation |
| | 2. | Establish a comprehensive program of improvements to the storm drain system, implement a maintenance program, and ensure that safety, property loss and the need for comprehensive planning be considered. | Drainage |
| **Policy** | 1. | Encourage underground installation of utilities in Lahaina town and in all new residential communities to enhance streetscape environments with the possible exception of the commercial section of Front Street to retain the flavor of old Lahaina. | Economic Activity |
| | 2. | Implement other related actions specified in the Transportation section of the Community Plan related to roadway, pedestrian, bikeway improvements for Lahaina town and the region. | Urban Design |
| | 3. | Reduce bus traffic on Front Street by designating drop-off points and enforcing parking regulations for businesses. | Transportation |
| | 4. | Install pedestrian crossings and other safety improvements or measures along Lower Honoapiilani Road in the vicinity of commercial developments. | Transportation |

56

## West Maui Community Plan Region
## Implementation Responsibilities

### DEPARTMENT: Department of Public Works and Waste Management (Con't.)

| Action Category | | Implementing Action | Planning Category |
|---|---|---|---|
| Project | 1. | Install signs clearly identifying public parking in Lahaina town. | Land Use |
| | 2. | Modify restrictive building code requirements to allow new buildings and renovations to be consistent with historic designs, such as balconies and canopies that protrude over the sidewalk. | Cultural Resources |
| | 3. | Modify Front Street and Wainee Street between Prison and Papalaua Streets for pedestrian/bicycle emphasis. Pedestrian connections through block interiors should be encouraged as part of larger development projects. | Transportation |
| | 4. | Design and construct improvements to expand the capacity of the Lahaina Wastewater Treatment Plant. | Liquid and Solid Waste |
| | 5. | Formulate or update a drainage master plan. | Drainage |
| | 6. | Construct Drain Line F situated makai of the Lahaina Aquatic Center and Honoapiilani Highway. | Drainage |
| | 7. | Develop incentives and requirements for energy efficient building design and site development practices, including modifications to building, zoning, and subdivision codes. | Energy |
| | 8. | Adopt standards for housing design and construction to reduce energy and water consumption. | Housing |
| | 9. | Review and amend building and subdivision codes and zoning standards such as minimum lot sizes, and compact parking ratios as a way to reduce the cost of development. | Government |

### DEPARTMENT: Office of the Mayor

| Action Category | | Implementing Action | Planning Category |
|---|---|---|---|
| Program | 1. | Evaluate, formulate and implement strategies for economic diversification in West Maui. | Economic Activity |
| Policy | 1. | Pursue restoration of the Lahaina Courthouse as an interpretive center and museum. | Cultural Resources |
| | 2. | Seek to provide adequate staffing for a Maui County Arborist and Coordinator, in order to improve the maintenance and enhancement of Maui County's tree and planting assets. | Urban Design |
| | 3. | Continue to appropriate adequate funds for park acquisition and expansion consistent with the Community Plan, County's beach access plan and other State and County recreational master plans. | Recreation and Open Space |

57

## West Maui Community Plan Region
## Implementation Responsibilities

| Action Category | | Implementing Action | Planning Category |
|---|---|---|---|
| **DEPARTMENT: Office of the Mayor (Con't.)** | | | |
| Project | 1. | Seek to quantify the economic value of agricultural lands and open space as a factor in resident and visitor satisfaction and as appropriate, incorporate this data in regional socio-economic assessments. | Economic Activity |
| | 2. | Continue to fund and operate mobile/satellite government facilities. | Government |
| **DEPARTMENT: State Department of Transportation** | | | |
| Policy | 1. | Implement other related actions specified in the Transportation section of the Community Plan related to roadway, pedestrian, bikeway improvements for Lahaina town and the region. | Urban Design |
| Project | 1. | Improve the existing highway through Lahaina town and Kaanapali by establishing or further improving turning lanes and coordinated traffic signals at key intersections noted within the West Maui Community Plan. | Transportation |
| | 2. | Construct left turn lanes on the Lahainaluna Road at its intersection with Honoapiilani Highway. | Transportation |
| | 3. | Widen the existing highway from the pali to Lahaina town and from Kaanapali Parkway to Office Road. | Transportation |
| | 4. | Provide a landscaped buffer area along Honoapiilani Highway to enhance both pedestrian and vehicular circulation, as well as to soften the effects of the built environment. | Transportation |
| | 5. | Signalize Front Street at its intersection with Honoapiilani Highway near Puamana. | Transportation |
| **DEPARTMENT: U. S. Army Corps of Engineers** | | | |
| Project | 1. | Plan, design, construct and regularly maintain siltation basins within major drainage ways to enhance stream and offshore water quality. | Environment |
| **DEPARTMENT: Department of Housing and Human Concerns** | | | |
| Program | 1. | Develop a comprehensive plan for housing assistance programs which coordinates all available public and private financial resources and incorporates appropriate regulatory measures. | Housing |
| | 2. | Establish a housing rehabilitation program, including loans, grants and/or technical assistance, and community outreach. | Housing |
| **West Maui Community Plan Region Implementation Responsibilities** | | | |
| **DEPARTMENT: Department of Fire Control** | | | |

58

| Action Category | Implementing Action | Planning Category |
|---|---|---|
| Project | 1. Expand the fire fighting capabilities at the existing fire station by providing ladder company equipment for multi-story fire fighting. | Health and Public Safety |
| **DEPARTMENT: Office of State Planning - CZM Program** | | |
| Program | 1. Establish and maintain an ocean resources management program, including the conduct of baseline studies, to ensure the sustainability of the region's ocean resources. | Environment |
| **DEPARTMENT: Department of Agriculture** | | |
| Program | 1. Establish and maintain programs which control invasive alien plant and animal species. | Environment |
| **DEPARTMENT: Department of Water Supply** | | |
| Project | 1. Update the County's Water Use and Development Plan and estimated water use for the Lahaina region. | Water & Utilities |
| **DEPARTMENT: Department of Police** | | |
| Program | 1. Provide resources to assist residential areas in implementing Neighborhood Watch programs. | Health and Public Safety |
| Project | 1. Expand police patrols. | Health and Public Safety |
| **DEPARTMENT: State Department of Health** | | |
| Program | 1. Periodically maintain and monitor outfall systems, streams and drainage ways for compliance with water quality standards. | Environment |
| | 2. Continue to investigate and monitor algae bloom conditions in West Maui's offshore waters and implement appropriate mitigative measures. | Environment |
| Project | 1. Determine the needs and feasibility for an emergency medical care facility for the West Maui region. | Health and Public Safety |

**West Maui Community Plan Region**
**Implementation Responsibilities**

| Action Category | Implementing Action | Planning Category |
|---|---|---|
| Program | 1. Monitor needs for expanded Intermediate and High School facilities and programs to assure that facilities and services are in place. | Education |
| Project | 1. Construct cafeteria facilities at Princess Nahienaena Elementary School and Lahaina Intermediate School. | Education |
| **DEPARTMENT: State Commission on Water Resource Management** | | |

59

| Action Category | Implementing Action | Planning Category |
|---|---|---|
| Program | 1. Address and resolve concerns over water rights when private interests conflict with Native Hawaiian or traditional uses consistent with Article XII, Section 7, Hawaii State Constitution, and Section 1-1, Hawaii Revised Statutes. | Land Use, Cultural Resources |

60

# PART V

# LAND USE MAP

## A. Land Use Categories and Definitions

### Conservation (C)

This category primarily recognizes the designation of lands in the State Conservation District and is used to protect and preserve wilderness areas, beach reserves, scenic areas and historic sites, open ranges, wetlands, and watersheds; to conserve fish and wildlife; and to promote forestry and grazing.

### Agriculture (AG)

This use indicates areas for agricultural activity which would be in keeping with the economic base of the County and the requirements and procedures of Chapter 205 H.R.S, as amended.

### Rural (R)

This use is to protect and preserve areas consisting of small farms intermixed with low-density single-family residential lots. It is intended that, at minimum, the requirements of Chapter 205 H.R.S, as amended, shall govern this area.

### Single-Family (SF)

This includes single-family and ohana dwellings.

### Multi-Family (MF)

This includes apartment and condominium buildings having more than two dwellings.

## Hotel (H)

This applies to transient accommodations which do not contain kitchens within individual units. Such hotel facilities may include permissible accessory uses primarily intended to serve hotel guests.

## Business/Multi-Family (BMF)

This includes a mixture of retail, office, and commercial services which are oriented to neighborhood service and single family and multi-family residential uses.

## Service Business/Single Family Residential (SBR)

This includes single family dwellings with small scale service and neighborhood oriented business which are primarily established in previously utilized residential dwellings or other existing structures. The business use should be compatible with the physical character of the residential neighborhood.

## Business/Commercial (B)

This includes retail stores, offices, entertainment enterprises and related accessory uses.

## Business/Industrial (BI)

This includes a mixture of warehousing, distribution, service operations, retail and offices uses.

## Light Industrial (LI)

This is for warehousing, light assembly, service and craft-type industrial operations.

## Heavy Industrial (HI)

This is for major industrial operations whose effects are potentially noxious due to noise, airborne emissions or liquid discharges.

## Airport (AP)

This includes all commercial and general aviation airports, and their accessory uses.

Public/Quasi-Public (P)

This includes schools, libraries, fire/police stations, government buildings, public utilities, hospitals, churches, cemeteries, and community centers.

Project District (PD)

This category provides for a flexible and creative planning approach rather than specific land use designations for quality developments. The planning approach would establish a continuity in land uses and designs while providing for a comprehensive network of infrastructural facilities and systems. A variety of uses as well as open space, parks and other project uses are intended in accord with each individual project district objective.

Future Growth Reserve (FGR)

This designation recognizes possible areas of urban growth that would occur beyond the 10-year time frame for the comprehensive review and update of the community plan. The Future Growth Reserve designation would encourage planning for infrastructure development and use allocations.

Park (PK)

This designation applies to lands developed or to be developed for recreational use. This includes all public and private active and passive parks. Golf courses are further identified as "PK (GC)" on the land use map in order to differentiate golf courses and related accessory uses from other kinds of park uses.

Open Space (OS)

This use is intended to limit development on certain urban and non-urban designated lands which may be inappropriate for intensive development due to environmental, physical, or scenic constraints; this category would include but not be limited to shoreline buffer areas, landscape buffers, drainage ways, viewplanes, flood plains, tsunami prone areas. Other appropriate urban and non-urban uses may be allowed on a permit basis.

COMMUNITY PLAN
LAND USE MAP

64

## Proposed Revisions to the West Maui Community Plan Land Use Map

| I.D. No. and Name | Current Designation | Zoning | Approx Acre | CAC Recommendation | Planning Department Revision | Planning Commission Recommendation | Planning Committee Recommendation | Comments |
|---|---|---|---|---|---|---|---|---|
| 1 Lahaina Bypass Highway | Various | Ag R-1 | N/A | Show approximate alignment on the map | Same | Same | Concur with CAC, Department and Commission | Supported by the landowner |
| 2 Churches and other public uses | Various | Various | Various | Housekeeping change proposed after the CAC process | Proposed changes to Public/Quasi-Public (P/QP) | Concurred with the Department | Concur with Department and Commission | |
| 3 Bikeway and one-way streets | Various | Various | N/A | Recommended in the text portion of the plan by the CAC | Department also proposed identification on the map | Concurred with the Department | Concur with CAC, Department and Commission | |
| 4 Plantation Golf Course | Ag | Ag | 230 | Change proposed after the CAC process | Change to Park (golf course) | Concurred with the Department | Concur with Department and Commission | TMKs: 4-2-05:39, 44, 45 & 49. Recognizes existing use. |
| 5 Burial Complex | Hotel Business | P/OS | 12 | Change proposed after the CAC process | Change to Open Space (OS) | Concurred with the Department | Concur with Department and Commission | Recognizes that the area is no longer proposed for development (TMK: 4-2-04:14) |
| 6 Kapalua Tennis Center | MF | GC and Open | NA | Housekeeping change proposed after the CAC process | Minor map change to Park | Concurred with the Department | Concur with Department and Commission | |
| 7a Napili Regional Park | OS PD SF | MF | 50 | CAC recommended change to Park | Same | Same | Designate Park at 50-acre airport site, 38-acre State site, 8-acre employee housing site. 16 acres to remain P.D. 1., and 3 acres to remain SF. Redesignate 6 acres from Park to Park (GC). | TMKs: 4-2-04: por. 24 and 4-3-01:3 & 5 TMKs: 4-3-18:40 & 41, and 4-3-01: por. 31 |

| I.D. No. and Name | Current Designation | Zoning | Approx Acre | Proposed by Planning Committee Chair | | | Planning Committee Recommendation | Comments |
|---|---|---|---|---|---|---|---|---|
| | | | | CAC Recommendation | Planning Department Revision | Planning Commission Recommendation | | |
| 7b Napili Regional Park Employee Housing | Park | State AG | | | | | Designate parcel Single-Family, so employee housing at Napili can be used for Park | TMK: 4-3-9-52 |
| 8 P.D. No. 1 | PD | Various | 245 (old) 220 (new) | Proposed after the CAC process | Reconfiguration due to changes to Park and PQP | Concurred with the Department | Concur with Department and Commission | TMKs: 4-2-03 and 4-2-04:21 & por. 24 |
| 9 P.D. No. 2 | PD Ag | Ag | 275 & 200 (old) 450 (new) | CAC recommended no change in designation | Relocation of P.D. No. 2 and consolidation with P.D. No. 1A | Concurred with the Department | Concur with Department and Commission, but insert in text 6-acre school and 34-acre Park/Open Space/Buffer, and Mailepai designated Rural, 1 acre limit | TMKs: 4-3-01: por. 1, 2 & 20 and 4-3-04:9, 11, 17, 19, 20, 21, 22, 26 |
| 10 Kahana infill | Ag | Ag | 10 | Proposed after the CAC process | Change to SF | Concurred with the Department | Concur with Department and Commission | TMKs: 4-3-05:16 & 18; supported by landowner. |
| 11 West Maui Airstrip | Ag AP | Airport | 50 | Reconfiguration to reflect SLUC urban district boundary | Same | Same | Concur with CAC, Department and Commission | TMK: 4-3-01: por. 31 & 68 |
| 12 ABC Store | MF | A-2 | >.5 | CAC recommended change to Business (Commercial) | Same | Same | Concur with CAC, Department and Commission | Requested by landowner |
| 13 Nunes property | Hotel | R-3 | 1.5 | CAC recommended change to Business (Commercial) | Same | Same | Concur with CAC, Department and Commission | Requested by landowner (TMK: 4-4-01:10) |

| I.D. No. and Name | Current Designation | Zoning | Approx Acre | CAC Recommendation | Planning Department Revision | Planning Commission Recommendation | Planning Committee Recommendation | Comments |
|---|---|---|---|---|---|---|---|---|
| 14 North Beach Makai | Hotel OS | H-2 H-M | 90 | CAC recommended 66 acres to Park | Department proposed redefinition of Park and Open Space (OS) | Commission recommended no changes in designation | Concur with Commission. Amfac to dedicate 8.4 acres of canoe beach land and highway relocation engineering. | Landowner prefers no changes in designation (TMKs: 4-4-013, 6, 8 & 9 and 4-4-06:5) |
| 15 North Beach Mauka | PD Ag | R-3 | 310 | CAC recommended deletion of P.D. No. 3 (PD to Ag) | Department proposed reconfiguration of P.D. and designation of additional Open Space | Concurred with the Department | Concur with Department and Commission | Reconfiguration requested by the landowner (TMKs: 4-4-02: por. 2 & 25) |
| 16 Puukolii Village | Ag | Ag | 260 | CAC recommended identifying project as Act 15 with no change to underlying designation | Ag to SF and MF (50 acres) for those uses makai of proposed bypass; entire project described in text | Ag to SF and MF for those uses makai of proposed bypass; FGR for those uses mauka of the proposed bypass | Concur with CAC | Landowner requested designation of entire project (TMK: 4-4-02: por. 2) |
| 17 South Beach Mauka | Park | R-3 Ag | 70 | CAC recommended no change | Department proposed change to SF | Same | Concur with Department and Commission | Requested by landowner (TMK: 4-4-06: por. 58) |
| 18 Old STP Site | MF | R-3 | 11 | Change proposed after the CAC process | Change to Light Industrial (LI) | Concurred with the Department | Concur with Department and Commission | Supported by landowner (TMKs: 4-4-06:13 & 56) |
| 19 Driving Range | MF | H-1 | 7 | Change proposed after the CAC process | Change to Park (golf course) | Commission recommended no change in designation | Concur with Commission | Landowner opposes change in designation (TMK: 4-4-08: por. of 18) |
| 20 Luigi's | Park | R-3 | >1 | Change proposed after the CAC process | Change to Business (Commercial) | Concurred with the Department | Concur with Department and Commission | Recognizes existing use (TMK: 4-4-06: por. of 32) |

-3-

| I.D. No. and Name | Current Designation | Zoning | Approx Acre | CAC Recommendation | Planning Department Revision | Planning Commission Recommendation | Planning Committee Recommendation | Comments |
|---|---|---|---|---|---|---|---|---|
| 21 Tennis courts and parking | Commercial | B-R | 18 | Change proposed after the CAC process | Change to Park | Concurred with the Department | Committee voted no change in designation due to existing business zoning | TMKs: 4-4-13:4 & 5 |
| 22 Civic Center | Ag P/QP | | 23 (+10) | Change proposed after the CAC process | Change to P/QP at existing Civic Center site; relocate 10 acres parking to Civic Center | Concurred with the Department | Concur with Department and Commission | TMKs: 4-5-21: por. 3, 10, 11, 14, 15 & 16 |
| 23 Leiali'i (HFDC) | Ag PD SF | Ag | 1,120 | CAC recommended identifying project as Act 15 with no change to underlying designation | Ag and PD to SF, MF and PK (golf course) for those uses makai of proposed bypass; entire project described in text | Concurred with the Department | Concur with CAC | TMK: 4-5-21: por. 3 |
| 24 P.D. No. 4 | PD | Ag | 116 | CAC recommended deletion (change to Ag) | Same | Same | Concur with CAC, Department and Commission | TMKs: 4-5-21: por. 3, 10, 11, 14, 15 & 16 |
| 25 Crater Village | SF | Ag | | CAC recommended no change in designation | Change to Agriculture | Concurred with the Department | Concur with Department and Commission | TMKs: 4-5-21: por. 2 & por. 3 |
| 26 Lands adjacent to Kahoma Stream | Ag | Ag | 38 | CAC recommended change to LI | Same | Same | Concur with CAC, Department and Commission | TMK: 4-5-10:7 |
| 27 Kapunakea Alignment | Ag LI | Ag M-I | NA | Change proposed after CAC process | Identify approx. alignment and new makai connection | Concurred with the Department | Concur with Department and Commission | Not opposed by landowners. (TMKs: 4-5-10: por. 7, 4-5-11: por. 11 and 4-5-21: por. 3) |
| 28 Cannery | LI | M-I | 16 | Change proposed after CAC process | Change to Business (Commercial) | Concurred with the Department | Concur with Department and Commission | TMKs: 4-5-11:2, 3 & 4 |

| I.D. No. and Name | Current Designation | Zoning | Approx Acre | CAC Recommendation | Planning Department Revision | Planning Commission Recommendation | Planning Committee Recommendation | Comments |
|---|---|---|---|---|---|---|---|---|
| 29 Kahoma Stream | Ag OS | Ag | | Maintain Open Space south of new stream alignment stated in text | New stream alignment shown on map and OS maintained along South bank | Concurred with the Department | Concur with CAC, Department and Commission | TMK: 4-5-10: por. 5 |
| 30 Weinberg Property | MF Park | A-1 | 24 | CAC recommended reconfiguration of Park (no change in acreage) | Same | Same | Committee voted for Project District as requested by landowner | Change to Project District requested by developer; other requests also made (TMK: 4-5-08:1) |
| 31 Mala Wharf Road | Commercial | R-2 Church | 2 | CAC recommended changes to LI and Business (Commercial) | Same | Same | Concur with CAC, Department and Commission | Requested by landowners (TMKs: 4-5-05:4-8 & 14-18) |
| 32 'Coral Redesign | MF | A-1 R-1 | >1 | CAC recommended changes to Business (Commercial) | Same | Same | Concur with CAC, Department and Commission | Requested by landowners (TMKs: 4-5-07:4 and 4-6-09:47, 48 & 49) |
| 33 Louis Property | P/QP | R-1 B-2 | 1.5 | Change proposed by landowner at Commission hearing | Landowner proposal; Department had no objections | Change Louis property and adjacent property to Commercial | Concur with Commission | TMKs: 4-6-09:14 & 28 |
| 34 Maui Islander | MF | A-1 | 8.6 | Change proposed after the CAC process | Change to Hotel | Concurred with the Department | Concur with Department and Commission | Recognizes existing use (TMK: 4-6-11:8) |
| 35 Library | Commercial | Hist. Dist. | | CAC recommended change to PQP | Same, with clean up of Park designations | Concurred with the Department | Concur with CAC, Department and Commission | Recognizes existing use (TMKs: 4-6-01:4, 7 & 10) |
| 36 Dickenson Street | MF | Dup. | 1+ | Change proposed after CAC process | Change to Business (Commercial) | Concurred with the Department | Disapprove. Parcel to remain MF | Requested by landowner (Archangel property) TMKs: 4-6-11:9, 10, 11, 27 & 33 |
| 37 Wainee Makai | Commercial | R-2 | 5.7 acre approx. | Change proposed after CAC process | Change to Service Business Residential (SBR) | Change to SBR except for properties along Dickenson Street. | Disapprove SBR. Instead, TMK: 4-6-8:24, 25, 63, 66, 83, and B-2 zoned parcels are Bus/Commercial, and all others SF | Includes all parcels not PQP or already zoned B-2. (TMKs: 4-6-08:14-26, 31-40, 46, 52, 63, 66, 75-85) |

| I.D. No. and Name | Current Designation | Zoning | Approx Acre | CAC Recommendation | Planning Department Revision | Planning Commission Recommendation | Planning Committee Recommendation | Comments |
|---|---|---|---|---|---|---|---|---|
| 38 Sullivan property | SF | R-1 | 4.7 | CAC recommended change to MF | No change in designation (leave as SF) | Concurred with CAC | Concur with Department and Commission | TMK: 4-6-12;2, requested by landowner; opposed by neighbors |
| 39 Mill | HI LI | M-2 | 6 acre approx | Change proposed after CAC process | Change to Ag | No change in designation | Concur with Commission | Change opposed by landowner |
| 40 Texaco | LI | M-2 | .3 | Change proposed after the CAC process | Change to Business (Commercial) | Concurred with the Department | Concur with Department and Commission | Recognizes existing use |
| I.D. No. and Name | Current Designation | Zoning | Approx Acre | CAC Recommendation | Planning Department Revision | Planning Commission Recommendation | Planning Committee Recommendation | Comments |
| 41 David Malo | Commercial | R-2 | 1.5 | Change proposed after the CAC process | Change to Multi-Family (MF) | Concurred with the Department | Concur with Department and Commission | Recognizes existing use (TMK: 4-6-10:28) |
| 42 Puunau Dickenson | SF | M-2 Ag | | Change proposed after CAC process | Change to Ag | Concurred with the Department | Concur with Department and Commission | TMKs: 4-6-16: por. 4, 5, 32, 38 & 39 |
| 43 Ikena Housing | Ag | Ag | 8 | Not recommended by CAC | Department proposed changed to SF | Same | Concur with Department and Commission | For the relocation of residents of Ikena Ave. displaced by development of the bypass highway |
| 44 Wainee Village | SF MF | Ag | | CAC recommended change to Ag | Same | Same | Entire Village to be designated SF | TMK: 4-6-15: por. 1 |
| 45 Wainee Park | Ag MF | Ag | Various | CAC recommended 13 acres to Park | Department proposed 20 acres to Park | Commission could not sustain a majority vote | Concur with Department | Landowner supports 13 acres for park use. (TMK: 4-6-15: por. 1) |
| 46 Lahaina drainage | Ag | Ag | | CAC recommended change to OS to recognize approx. channel alignment | Same | Same | Concur with CAC, Department and Commission | TMKs: 4-6-13: por. 1 4-6-15: por. 1 and 4-6-18: por. 3 |
| 47 Gateway park | Ag | Ag | 7 | CAC recommended change to Park | Department proposed no change in designation | Concurred with CAC | Concur with Department | TMK: 4-6-13: por. 1 |

| I.D. No. and Name | Current Designation | Zoning | Approx Acre | CAC Recommendation | Planning Department Revision | Planning Commission Recommendation | Planning Committee Recommendation | Comments |
|---|---|---|---|---|---|---|---|---|
| 48 Olowalu | Ag | B-3 A-3 R-2 R-3 Hotel | various | CAC recommended recognizing existing uses | Same | Same | Concur with CAC, Department and Commission | TMKs: 4-8-3:2, 31 & 33 and 4-8-04:1-19. Zoning is included for informational purposes only and is based on a map dated in May 1961. This map is not consistent with current SLUC and CP designations. Use of this information in this summary (for this item and the next item) does not constitute legal recognition of the validity or invalidity of said map. |
| 49 Olowalu Beach Park | Ag OS | R-3 A-3 | 10 | CAC recommended no change | Department proposed change to Park | Commission concurred with redesignation with consultation with landowner over final configuration of the beach park | Concur with Commission | TMK: 4-8-03: por. 5. Landowner supported text change for 10-acre park with consultation. Zoning is included for informational purposes only. See note above. |
| 50 Omori Existing Puunoa Beach Estates (Multi-family request) | SF | A-1 | 1.2 acre | Change proposed after the CAC process | Did not review | Did not review | Approve MF due to existing use and A-1 zoning | TMK: 4-5-04:02 |

| I.D. No. and Name | Current Designation | Zoning | Approx Acre | CAC Recommendation | Planning Department Revision | Planning Commission Recommendation | Planning Committee Recommendation | Comments |
|---|---|---|---|---|---|---|---|---|
| 51 Omori Existing 1189 Halepuka Place (Single Family request) | Public/Quasi-Public and Park | Public/Quasi-Public and R-2 | 0.3 acre | Change proposed after the CAC process | Did not review | Did not review | Approve SF due to existing use and R-2 zoning | TMK: 4-5-04-48 |
| 52 Omori Existing (Heavy Industrial request) | Light Industrial | M-2 Heavy Ind. | West Maui Center 3.5 acre Tanabe 0.5 acre | Changes proposed after the CAC process | Department opposes Heavy Industrial designation | Did not review | Disapprove HI designation. Parcels to remain LI | TMK: 4-5-07.2  TMK: 4-5-09.2 |
| 53 Plantation Inn (Hotel request) | Business | B-2 | 0.5 acre | Change proposed after the CAC process | Did not review | Did not review | Disapprove Hotel designation. Parcel to remain Business | TMK: 4-6-09-37 |
| 54 MacInnes property (Multi-family request) | 1.5 acre SF 1.5 acre OS | R-3 | 3.0 acre | Changes proposed after the CAC process | Did not review | Did not review | Approve applicant's request for redesignation from Single Family to Multi-Family | TMK: 4-3-06.70 |
| 55 Ng property (Business request) | Public/Quasi-Public | Historic District | 0.4 acre | Changes proposed after the CAC process | Did not review | Did not review | Disapprove Business designation. Parcel to remain Public/Quasi Public | TMK: 4-6-07.03 |

| # | | | | Changes proposed after the CAC process | Did not review | Did not review | | |
|---|---|---|---|---|---|---|---|---|
| 56 Ziqun Folvarko property (Business request) | SF | R-1 | 0.4 acre | Did not review | Did not review | Did not review | Disapprove Business designation. Parcel to remain SF | TMK: 4-5-13:15 & 16 |
| 57 West Maui Plaza | Business | Interim | 3.3 acre | Did not review | Did not review | Did not review | Redesignate from Business to Ag | TMK: 4-6-11:12 & 34 |
| 58 Zack Property | MF | R-2 | 0.2 acre | Did not review | Did not review | Did not review | Redesignate from MF to Business/Multi-Family | TMK: 4-5-03:14, lot 1 |

pc:complans:westmtrfc:wab

- 9 -

# Index

# ABOUT THE AUTHOR

LISA HUYNH ELLER is a longtime writer and communications professional based out of Hilo, Hawai'i. She owns Big Blue Studio, a small business providing communications support to nonprofits and businesses. She is a regular contributor to *Ka Wai Ola,* the Office of Hawaiian Affairs monthly newspaper. She served as the communications director for the Nature Conservancy in Idaho between 2012 and 2020. Prior to that, she worked as full-time reporter for *West Hawaii Today* and the *Montrose Daily Press,* earning awards from the Society of Professional Journalists and the Associated Press for her coverage of public affairs and education. Lisa graduated from the University of Hawai'i at Mānoa with a degree in journalism in 2004.